110+ *in* GS 2

For Civil Services Main Examination

110+ *in* GS 2

For Civil Services Main Examination

Manuj Jindal, IAS

Published by
OakBridge Publishing Pvt. Ltd.
M 35, 1st Floor, Old DLF, Gurugram, 122001, Haryana, India
Tel.: +91 124 4305970, E-mail: info@oakbridge.in
www.oakbridge.in

ISBN: 978-81-939171-5-2

Printed and bound at Saurabh Printers Pvt. Ltd.

PREFACE

I have written this book 110+ in GS 2 from Civil Services aspirants' point of view. This has helped me figure out the questions I faced when I was preparing myself for the Civil Services Exam. Only then could I attempt to guide the aspirants to answer those questions to the best of my ability.

The top question for me, almost always, has been: **How do I write answers that will fetch me good marks?** What is a UPSC examiner looking for? How do I cross the threshold of getting 3–4 marks per question to getting 5–6 marks per question?

Without getting 110+ in every GS paper, I could not see myself bagging a rank within the top 100. Therefore, answer writing and conceptual clarity of issues was my key focus during my preparation. I have tried to answer the above questions by providing over 100 answers (good and bad :)) and also the specific 'approaches' I followed during the preparation. It is my sincere hope that this book would help aspirants answer their questions! I also hope that every student reading my book uses his or her common sense and critical thinking. If you do not agree with what I say, please feel free to improvise!

In the end, I would like to sincerely thank thousands of students whose emails served as a guiding light while I was writing this book. It has been my dream to clear the UPSC and write a book, and I have done both within a year! This could not have happened without the support system I have had in my life. For this, I would like to high-five my brothers, Anuj and Puru, who have never shied away from lending a critical hand of advice and support. Finally and most importantly, I am grateful to my parents, whose consistent belief in me puts even my wits to surprise.

Jai Hind!

Manuj Jindal, IAS

Brief Contents

Scheme of Civil Services Examination xv
Syllabus of General Studies Paper II xvi
Features - At a Glance *xviii*

1. Understanding the Constitution of India 2
2. Elections in India 32
3. Judiciary and Its Issues 44
4. NGOs, SHGs 70
5. Governance 90
6. Social Justice 106
7. India's International Relations 152

Appendix A: Important Supreme Court Judgements 174
Appendix B: Approach & Framework for Answer Writing 184
Appendix C: Solved Practice Sets: Main Examination 214
Appendix D: Additional Reads for Main Examination 260

Contents

1. Understanding the Constitution of India 2

Functions of the Constitution 3
Evolution of the Constitution 5
The Preamble 6
Provisions Adopted from Other Constitutions 6
Structure of the Indian Constitution 7
Basic Structure Doctrine of Indian Constitution 7
Cases and Amendments related to Basic Structure doctrine 9
Features of the Indian Constitution 11
Fundamental Rights 13
Importance of Fundamental Rights 13
Evolution of Fundamental Rights 13
Procedure for Amendments to the Constitution 15
Types of Amendments 16
Unamendable Parts of the Constitution 17
The 42nd Constitutional Amendment Act, 1976 17
Judicial review of ordinary laws 17
Federalism 18
Early Years of Independence 18
Federal features of the Constitution of India 18
Unitary features 18
Cooperative federalism 19
Removal of Governor 19
Rules and Recommendations 19
Important Amendments to the Constitution 20
President's Rule 26
Need for President's Rule 26
Sarkaria Commission Recommendations 27
Punchhi Commission 27

2. Elections in India 32

Introduction 32
First-Past-the-Post System 32
Merits and Demerits of FPTP System 33
Proportional Representation System 34
Electoral Reforms 35
Criminalization of politics 37
Immediate Disqualification 37
Relevant Case Laws 38
Attempts to dilute provisions to favour legislators 38
Model Code of Conduct 39
Voter Education in India 39

National Voters' Day 39

3. Judiciary and Its Issues 44

The Judiciary in India 44
Features of Indian Judiciary 45
Supreme Court of India 45
Jurisdiction of Supreme Court 45
Independence of Judiciary 46
Kesavananda Bharati Case 47
Appointment of Judges to the Supreme Court 47
The Collegium 49
National Judicial Appointments Commission 49
Appointing Judges: UK Process 52
Appointing Judges: US Process 52
Reforms in the Judiciary 52
Highlights from Law Commission Report 53
Judicial Activism 54
Abuse of PIL 54
Indian Judiciary Issues 55
Steps Taken to Address These Issues 56
Reforms Required 56
Challenges of Criminal Justice System in India 57
Strategy for Reform 57
Alternative Dispute Resolution 58
ADR and Constitution 58
Advantages of ADRs 59
Lok Adalats 59
Increasing Tribunalization in India 59
Legal Services Authorities Act, 1987 60
National Legal Services Authority 61
The Role of Lok Adalats 62
The Role of Gram Nyayalayas 63
Judicial Review in India 63
Importance of judicial review 63
Disadvantages of Judicial Review 63
Tribal Justice System 64
Condition of Undertrials 65
Reasons for Huge Number of Undertrials 65
Government Steps in this direction 65
Recommendations for improving the Conditions of undertrials 65

4. NGOs, SHGs 70

NGOs, SHGs -- The Third Sector 70
Various Roles of Voluntary Sector Organisations 71
Advantages/Importance 72
Civil Society as a Major Economic Force 72
Funding Sources 73
Government NGO interface 73
Self-help Groups 73

Beginning 74
Functions 74
Advantages/Benefits 74
Impact: 75
E-Shakti [SHGs] — NABARD's SHG-Bank Linkage Program 75
Organizations involved: 76
Success Stories 77
Impact of Self-help Groups on financial inclusion in India 77
Bank Sakhi Program 77
Self-Help Promoter Institutions (SHPIs) 78
Role of SHPI 79
Challenges 79
Waqf 79
Charities 80
CSR (Corporate Social Responsibility) 81
Self-Regulatory Authorities 82
Social capital — SHGs and Cooperatives — a Gandhian idea of self-reliance 83

5. Governance 90

Good Governance 91
Features of Effective Governance 92
Accountability 92
Transparency 92
Regulation 92
Single Window System for Delivery of Services 93
Bottlenecks 93
e-Governance 93
National e-Governance Plan 94
e-Kranti 94
Digital India 96
Problems in e-Governance 97
Consumer Protection 98
Financial Inclusion 98
Nachiket Mor Committee on Financial Inclusion 98
Important Developments 100
Citizen's Charter 101
Citizen Participation 102

6. Social Justice 106

Historical Underpinnings of Social Justice 106
Origin of the Concept of Social Justice 107
Social Justice in Indian Political System 107
Capabilities Approach' of Social Justice 107
Justice v. Social Justice 108
Constitution of India and Social Justice 108
Social Justice Post Liberalization 112
Categorization of Social Justice Schemes 112
B. R. Ambedkar and Social Justice 113

Views on Social Justice and Socio-cultural Rights 113
View on Political Rights 115
Achievements of Ambedkar 115
Rights Based Approach to Social Policy 116
Health 116
Social Importance of Health 116
Economic Importance of Health 117
Major Health Care Schemes 117
Features of RSBY 119
Integrated Child Development Schemes 120
National Rural Health Mission 120
12th FYP on Health 123
Problems in the Public Healthcare Domain in India 123
Goals 126
Challenges faced by current healthcare programmes 127
General Issues with Healthcare in India 128
Private Healthcare Industry 129
The (successful) example of Tamil Nadu Healthcare 131
Suggested Focus Areas 132
Steps already taken 133
Universal Health Coverage Models 133
Disease Control Programmes 134
Food Safety 134
Early Childhood Development 135
Education 135
Broad Objectives of Education 135
Benefits of Education 135
Relationship between education and development 136
Achievements 136
Issues with private schools as an alternative 137
Government Schemes in Education 138
Sarva Shiksha Abhiyan 138
Shala Programmes 138
Some other Schemes and Initiatives 139
Problems with Education in India 140
New Education Policy in India 140
Recommendations of the TSR Subramanian Committee 140
National Skill Development Mission 141
Focus of National Skill Development Mission 141
National Skill Development Corporation (NSDC) 142
UDAAN 142
Pradhan Mantri Kaushal Vikas Yojana 142
NSFQ 143
Poverty Reduction 144
Poverty Line Evolution in India 144
Post-Independence 145
First Planning Commission working group 145
YK Alagh Committee 145
Lakdawala Formula 145
Suresh Tendulkar Committee 146

Current Status 146
Why defining poverty line is a controversial issue 147
Poverty definition in other countries 147
Social Audit 147
Benefits 147
Problems 148
Practice Question (Main Examination) 148
Gram Panchayat 148

7. India's International Relations 152

Objectives of India's Foreign Policy 152
Overview of India's Foreign Policy since Independence 152
Promotion of International Peace 152
Anti-Colonialism 153
Anti-Racialism 154
Non-Alignment 154
Panchsheel 155
Afro-Asian Bias 155
Links with the Commonwealth 156
Support to the UNO 156
Disarmament 156
Look East Policy 156
Gujral Doctrine 157
Nuclear Policy of India 157
India's relation with her Neighbours 158
India and Pakistan 158
Issues between India and Pakistan 158
India and Bhutan 162
Geopolitical and Cultural Significance of Bhutan 162
Bhutan's Response to India's International Position 163
Indo-Bhutan Friendship Treaty 163
Challenges in Indo-Bhutan Relations 164
Chinese Engagement in Bhutan 165
Hydroelectricity 166
India-Bhutan Foundation 166
Concept of Gross National Happiness 166
India and SAARC 166
Why SAARC?[3] 167
SAARC's achievements 168
Where SAARC failed 168
Reasons for failure 169
Suggestions for the future 169
India and ASEAN 170
Act East Policy 170
Challenges and Opportunities 171

Appendix A: Important Supreme Court Judgements 174
Appendix B: Approach & Framework for Answer Writing 184
Appendix C: Solved Practice Sets: Main Examination 214
Appendix D: Additional Reads for Main Examination 260

Scheme of Civil Services Examination

Civil Services Preliminary Examination			
Paper	**Subject**	**Duration**	**Marks**
Paper I	General Studies Paper I	2 Hours	200
Paper II	General Studies Paper II	2 Hours	200*
Total			400

**Paper II is qualifying in nature.*

Civil Services Preliminary Examination			
Paper	**Subject**	**Duration**	**Marks**
Compulsory Papers			
Paper I	Essay	3 Hours	250
Paper II	General Studies Paper I (Indian Heritage and Culture, History and Geography of the World and Society)	3 Hours	250
Paper III	General Studies Paper II (Governance, Constitution, Polity, Social Justice and International relations)	3 Hours	250
Paper IV	General Studies Paper III (Technology, Economic Development, Bio-diversity, Environment, Security and Disaster Management)	3 Hours	250
Paper V	General Studies Paper IV (Ethics, Integrity and Aptitude)	3 Hours	250
Optional Paper (One optional Subject to be chosen from the given list)			
Paper VI	Optional Paper I	3 Hours	250
Paper VI	Optional Paper II	3 Hours	250
Total (Written)			**1750**
Language Papers**			
Paper A	(One of the Indian Language to be selected by the candidate from the Languages included in the Eighth Schedule to the Constitution)	3 Hours	300
Paper B	English	3 Hours	300

*** Qualifying in nature and not counted in the merit*

Personality Test	275 Marks
Grand Total (Written+Personality Test)	**1750+275=2025 Marks**

Syllabus of General Studies Paper II

Indian Political System

- Indian Constitution- historical underpinnings, evolution, features, amendments, significant provisions and basic structure.
- Functions and responsibilities of the Union and the States, issues and challenges pertaining to the federal structure, devolution of powers and finances up to local levels and challenges therein.
- Separation of powers between various organs dispute redressal mechanisms and institutions.
- Comparison of the Indian constitutional scheme with that of other countries Parliament and State Legislatures – structure, functioning, conduct of business, powers & privileges and issues arising out of these.
- Structure, organization and functioning of the Executive and the Judiciary Ministries and Departments of the Government; pressure groups and formal/informal associations and their role in the Polity.
- Salient features of the Representation of People's Act.
- Appointment to various Constitutional posts, powers, functions and responsibilities of various Constitutional Bodies.
- Statutory, regulatory and various quasi-judicial bodies

Governance in India

- Government policies and interventions for development in various sectors and issues arising out of their design and implementation.
- Development processes and the development industry- the role of NGOs, SHGs, various groups and associations, donors, charities, institutional and other stakeholders.
- Welfare schemes for vulnerable sections of the population by the Centre and States and the performance of these schemes; mechanisms, laws, institutions and Bodies constituted for the protection and betterment of these vulnerable sections.
- Issues relating to development and management of Social Sector/Services relating to Health, Education, Human Resources.
- Issues relating to poverty and hunger.
- Important aspects of governance, transparency and accountability, e-governance- applications, models, successes, limitations, and potential; citizens charters, transparency & accountability and institutional and other measures.
- Role of civil services in a democracy.

International Relations

- India and its neighbourhood- relations.
- Bilateral, regional and global groupings and agreements involving India and/or affecting India's interests
- Effect of policies and politics of developed and developing countries on India's interests, Indian Diaspora.
- Important International institutions, agencies and fora- their structure, mandate.

Features - At a Glance

Subject related Quotes

Every chapter begins with a quote related to the chapter.

"In this life we cannot do great things, we can only do small things with great love"
-Mother Teresa

Learning Objectives

At the start of every chapter, overview of the chapter has been given to facilitate the better understanding.

Overview of the Chapter

- Development processes and the development industry- the role of NGOs, SHGs, various groups and associations, donors, charities, institutional and other stakeholders

Flowcharts and Diagrams

In order to facilitate better understanding, Flowcharts and diagrams have been used to illustrate the topics.

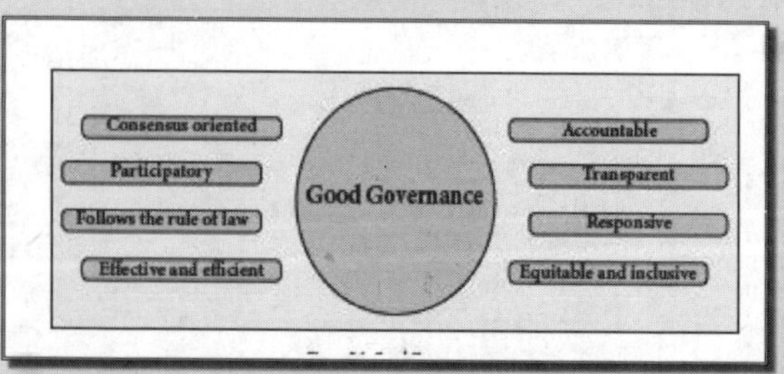

Answer Writing Tips

For every chapter, answer writing tips are given to help the students in framing the answers.

Answer Writing Tips:

- Do not try to 'stand out'. Lot of students try to be t
creative. The key is to be creative but within the accept
norms. Please remember that UPSC examiners a
provided a framework within which they check t

Tables and Boxes

Tables and boxes have been provided to compile the important information from the texts.

SIX VISIONS STATEMENTS		
Topic	**What will we do?**	**Vision Statement**
3. Easy loans	• Banks don't easily give loans to poor people and small businessman–100% financial inclusion not achieved. • So, for that, I'll suggest reforms in Priority sector lending (PSL), NBFC, RRB etc. But they too have their problems of NPA, liquidity and loan defaults. We'll setup special "Wholesale banks" to help them out.	3. Sufficient Access to Affordable, Formal Credit by 1/1/2016
4. Investment	• IF you deposit money in bank, at max you can get ~9% return (on fixed deposit/FD).	4. Universal Access to Investment Products at

Practice Question

For the purpose of self assessment, every chapter ends with the practice questions related to main examinations.

Practice Questions (Main Examination)

1. Do you think partisan federalism is acting as impediment to cooperative federalism? Examine how the Supreme Court can end partisan federalism in India.

Ans: Federalism can be defined as the form of government in which the Central or Federal Government is merged with regional or state governments in a single political system. Federalism is a part of the basic structure of the Constitution of India (as provided by the Supreme Court).

Overview of the Chapter

1

UPSC Syllabus Covered:

- Indian Constitution- historical underpinnings, evolution, features, amendments, significant provisions and basic structure.
- Functions and responsibilities of the Union and the States, issues and challenges pertaining to the federal structure, devolution of powers and finances up to local levels and challenges therein.
- Separation of powers between various organs dispute redressal mechanisms and institutions.
- Comparison of the Indian constitutional scheme with that of other countries.
- Parliament and State Legislatures – structure, functioning, conduct of business, powers & privileges and issues arising out of these.

Answer Writing Tips:

- Answer in short sentences of maximum 2 lines. Do not use extremely long sentences as they confuse the examiner about the point you are making.
- Use flow charts, tables and diagrams to enhance the quality of your answer. Be sure to provide a title for that diagram or table.
- Do not use flowery language and complicated words. Use of simple language with 'key words' that add value to the answer is expected.

1

Understanding the Constitution of India

"The Indian Constitution is first and foremost a social document."

— Granville Austin

Introduction

The Constitution of India has been brought into force for creating a framework for the functioning of the democracy, creating opportunities for everyone, and changing the social, political, economic, and psychological landscape of India. There are two important concepts to understand at the outset about the Constitution and its basic role in the Indian democracy.

First, the constitution works as a "framework". It is an overarching document, which guides the functioning of ourmodern liberal democracy. You can visualize it as a frame of a painting. Without the frame, the painting will not look beautiful and will do injustice to the painter's hard work. Similarly, without a Constitution, a liberal democracy might not have the right direction and vision to build a political, social and economic unit. Second, the constitution limits the ability of the government from violating some basic rights. Hence, the Constitution provides a check on the government. To do so, the Constitution has divided the Government into three branches: legislative, executive, and judicial. That was an important decision because it gave specificpowers to each branch and set up a system of checks and balances. Checks and balances means that each of the three branch of the government mentioned above has some influence over the other in order to limit the concentration of powers in one branch. The laws made by the legislature can be reviewed by the judiciary on the grounds of their Constitutional validity. Similarly, the President, an Executive head, has veto power to check the legislature. The legislature also has the power to remove judges and the President according to Constitutional procedures.

Functions of the Constitution[1]

The Constitution is a critical component of democratic functioning of a country. It is a grand document (written or spoken, i.e., by convention) that provides a general direction and vision to a political unit. Broadly speaking, the functions of the Constitution of India are as follows:

1. The first function of the Constitution is to provide a set of basic rules that allow for minimal coordination amongst members of a society: The Preamble provides for the overall vision of the Constitution and the structure of government in India (centre-states-citizenship).
2. The second function of the Constitution is to specify who has the power to make decisions in a society. It decides how the government will be constituted;it provides for the positions of President and Governor and also the process of an elected government and adult franchise.
3. The third function of the Constitution is to set some limits on what a government can impose on its citizens. These limits are fundamental in the sense that the government may never trespass them. This is done through the provision of fundamental rights in the Constitution. For example, the government cannot order any citizen to follow or not to follow any religion. The Fundamental Right to Practice One's Religion sets limitations on the power of the government to do so.
4. The fourth function of the Constitution is to enable the government to fulfil the aspirations of the society and create conditions for a just society:

   This is done through the provision of Directive Principles of State Policy and other enabling laws.

> *"The Constitution is not an instrument for the government to restrain the people, it is an instrument for the people to restrain the government."*
>
> — Patrick Henry, American politician

The Constituent Assembly was formed by the Cabinet Mission Plan in November 1946 to create the Constitution. M.A. Jinnah and M.K.Gandhi were not part of the Constituent Assembly. Members were elected by the legislative assembly (equivalent to the Lok Sabha today) members through proportional representation by means of the single transferable vote (the same procedure as used presently for the President's election). The princely states' members were nominated by the heads of the states, but these princely states decided to stay away from the Constituent Assembly.

[1]Uppal, Shveta(ed.). (2006). Indian Constitution at Work, NCERT, pp. 1–25

Formation of the Constituent Assembly: Jawaharlal Nehru and other leaders taking pledge during the midnight session of the Constituent Assembly of India held on 14 and 15 August 1947.

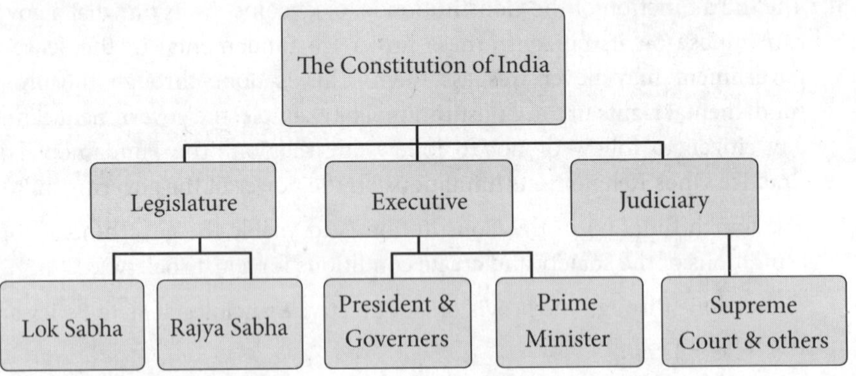

Figure 1.1 depicts the constitutional framework of democratic India.

The first meeting of the Constituent Assembly took place on 9 December 1946. Dr. Sachidanand Sinha was appointed as the temporary President, as he was the oldest member. The Muslim League boycotted the meeting in demand of Pakistan. Dr Rajendra Prasad was elected the President, H.C. Mukherjee as Vice-President, and Sir B.N. Rau as Constitutional Advisor of the Constituent Assembly. Decision-making in the Constituent Assembly was by consensus, accommodation, and by the art of selection and modification.

On 13 December 1946, Jawaharlal Nehru moved the Objectives Resolution in the Assembly. The Assembly adopted the motion to guarantee social, political, and economic justice; freedom of thought, expression, belief, faith, worship, and vocation; equality before law; equality of opportunity; freedom of association and action, subject to law and public morality; etc. for the people. This was passed unanimously on 22 January 1947.

The princely states started joining and by 28 April 1947, a total of 6 states had joined. The Mountbatten Plan was accepted on 3 June 1947 for partition of the country and the India Independence Act was passed. It made the following three changes in the position of the Constituent Assembly:

The Assembly was made a fully sovereign body, which could frame the Constitution as it pleased. It could alter or abrogate any law made by the British Parliament in relation to India.

The Assembly also became a legislative body. Therefore the functions of the Assembly included:

(i) Drafting the Constitution

(ii) Making ordinary laws for free India

Thus, it became the first Parliament of free India (Dominion Legislature). The constituent body was headed/chaired by Dr Rajendra Prasad and the legislative body was chaired by G.V. Mavalankar. This continued till 26 November 1949, until the making of the Constitution was over. The Muslim League members (hailing from areas included in Pakistan) withdrew from the Constituent Assembly.

Some other functions performed by the Constituent Assembly are as follows:

1. Ratified India's membership of the Commonwealth in May 1949.
2. Adopted the National Flag on 22 July 1947.
3. Adopted the National Anthem on 24 January 1950.
4. Adopted the National Song on 24 January 1950.
5. Elected Dr Rajendra Prasad as the first President of India on 24January 1950.

Evolution of the Constitution

The Constitution did not come into existence overnight. Many years and various events led to its culmination. These are as follows:

1922: In the magazine Young India, Mahatma Gandhi talked about self-determination.This was the first time a leader (at a mass scale) talked about the Right to Determine our own political formation as Indians, fully independent from the British.

1928: This was the year the first draft of a document by Motilal Nehru,'Nehru Report', was released. This report was sort of a mini-Constitution, as it outlined the various provisions of self-governance of India by Indians.

1938: Haripura Session of Congress: Here for the first time, Indians made a declaration demanding the formation of a constituent assembly.

1940: August offer: The British for the first time agreed to devising of a constitution for the Indians, partly by Indians.

1942: Cripps offer: This was the first time that the British agreed to devising of a constitution for the Indians by the Indians (fully by Indians).

The Preamble

The Preamble serves two functions:

1. It specifies the source from which the Constitution derives its authority.
2. It states the objects that the Constitution seeks to achieve.

The source of authority of the Constitution, according to the Preamble, are the people of India. It also provides for the nature of Indian state—sovereign, socialist, secular, democratic, republic.

The objectives of the Indian Constitution are justice, liberty, fraternity, and equality, which are mentioned in the Preamble. Preamble is not a source of power to the Legislature nor a prohibition of the powers of the Legislature, hence it plays the role of a guide to the political democratic setup in India. It is not justiciable, that is, it cannot be used in the court of law as a basis for a judgement. The Preamble provides the adoption date of the Constitution as 26 November 1949.

Provisions Adopted from Other Constitutions

The Constitution of India is humongous and borrows many of its provisions from many other such documents across countries. Here are some major borrowings from other countries.

British Constitution

1. First past the post system of voting
2. Parliamentary form of government
3. The idea of the rule of law
4. Institution of the speaker and her/his role in the law-making procedure

United States Constitution

1. Charter of fundamental rights
2. Power of judicial review and independence of the Judiciary

French Constitution

1. Principles of liberty, equality, and fraternity

Canadian Constitution

1. Quasi-federal form of government (a federal system with a strong central government)
2. The idea of residual powers

Irish Constitution

1. Directive Principles of State Policy

Structure of the Indian Constitution

Figure 1.2 shows the structure of the Indian Constitution. The six constituents are described in the following:

1. Preamble: It is a brief opening or introductory statement that lays out the main purpose and guiding principles of the Constitution.
2. Parts: There are a total of 25 parts in the Constitution. For example, Part I—Union and its Territory, Part II—Citizenship, and so on.

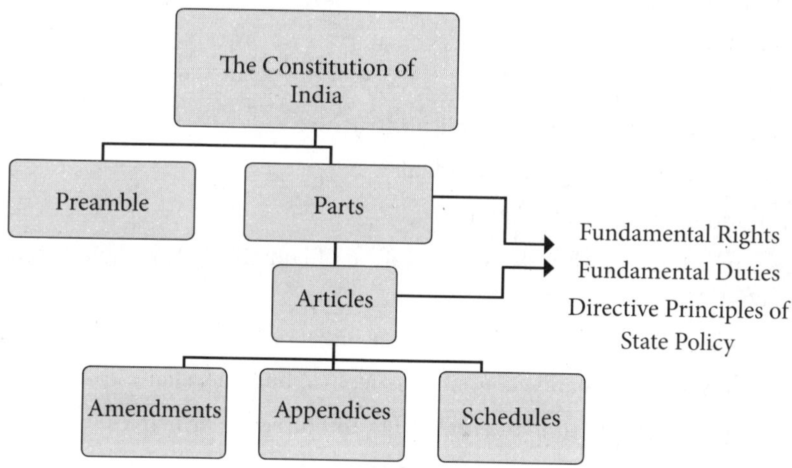

Figure 1.2: Structure of the Indian Constitution

3. Articles: Individual articles are grouped together under the various parts. There are a total of 448 articles at present.
4. Amendments: There have been 100 amendments since Independence. These represent changes in the Constitution through the Parliament.
5. Schedules: These are lists in the Constitution that tabulate the bureaucratic activity and policy of the government.
6. Appendices: These are extensions to the Constitution.

Basic Structure Doctrine of Indian Constitution

In the 1973 Kesavananda Bharati vs. State of Kerala case, the Supreme Court of India adjudicated that the Legislature of India can amend the Constitution of India but cannot destroy the very basic elements or the fundamental features of the Constitution.

Article 368 of the Constitution of India provides for the constituent powers of the Parliament, and lays down the procedure for amendments to the Constitution. As opined by the Supreme Court, the following features seem to emerge as the 'basic structure', so as to be immune from the amending power of the Parliament under Article 368 (However, the Supreme Court has not provided any list. These are just widely accepted components of the basic structure, but are not limited to these only):

1. Supremacy of the Constitution
2. Rule of law
3. The principle of separation of powers
4. The objectives specified in the Preamble to the Constitution
5. Judicial review
6. Articles 32 and 226
7. Federalism
8. Secularism
9. The sovereign, democratic, republican structure
10. Freedom and dignity of the individual
11. Unity and integrity of the nation
12. The principle of equality, not every feature of equality, but the quintessence of equal justice
13. The 'essence' of other fundamental rights in Part III
14. The concept of social and economic justice—to build a welfare state: Part IV in toto
15. The balance between fundamental rights and directive principles
16. The Parliamentary system of government
17. The principle of free and fair elections
18. Limitations upon the amending power conferred by Article 368
19. Independence of the Judiciary
20. Effective access to justice
21. Powers of the Supreme Court under Articles 32, 136, 141, 142
22. Legislation seeking to nullify the awards made in the exercise of the judicial power of the State through the Arbitration Tribunals constituted under an Act.

> *"Basic structure of the Constitution means structural pillars on which the Constitution rests and that if these structural pillars are demolished the entire constitutional framework will crumble."*
>
> — Judge, Anwar Hossain Chowdhury Vs. Bangladesh

Shri Kesavananda Bharthi VS. The State of Kerala [1973]

Background

In the Golaknath vs. State of Punjab case, the judges maintained that the fundamental rights were sacrosanct and transcendental in importance that they could not be restricted even if such a move were to receive unanimous approval of both houses of Parliament. In other words, the Supreme Court held that some features of the Constitution lay at its core.

Did You Know?

The phrase ' basic structure' was introduced for the first time by M.K. Nambiar and other counsels while arguing for the petitioners in the Golaknath Case. But it was only in 1973 that this idea of a 'basic structure' surfaced in the text of the 'Supreme Court's verdict.

Outcomes

- The final verdict was that Parliament's constituent power was the subject to inherent limitations.
- Parliament could not use its amending power under Article 368 to 'damage', 'emmaculate', 'destroy', aboragate', 'change' or 'alter' the 'basic structure' of the frame of the Constitution.
- The judges held the view that the preamble of the Constitution of India is a part of the Constitution.
- The preamble has a significant role to play in the interpretation of statues and also in the interpretation of the powers of the Constitution.

Cases and Amendments related to Basic Structure doctrine

1. **Shankari Prasad Case (1951)**
   - Supreme Court ruled that Parliament can abridge or take away any of the FRs by enacting a constitutional amendment act.
   - This was after first Amendment was passed to curtail Right to property.
   - SC advised so because it remarked that the provision for 'Law' in Article 13 only for ordinary laws and not constitutional amendment act (Constitutional Laws).

2. **Golak Nath Case(1967)**
   - Supreme Court revised its stand (Constitutional validity of 17th amendment act challenged).
   - FRs are of 'transcendental and immutable' position.
   - Parliament cannot abridge or take away any of these rights.

3. **Parliament reacted to this and enacted 24th amendment:** Parliament does have the power to take away any FR through under article 368

Important observations of the makers of the Constitution

"We must make our political democracy a social democracy as well. Political democracy cannot last unless there lies at the base of it social democracy. What does social democracy mean? It means a way of life, which recognises liberty, equality and fraternity as the principles of life. These principles of liberty, equality and fraternity are not to be treated as separate items in a trinity. They form a union of trinity in the sense that to divorce one from the other is to defeat the very purpose of democracy. Liberty cannot be divorced from equality, equality cannot be divorced from liberty. Nor can liberty and equality be divorced from fraternity. Without equality, liberty would produce the supremacy of the few over the many. Equality without liberty would kill individual initiative. Without fraternity, liberty and equality could not become a natural course of things..."

—Dr B.R. Ambedkar
CAD, Vol. XI, p.979
25 November 1949

"... I have realised as nobody else could have, with what zeal and devotion the members of the Drafting Committee and especially its Chairman, Dr. Ambedkar in spite of his indifferent health, have worked. We could never make a decision which was or could be ever so right as when we put him on the Drafting Committee and made him its Chairman. He has not only justified his selection but has added lustre to the work which he has done. In this connection, it would be invidious to make any distinction as among the other members of the Committee. I know they have all worked with the same zeal and devotion as its Chairman, and they deserve the thanks of the country."

—Dr Rajendra Prasad
CAD, Vol. XI, p.994
26 November 1949

4. **Keshvananda Bharti Case (1973) [Origin of Basic Structure doctrine]**
   - SC upholds the 24th amendment act 1971 but activates or introduces a new doctrine of " The Basic Structure" of the constitution .
   - Article 368 does not enable the Parliament to alter the "Basic structure". Parliament cannot take away FRs (fundamental rights) that form its Basic Structure.
5. 42nd Amendment: Parliament reacted to 1973 ruling and declared that amendments under (1970) Article 368 cannot be questioned or challenged in any court
6. **Minerva Mills Case (1980)**
   - SC invalidated this as judicial review is ' Basic Feature' of the constitution
   - Parliament introduced new clauses into Article 368 that transgressed with the judicial review powers of the judiciary and took away the limitations on the amending power of Parliament
   - SC reiterated the principles of the Keshavanand Bharti Case

However there is no specific clarity on the "Basic Structure" itself yet, as the SC has not provided any list or definition of the "Basic Structure"

Features of the Indian Constitution

1. **Lengthiest written constitution in the world:**
    - It is one of the few constitutions in the world which contains fundamental principles of governance as well as administrative details to do so.
    - It has 448 articles in 25 parts, 12 schedules, 5 appendices and 98 amendments.

2. **Drawn from a multitude of sources, including other constitutions:**
    - Dr Ambedkar proudly called the Indian Constitution as being the "ransacking of all the other known constitutions in the world" thereby showcasing the fact that it adopted some of the best features suitable for Indian conditions.

3. **Both rigid and flexible in nature:**
    - Article 368 allows amendment of the Constitution:
        (i) It is rigid in the sense that some provisions can only be amended by two-thirds majority of the members of each House present and voting, and a majority of the total membership of both the Houses.
        (ii) Some provisions need special majority as well as ratification by 50% of the states as well. For example, the GST Act required such an amendment in the Constitution.
    - It is flexible because some amendments do not need Article 368 to be invoked. Some of its provisions can be amended by a simple majority of the Parliament through the ordinary legislative process.

4. **Federal system of government with unitary bias:**
    - The Indian Constitution describes India as a 'Union of States' (Article 1), which implies that the Indian federation is not the result of any agreement among the units, and the units cannot secede from it.

5. **Provides for a Parliamentary form of government:**
    - The Indian Constitution provides for a Parliamentary system of government, i.e., the real executive power rests with the council of ministers and the President is only a nominal ruler (Article 74).

6. **Provides for Parliamentary sovereignty and judicial supremacy:**
    - Parliamentary sovereignty is a feature of the British Constitution while judicial supremacy is a feature of the American Constitution. The Indian constitution provides for both to ensure balance of power.

7. **Provides for an independent judiciary:**
    - Article 76 of the Constitution provides for an independent judiciary to ensure justice for the citizens.

8. **A comprehensive set of fundamental rights:**
    - The Indian Constitution provides an elaborate list of fundamental rights to the citizens of India, which cannot be taken away or abridged by any law made by the states (Articles 12–35).

9. **A strong set of non-justiciable directive principles of state policy:**
    - Articles 36–51 provide a list of principles that the government must keep in mind when formulating any policy.

10. **Fundamental duties:**
    - Article 51A of the Constitution also provides a list of 11 duties of the citizens.

11. **Single citizenship:**
    - Indian citizens can hold only one citizenship. This also makes our constitution unitary in nature.

12. **Universal adult franchise:**
    - Article 326 provides that elections to the House of the People and to the legislative assemblies of the states should be on the basis of adult suffrage. Every person who is a citizen of India and who is not less than eighteen years of age shall be entitled to be registered as a voter at any such election. (Exceptions are there.)

13. **Provision for three-tier government, which eventually manifested in the 73rd and 74th Amendments:**
    - This includes governance institutions at the village and urban levels.

14. **Emergency provisions:**
    - The Constitution vests extraordinary powers, known as Emergency Powers, in the President during emergencies out of armed rebellion or external aggression or due to failure of constitutional machinery in the state (Articles 352–360).

15. A secular state

- It establishes a fully secular state that respects all religions and religious practices.

Fundamental Rights

Fundamental rights are certain basic and inalienable rights that people need in order to live a fulfilling and happy life. In the Indian Constitution, a comprehensive list of fundamental rights has been provided under the charter of rights contained in Part III (Articles 12 to 35). This charter guarantees various civil liberties and enables citizens to lead their lives in peace and harmony. These include rights such as equality before law, freedom of speech and expression, religious and cultural freedom, peaceful assembly, freedom to practice religion, and the right to constitutional remedies for the protection of civil rights.

The right to constitutional remedies (Article 32) has been often termed as the most important right. Dr B.R. Ambedkar called this right the 'heart and soul of the Constitution'. This is because Article 32 provides that any citizen who feels deprived of his or her fundamental right can move the Supreme Court directly by means of writs such as habeas corpus, mandamus, prohibition, certiorari, and quo warranto. Violation of these rights results in punishments as prescribed in the Indian Penal Code or other special laws, subject to the discretion of the Judiciary.

Importance of Fundamental Rights

These rights enable humans to achieve the very basic component of development—freedom. Freedom against debilitating interference from the government and misuse of power by the government against an ordinary citizen, which allows for harmonious development of personality.

Evolution of Fundamental Rights

The rights have their origins in many sources, including England's Bill of Rights, the United States Bill of Rights, and France's Declaration of the Rights of Man.

In England, there is no written constitution and no Bill of Rights. The fundamental rights are more negative in the UK, in that a citizen enjoys all the basic human rights as long as she does not violate any ordinary law of the land. The Judiciary protects the legal rights of citizens in the UK, and protects their rights from the tyranny of the Executive. However, the Judiciary has no power over the Legislature. The Legislature has full power to thwart any of the rights as it pleases. Hence, the supremacy of the Parliament or its 'omnipotence' exists in the UK. Therefore, there is no right that can be said to be 'fundamental' in the proper sense of the word. Another vital consequence of the supremacy of the UK Parliament is that the English Court has no power of judicial review over the legislation at all.

In the US, a Bill of Rights guarantees the fundamental rights to citizens. Here, unlike the UK, the makers of the constitution were apprehensive not only of the tyranny of the Executive but also the Legislature. Therefore, both the Executive and the Legislative cannot change any features of the fundamental rights there. Hence, while in the UK there is 'Parliamentary supremacy', in the US, there is 'Judicial supremacy'. Only the Judiciary is empowered to change the Bill of Rights in face of any emergency or danger to the state.

In India, the Fundamental Rights (Part III) are ensured by the Constitution, and they are explicitly written down. The Indian Constitution affects a compromise between the judicial supremacy and the Parliamentary sovereignty. The fact that India has a written Constitution and its Parliament is subject to limitations imposed by this written Constitution make it different from the British practice. Additionally, there are provisions enshrined in the Constitution of India that enable the judiciary to declare any transgressions of the Parliament as unconstitutional and void. This is laid out in Article 13(2), which says: "The State shall not make any law which takes away or abridges the rights conferred by the Part and any law in contravention of this clause shall, to the extent of the contravention, be void."

The American Bill of Rights does not lay down any limitations to fundamental rights within the Bill itself. The limitations are governed by the Judiciary, for which it has given doctrines such as the Police Power of the State. Unlike that, in India, the Constitution lays down various limitations to fundamental rights next to the rights themselves. Hence, our Constitution follows the American model rather than the English one. However, judicial supremacy in India is weaker than the American model because of the following:

1. Fundamental Rights to Property was made a legal right by the 44th Amendment Act in 1978, hence bringing it under the authority of the Legislature, not the Judiciary.
2. Introduction of Fundamental Duties by the 42nd Amendment Act in 1976 (Article 51A). Though these are not enforceable in the court, a court, in front of which a fundamental right is sought to be enforced, has to read all parts of the Constitution. This means that the court may refuse to enforce the fundamental right in that instance if the individual has patently violated any of the duties specified in Article 51A. Therefore, the original provision of fundamental rights has been effectively minimized.

The American Constitution expressly says that the enumeration of certain rights in the Bill of Rights shall not be construed to deny or disparage others retained by the people. Therefore, it introduces the concept of natural rights that people have, regardless of whether mentioned in the Bill of Rights. There is no such provision in the Indian Constitution. This means that Article 32 can be applied only to seek judicial review of the fundamental rights mentioned in Part III, and this article cannot be applied to other interpretations of 'rights' if brought to the court.

Know Your Fundamental Rights and Learn to Use them	
Right to Equlity	Article 14:- Equality before law and equal protection of law Article 15:- Prohibition of discrimination on grounds only of religion, race, caste, sex or place of birth. Article 16:- Equality of opportunity in matters of public employment Article 17:- End of untouchability Article 18:- Abolition of titles, Military and academic distinctions are however, exempted

Know Your Fundamental Rights and Learn to Use them	
Right to Freedom	Article 19:- It guarantees the citizens of India the following six fundamental freedoms: Freedom to Speech and Expression Freedom to Assembly Freedom to form Associations Freedom to Movement Freedom to Residence and Settlement Freedom to Profession, Occupation, Trade or Business Article 20:- Protection in respect of conviction for offences Article 21:- Protection of life and personal liberty. Article 22:- Protection against arrest and detention in certain cases.
Right Against Exploitation	Article 23:- Trafficking in human beings is prohibited. Article 24:- No child below the age of 14 can be employed.
Right to freedom of Religion	Article 25:- Freedom of conscience and free profession, practice and propagation of religion. Article 26:- Freedom to manage religious affairs. Article 27:- Prohibits taxes on religious grounds. Article 28:- Freedom as to attendance at religious ceremonies in certain educational institutions.
Cultural and Educational Rights	Article 29:- Protection of interests of minorities. Article 30:- Right of minorities to establish and administer educational institutions. Article 31:- Omitted by the 44th Amendment Act.
Right to Constitutional Remedies	Article 32:- The right to move to Supreme Court in case of the violation of FRs (called soul and heart of the Constitution by BR Ambedkar) .

Constitutional Amendments

The basic structure of the Constitution is unchangeable. The amendments that do not affect the basic structure can be carried out in the following ways:

1. By simple majority of the Parliament.
2. By special majority of the Parliament.
3. By special majority of the Parliament and ratification by the states.

Procedure for Amendments to the Constitution

Article 368 of the Constitution provides for the Constitutional Amendment Act in the Parliament and the rules related to it. It stipulates certain conditions:

- An amendment can be initiated in any House of the Parliament, not in state legislatures, by the introduction of a bill.
- It can be introduced by any member of the Parliament and does not need prior recommendation of the President.

- Each house must pass the bill separately and no provision for joint sitting is provided under this amendment procedure. The provision for joint sitting of the Houses is only for ordinary bills via Article 108 but not for constitutional amendment bills.
- After the two Houses pass an amendment, the President must give his assent to it. He cannot withhold his assent nor return the bill for reconsideration of the Houses.
- It is obligatory for the President to give his assent to a constitutional amendment bill under Article 368.

Types of Amendments

Article 368 provides for only two types of amendments.

Amendments needing Special Majority

The amendable parts of the Constitution under this type are

- Fundamental rights
- Directive Principles of State Policy

Such amendments need the majority of the total membership of each House (50% membership) separately and a majority of two-thirds of those present and voting in each House separately.

Amendments Needing Special Majority and ratification by at Least 50% of the States

Amendments dealing with the federal nature of the Constitution require special majority of the Houses and also consent of at least 50% of the states. This means that at least 50% of the state legislatures must pass the bill as well by simple majority. Examples are

- Election of the President
- Extent of the executive powers of the states and the Union
- Supreme and high courts
- Distribution of legislative powers between states and the Union
- Any item on the list in the 7th Schedule
- Representation of states in the Parliament
- Power of the Parliament to amend the Constitution and its procedures (Article 368 itself)

An amendment can also be made by simple majority of the Houses, but such an amendment does not fall under Article 368 (i.e., not under the Constitution). Some examples are as follows:

- Admission or establishment of new states.
- Formation of new states and alteration of areas, boundaries, or names of existing states.
- Abolition or creation of legislative councils in states.
- Second schedule—emoluments, allowances, privileges, and so on of the President, governors, Speaker, and judges.

- Quorum in the Parliament.
- Salaries and allowances and privileges of the members of Parliament.
- Rules of procedure in the Parliament.
- Use of English in the Parliament.
- Number of puisne judges in the SC.
- Conferment of more jurisdiction to the SC.
- Use of official language.
- Citizenship.
- Elections to the Parliament and state legislatures.
- Delimitation.
- Union territories.
- 5th Schedule—Scheduled areas and STs.
- 6th schedule—Tribal areas.

Unamendable Parts of the Constitution

Until the Golaknath case, the Supreme Court (SC) held that no part of the Constitution of India was unamendable. The word 'law' in Article 13 referred to ordinary laws made by the Parliament in its legislative capacity and not to constitutional amendment acts made under its constituent capacity. In the Golaknath case, the SC held that constitutional amending power was a legislative power conferred upon the Parliament by Article 245. So a constitutional amendment act is also a law under Article 13. This meant that the fundamental rights cannot be amended by the Parliament as they have been given a transcendental position under the Constitution.

After the Golaknath verdict, the Parliament sought to supersede it via the 24th Constitutional Amendment Act, 1971, by specifying in Article 368 that a constitutional amendment act under Article 368 will not be a 'law 'with respect to Article 13. The validity of the 24th Constitutional Amendment Act was challenged in the Kesavananda case, where it was held valid. However, the doctrine of basic features was propounded.

The 42nd Constitutional Amendment Act, 1976

Judicial review of ordinary laws

For the first time, a distinction was made between union laws and state laws for challenging their validity on the grounds of unconstitutionality. It was provided that a high court cannot pass judgements on a central law and the SC cannot pass judgements on a state law unless a central law had also been questioned in the same proceedings.

Judicial review of constitutional amendment acts

It was provided that a constitutional amendment act will be completely immune from a judicial review whether on substantive or procedural grounds. The procedural provision was absurd. It introduced fundamental duties. It devalued fundamental rights by expanding the scope of Article 31C to include any law to implement any of the directives.

Federalism

Article 1 of the Indian Constitution says, "India, that is Bharat, is a Union of States." The fact that the Indian Constitution has declared Indian polity as a 'unitary' one instead of a federal one raises questions about the exact nature of our Constitution. On the contrary, the Supreme Court has declared in its judgement that the Indian Constitution is a federal one. There are various features that make the Indian Constitution a federal structure rather than a unitary one.

Early Years of Independence

Dr B.R. Ambedkar had clearly argued in the constitutional amendment debates that the word 'union' has been deliberately used because India was not created by an agreement of different states. Infact, the Union is indestructible but the states are not. However, federalism was promoted in the early years of Independence by:

1. Setting up of a National Development Council in 1952
2. Setting up of a National Integration Council in 1962
3. Holding annual conferences between the Centre and state chief ministers on finance, labour, food, and other functional areas.

Federal features of the Constitution of India

1. Written constitution
2. Rajya Sabha
3. Distribution of power between the Centre and the states vide the 7th Schedule of the Constitution
4. Independent Judiciary
5. Dual system of governance with a government at the Centre as well as a government at the state level
6. Supremacy of the Constitution

Unitary features

1. Residuary powers lie with the Centre and not the states, as in the US
2. Overwhelming taxation powers of the Centre
3. Single citizenship

4. Integrated Judiciary with the Supreme Court at the apex level.
5. Position of governor vis-à-vis the state executive
6. Emergency powers of the Centre under Articles 356, 352, and 365
7. All-India services

Hence, it can be said that Indian polity is federal with peculiar unitary features.

Cooperative federalism

Indian federalism can be more accurately described as 'cooperative' federalism. It has all the features of a federal structure as described already and gives ample power to the states to run their governments, impose taxes, and decide on various policies on development. In this matter, the Central Government assists the states in carrying out these plans through grants, and also ensures that the integrity of the nation is maintained.

More recently, cooperative federalism has become even more relevant, as the Planning Commission has been scrapped and the National Institution for Transforming India (NITI Aayog) has been established.

Removal of Governor

In 2010, the then Chief Justice of India, K.G. Balakrishnan, ruled that no governor can be removed on the basis of being "out of sync with policies and ideologies of Union Government." This decision also states that governors can be removed, but there must be 'compelling' reasons for doing so. The principle of natural justice must be followed, and the governor must be given a chance to explain his/her position.

Rules and Recommendations

The Constitution of India says, as per its Articles 155 and 156, that a governor is appointed on the pleasure of the President. This 'pleasure doctrine' has been used by the Central Government to cut down the tenures of governors without giving any reasons on too many occasions. This ugly practice of sacking governors without any reason has been the subject matter of three important commissions. Each commission has come up with their recommendations in this regard.

1. The Sarkaria Commission (1988) recommended that governors must not be removed before completion of their five-year tenure, except in rare and compelling circumstances. This was meant to provide governors with a measure of security of tenure, so that they could carry out their duties without fear or favour. If rare and compelling circumstances warranting the removal of governors did exist, the Commission said that the procedure of removal must allow the governors an opportunity to explain their conduct, and the Central Government must give fair consideration to such explanation. It was further recommended that governors should be informed of the grounds of their removal.

2. The Venkatachaliah Commission (2002) similarly recommended that ordinarily governors should be allowed to complete their five-year term. If they have to be removed before completion of their term, the Central Government should do so only after consultation with the chief minister of the state.
3. The Punchhi Commission (2010) suggested that the phrase "on the pleasure of the President" should be deleted from the Constitution, because a governor should not be removed at the will of the Central Government; instead he or she should be removed only by a resolution of the state legislature.

The B.P. Singhal v. Union of India case

The newly elected Central Government, under the prime ministership of Dr Manmohan Singh, had removed the governors of Uttar Pradesh, Gujarat, Haryana, and Goa in July 2004 after the 14th Lok Sabha election. When these removals were challenged in the B.P. Singhal vs. Union of India case, the Supreme Court held:

1. The President, in effect the Central Government, has the power to remove a governor at any time without giving him or her any reason, and without granting an opportunity to be heard.
2. However, this power cannot be exercised in an arbitrary, capricious, or unreasonable manner. The power of removing governors should only be exercised in rare and exceptional circumstances for valid and compelling reasons.
3. The mere reason that a governor is at variance with the policies and ideologies of the Central Government, or that the Central Government has lost confidence in him or her, is not sufficient to remove a governor. Thus, a change in the Central Government cannot be a ground for removal of governors, or to appoint more favourable persons to this post.
4. A decision to remove a governor can be challenged in a court of law. In such cases, first the petitioner will have to make a prima facie case of arbitrariness or bad faith on part of the Central Government. If a prima facie case is established, the court can require the Central Government to produce the materials on the basis of which the decision was made in order to verify the presence of compelling reasons.

In summary, this means that the Central Government enjoys the power to remove governors of states, as long as it does not act arbitrarily, without reason, or in bad faith.

Important Amendments to the Constitution

As of January 2018, there have been 123 Amendment Bills and 101 Amendment Acts to the Constitution of India since it was first enacted in 1950. Some of the important ones are given in brief here.

1st Amendment, 1951

- Empowered the State to make special efforts for the advancement of socially and economically backward classes.
- Provided for the saving of laws providing for the acquisition of estates, etc.(via Articles 31a, 31b, 31c)
- Added the 9th Schedule to protect land reform and other laws included in it from the judicial review.
- Added three more grounds of restrictions on freedom of speech and expression, namely, public order, friendly relations with foreign states, and incitement to an offence. Also made the restrictions 'reasonable' and, thus, justifiable in nature.
- Provided that state trading and nationalization of any trade or business by the state is not to be invalid on the ground of violation of the right to trade or business.

6th Amendment, 1956

- Included a new subject in the Union List, i.e., taxes on the sale and purchase of goods in the course of interstate trade and commerce, and restricted the state's power in this regard.

8th Amendment, 1960

- It extended the period of reservation of seats for Scheduled Castes and Scheduled Tribes and Anglo-Indians in the Lok Sabha and the state legislative assemblies till 1970.
- It amended Article 334 of the Constitution.

10th Amendment, 1961

- Incorporation of Dadra, Nagar, and Haveli as a union territory, consequent to acquisition from Portugal.
- It amended Article 240 of the Constitution.

13th Amendment, 1963

- Formation of the state of Nagaland, with special protection under Article 371A.
- It amended Article 170.

15th Amendment, 1963

- Enabled the high courts to issue writs to any person or authority even outside its territorial jurisdiction if the cause of action arises within its territorial limits.
- Increased the retirement age of high court judges from 60 to 62 years.
- Provided for appointment of retired high court judges as acting judges of the same court.

- Provided compensatory allowance to judges who are transferred from one high court to another.
- Enabled retired high court judges to act as adhoc judges of the Supreme Court.
- Provided for the procedure for determining the age of the Supreme Court and high court judges.

24th Amendment, 1971

- Affirmed the power of the Parliament to amend any part of the Constitution including the Fundamental Rights.
- Made it compulsory for the President to give his assent to a constitutional amendment bill.

36th Amendment, 1975

- By this amendment, Sikkim became the 22nd state of the Indian Union.

39th Amendment, 1975

- The Bill was passed by the Lok Sabha on August 7 and received Presidential Assent on 9 August1975.
- The Act places beyond challenge in courts the election to the Parliament of a person holding the office of Prime Minister or Speaker and the election of the President and Vice-President.

40th Amendment, 1976

- Empowered the Parliament to specify from time to time the limits of the territorial waters, the continental shelf, the exclusive economic zone (EEZ), and the maritime zones of India.
- Included 64 more central and state laws, mostly relating to land reforms, in the 9th Schedule.

42nd Amendment, 1976

- It was enacted during the period of internal emergency. It was passed by the Parliament on 11 November 1976 and received Presidential Assent on 18 December 1976.
- The amendment established beyond doubt the supremacy of the Parliament over the other wings of the Government; gave the Directive Principles precedence over the Fundamental Rights; enumerated for the first time a set of 10 Fundamental Duties.
- It further imposed limits on the power and jurisdiction of the Judiciary, raised the term of the Lok Sabha and the Vidhan Sabha from five to six years, authorized the use of the central armed forces in any state to deal with law and order problems, bound

the President by the advice of the Council of Ministers, and envisaged the establishment of administrative tribunals for service matters of government employees as well as other tribunals for economic offences.

- The Act also clearly laid down that no constitutional amendment could be questioned in any court of law.

43rd Amendment, 1978

- It received the Presidential Assent on 13 April 1978.
- This act repealed the provisions of the Constitution (42nd Amendment) Act passed during the Emergency. It restored civil liberties by deleting Article 3ID, which gave powers to the Parliament to curtail even legitimate trade union activity under the guise of legislation for the prevention of anti-national activities.
- The new law, which was ratified by more than half of the states in accordance with the Constitution, also restored legislative powers to the states to make appropriate provisions for anti-national activities consistent with the Fundamental Rights. Under the Act, the Judiciary was also restored to its rightful place.
- The Supreme Court now has the power to invalidate state laws, a power taken away by the 42nd Amendment Act. The high courts will also be able to go into the question of the constitutional validity of central laws, thereby enabling persons living in distant places to obtain speedy justice without having to come to the Supreme Court.

44th Amendment, 1978

- The Constitution (45th Amendment) Bill, renumbered as the 44th Amendment, came into force on 30 April 1979, when the President gave his assent.
- The Act removed major distortions in the Constitution introduced during the Emergency. The durations of the Lok Sabha and state legislative assemblies have been reduced from six to five years—the normal term, which was extended during the Emergency under the 42nd Amendment to achieve some political purposes.
- The Right to Property ceased to be a Fundamental Right and has become only a legal right.
- The Act also extended, for the first time since Independence, constitutional protection for publication of the proceedings of the Parliament and state legislatures, except in cases where it is proved to be 'malicious'. Another important feature of the Act is that, henceforward, any proclamation of Emergency can be issued by the President only after receiving the advice of the Cabinet as a whole in writing. The President will not be called upon to act on the basis of advice by the Prime Minister on his own without consulting his Cabinet. Other safeguards provide that the proclamation will have to be adopted by a two-thirds majority of the members of both houses of the Parliament within a month.

- The Amendment provides safeguards against future subversion of the Constitution for establishing an authoritarian regime. It contains provisions that are designed to make it impossible to impose the kind of emergency the country experienced for a 19-month period in 1975–77.

46th Amendment, 1982

- It sought to authorize the Government to prepare an authoritative text of the Constitution in Hindi.

52nd Amendment, 1985

- The Act made defection to another party, after elections, illegal. Any member defecting to another party after elections will be disqualified from being a member of the Parliament or state legislature.

61st Amendment, 1989

- It lowered the voting age from 21 to 18.

69th Amendment, 1991

- This Amendment designated Delhi as National Capital Territory of Delhi. The Act also made the provision for a legislative assembly and a council of ministers for Delhi.

71st Amendment, 1992

- The Act amended the 8th Schedule to the Constitution to include Konkani, Manipuri, and Nepali languages in it.

73rd Amendment, 1992

- Ensures direct election to all seats in panchayats, reserves seats for SCs and STs in proportion to their population, and secures reservation of not less than one-third of the seats in panchayats for women.

74th Amendment, 1992

- This Amendment ensures direct election to all seats in nagarpalikas and municipalities.

86th Amendment, 2002

- Provided for Right to Education until the age of 14 and early childhood care until the age of six.

87th Amendment, 2003

- Provided for readjustment and rationalization of territorial constituencies in the states on the basis of the population figures of 2001 census, and not the 1991 census as provided earlier by the 84thAmendment Act of 2001.

89th Amendment, 2003

- Bifurcated the erstwhile combined National Commission for Scheduled Castes and Scheduled Tribes into two separate bodies, namely, National Commission for SCs (Article338) and National Commission for STs (338A).

90th Amendment, 2003

- Provided for maintaining the erstwhile representation of the Scheduled Tribes in the Assam Legislative Assembly from the Bodoland Territorial Areas District [Article 332 (6)].

91st Amendment, 2004

- Restricted the size of the council of ministers to 15 percent of legislative members and strengthened anti-defection laws.

92nd Amendment, 2004

- Included Bodo, Dogri, Santhali, and Maithili as official languages.

93rd Amendment, 2006

- Provided for 27 percent reservation for other backward classes in government as well as private higher educational institutions.

97th Amendment, 2012

- Added the words "or co-operative societies" after the words "or unions" in Article 19(l) (c) and inserted Article 43B related to promotion of co-operative societies and added Part IX B, that is, "The Co-operative Societies".

98th Amendment, 2013

- Empowered the Governor of Karnataka to take steps to develop the Hyderabad-Karnataka region.

99th Amendment, 2014

- The amendment provided for the formation of a National Judicial Appointments Commission.

100th Amendment, 2015

- The Constitution (100th Amendment) Act, 2015, was in news in the fourth week of May 2015, as the President of India Pranab Mukherjee gave his assent to the Constitution (119th Amendment) Bill, 2013, that related to the Land Boundary Agreement between India and Bangladesh.

President's Rule

Article 356 of the Constitution enables the Centre to impose President's rule in states on the occasion of failure of constitutional machinery in the states. This matter was hotly debated in Constituent Assembly debates, as many members felt that this could lead to instability in the Indian federal system and cause irreparable harm to the functioning of state governments. Dr B.R. Ambedkar had referred to provisions related to President's Rule as a dead letter of the Constitution.

Need for President's Rule

India is a young polity with a diversity of languages, ethnicities, religions, and regional practices. The unity of the nation is of supreme importance and, hence, this provision allows the Centre to check any usurpation of power or unconstitutional actions by the states. The power under Article 356 can be used in order to ensure that the constitutional machinery is working as per the provisions of the Constitution in the states.

Unfortunately, India saw an unchecked and arbitrary use of this power by the Centre in the 1960s, 1970s, and 1980s. This period saw the Centre overthrowing many legitimately elected state legislatures and ruling the states by proxy by imposition of President's Rule. Eventually, it was the Supreme Court in the S.R. Bommai case in 1993that laid down the guidelines under which President's Rule could be imposed. These are as follows:

1. The Proclamation of President's Rule is subject to judicial review on grounds of mala fide intention.
2. The Proclamation shall be based on relevant material and the Centre has to justify the imposition of President's Rule.
3. The court has the power to revive a dissolved or suspended state government if the proclamation of President's Rule is found unconstitutional and invalid.
4. The state assembly cannot be dissolved before approval by the Parliament for the imposition of President's Rule, and only the President can suspend the assembly.
5. The grounds of serious allegations of corruption against the ministers of a state or a state's financial instability are not enough for the imposition of President's Rule.
6. The state government shall be given enough opportunities to correct itself in cases where directives are issued.
7. Secularism is the basic feature of our constitution and any measure or action, if taken by the state government for the security of this feature, cannot lead to the use of Article 356.

8. Power under Article 356 cannot be used to sort out intra-party problems of the ruling party.
9. If the ministry of a state resigns or is dismissed or loses majority, then the governor cannot advise the President to impose President's Rule until enough measures are taken by the governor for the formation of an alternative government.
10. The SC held that power under Article 356 is exceptional power, to be used only in case of exigencies.

Sarkaria Commission Recommendations

The Commission noted that this Article has been misused in more than 90% of the cases for political purposes. So it recommended as follows:

1. The President's Proclamation should include the 'reasons' why the state cannot be run as per the normal provisions of the Constitution.
2. As far as possible, the Centre should issue a warning to the state government before resorting to the use of Article 356.
3. It should not be used to serve political purposes.
4. Article 356 should be amended so that the President is empowered to dissolve the state legislature only after approval by the Parliament.

Punchhi Commission

1. On the question of invoking Article 356 in case of the failure of the Constitutional machinery in the states, the Commission recommended suitable amendments to incorporate the guidelines set forth in the landmark judgement of the Supreme Court in the S.R. Bommai v. Union of India (1994) case.
2. The Commission recommended a provision of 'localized emergency', which means that the Centre can tackle issues at the town/district level without dissolving the state legislative assembly while at same time carrying out the duty of the Union to protect the states under Article 355.
3. It is, however, necessary that a legal framework for exercising the power of 'localized emergency' is provided by an independent statute borrowing the model of the Disaster Management Act, 2005, and the Prevention of Communal Violence and Rehabilitation Bill, 2006.
4. Only exceptional situations that fall within the scope of 'external aggression' or 'internal disturbance' should be considered for the purposes of a separate legislation under the mandate of Article 355.

———XXXX———

Practice Questions (Main Examination)

1. Do you think partisan federalism is acting as impediment to cooperative federalism? Examine how the Supreme Court can end partisan federalism in India.

Answer: Federalism can be defined as the form of government in which the Central or Federal Government is merged with regional or state governments in a single political system. Federalism is a part of the basic structure of the Constitution of India (as provided by the Supreme Court). The manifestations of partisan federalism are as follows:

1. **Appointment of governors** : Despite the Supreme Court guidelines on the removal of the governor (B.P. Singhal v. UoI) and on the office of the governor (Hargobind Kaur v. Raghuku l), successive governments have undermined this office and created conditions averse to cooperative federalism.

2. **Application of President's Rule**: Article 356 deals with the imposition of President's Rule over the state of India. When a state is under President's Rule, the elected state government (led by the Chief Minister and the Council of Ministers) is dismissed, the Council of Ministers is suspended at the Legislature, and administration is conducted directly by the Governor of the state. The Governor is an appointee of the President and thus, effectively, a functionary of the Union Government. Article 356 has been used repeatedly by central governments to suspend state governments (mostly run by opposite political parties) based on genuine reasons or trumped-up excuses. This practice of invoking Article 356 to dismiss state governments for reasons fair or unfair came to be questioned in the S.R. Bommai case in the Supreme Court. (The Bommai-led Janta Dal Government in the state of Karnataka was dismissed by invoking Article 356 in April 1989.)The judgement in the S.R. Bommai case was a landmark one in regard to the application of Article 356.In its judgement in the Bommai case, the SC ruled that the President's Rule should be a measure of last resort. Though this judgement has laid out guidelines for the imposition of President's Rule and reduced the scope of its misuse, its very use is seen as denting the spirit of cooperative federalism.

Use of Governor's Office: The office of governor is at times used to reserve bills, mischievously, of state(s) governed by an opposition party for President's approval. This dents the spirit of cooperative federalism. To strengthen federalism, the Centre has taken the following steps to strengthen the rubric of cooperative federalism in the country:

1. The passage of the 101st Constitution Amendment Bill by an effective process of consultation with state governments and addressing their concerns through the Empowered Group of Finance Ministers is a shining example of cooperative federalism.
2. The implementation of the Report of the 14th Finance Commission, accepting greater devolution of taxes to the states, also indicates strengthening of fiscal federalism.
3. The present central government has laid emphasis on cooperative and competitive federalism and seeks the states' support in many of its key initiatives such as Make in India, Swachh Bharat Abhiyan, etc.

Implementing the guidelines issued by the Supreme Court in the S.R. Bommai case verdict with respect to the imposition of President's Rule, the recommendations made with respect to the appointment of governors as per the B.P. Singhal case should be followed, and other steps must be taken to strengthen the rubric of federalism and good governance.

2. Are Inter-State Council becoming irrelevant due to NITI Aayog? Should they be merged?

Answer: The Inter-State Council (ISC) was envisioned under Article 263 of the Constitution, but was made operational only since 1990 (on the recommendations of the Sarkaria Commission and the First Administrative Reforms Commission—First ARC).The ISC was set up as an instrument for cooperation, coordination, and evolution of common policies between the Centre and the states. The ISC was revived recently with a discussion on the following topics:

1. Direct benefit transfers using Aadhaar
2. Education
3. Internal security.
4. The Punchhi Commission report on centre-state relations

Problems:

1. The ISC has met just 11 times in the past 26 years.
2. The National Development Council (NDC), which was established to discuss planning issues with states, sidelined the ISC.
3. The ISC has not been given all the powers envisaged under the Constitution.

Solutions:

1. The ISC needs to be given all the powers contemplated under Article 263 of the Constitution, which gave the council the power to investigate issues of interstate conflict.
2. The ISC should provide greater opportunities to civil society institutions and the corporate sector to make their representations.
3. Merge the two: The ISC and NITI Aayog should be merged into one constitutional forum to improve the institutional participation of state governments. Such a merger will enhance the institutional status of the NITI Aayog by being attached to a constitutional body, i.e., the ISC.
4. Its secretariat should be shifted from the Union Home Ministry to the Rajya Sabha secretariat for better functioning.
5. Along with another constitutionally sanctioned entity—the Finance Commission (FC)—the ISC should be the body that puts the 'federation' back in the definition of 'Indian nation'. Together, the FC and the ISC should operationalize Parts XI and XII of

the Constitution, which ensure appropriate financial devolution and political decentralization.

3. The rights-based approach is giving rise to a new trend in Indian constitutional governance, that is, the DPSPs are getting preference over Fundamental Rights. Identify such trends and analyse their pros and cons.

Answer: The rights-based approach refers to fulfilling various economic, social, and political ends of a society by viewing them as inalienable and inseparable 'rights' and not just as obligations.

For instance, as provided by DPSP earlier, educational rights for 6 to 14 year old children were not fundamental in nature. The passage of the RTE Act has made this a fundamental right, which is justiciable.

Similarly, DPSPs such as legal aid for the poor, nutrition for all sections of the society, child rights, and so on are also viewed more and more to be fundamental rather than just as directive objectives to be fulfilled by the state.

This could even lead to a compromise of rights by the government. For instance, Aadhaar identification to deliver various services could compromise on citizens' basic right to privacy, as established in the R. Rajagopalan Case by the Supreme Court.

The need of the hour is for the state to be able to view fundamental rights as complementary to the directive principles that have to be fulfilled and protected side by side.

Overview of the Chapter

UPSC Syllabus Covered:

- Salient features of the Representation of People's Act.
- Appointment to various Constitutional posts, powers, functions and responsibilities of various Constitutional Bodies.
- Statutory, regulatory and various quasi-judicial bodies.

Answer Writing Tips:

- You are advised to start the paper as soon as you receive it in the examination hall. Do not read or go through the paper. Read the first question and start writing if you know it well. If you are not sure, quickly move to the second question and so on. This will save time.
- Time yourself really well. Keep a stop-watch to consistently see how much time you are spending on every question. Once you do this a lot in practice, you will become a master of timing the questions without worrying about the word limit.
- Read the question twice or three to four times if you do not understand it. Do not go too deep into the introductory statement UPSC makes in questions. Focus on more on the later part of the question where UPSC actually asks. Sometimes the introductory statements can be slightly misleading. UPSC actually asks the main part of the question.

2

Elections in India

"I mean to diminish no individual, institution or phase in our history when I say that India is valued the world over for a great many things, but for three over all others: The TajMahal; Mahatma Gandhi; and India's electoral democracy. "

— Gopalkrishna Gandhi (2013)

Introduction

India's has built one of the most robust election machineries seen in any democracy around the world. An independent Election Commission (the apex electoral body of India) along with a robust set of laws (Representation of People's Act 1950, 1951) ensures that elections in India are held through a transparent and accountable mechanism. In addition, several debates surround the efficacy of the current system and whether it is suited to serving the needs of an evolving democracy. This chapter covers various theoretical and practical aspects of India's election system. It aims to built a solid conceptual as well as working understanding of elections in India through a constitutional and judicial point of view, which is must for the UPSC civil services exam

First-Past-the-Post System

The first-past-the-post (FPTP) system, followed in the Lok Sabha elections in India, is regarded as one of the simplest forms of electoral systems, where each voter has a single vote and where a candidate wins if he/she receives the highest number of votes cast in a constituency. During the drafting of the Constitution, various systems of proportional representation were considered, but the FPTP system was eventually adopted to avoid fragmented legislatures and to facilitate the formation of stable governments.

Merits and Demerits of FPTP System

Simplicity

The most significant advantage of the FPTP system is its uncomplicated nature. The FPTP system is the simplest form of the plurality/majority system, using single-member districts and candidate-centred voting. Moreover, the FPTP system allows voters to choose between people as well as parties, with voters having the opportunity to assess the performance of a candidate rather than having to accept a list of candidates presented by a party, as under the list system. This system, however, is thought to result in an increase in election expenditure, since every candidate is required to reach out to the electors on an individual as well as at the party level.

Stability

The FPTP system has been the hallmark of stability in the electoral system of India. The Supreme Court in RC Poudyal v. Union of India had categorized the FPTP system as possessing "the merit of preponderance of decisiveness over representativeness." The system presents the advantage of producing a majority government at a general election by being decisive, simple and familiar to the electorate. This at least in theory, assures stable terms for the party in power, with the requisite representation in the House, to ensure the implementation of its policies. It also means better accountability for decision-making in the Parliament, since this system makes it easier for voters to identify who to vote for or not to vote for in the future. In practice, India has seen both stable majority and unstable coalition governments under the FPTP system, indicating that it is not this factor alone that assures the stability of the electoral system in India.

Representativeness

The principal criticism levelled against the FPTP system is that it leads to the exclusion of small or regional parties from the Parliament. There is generally a discrepancy between the vote share and seat share in the results, as the votes given to smaller parties are 'wasted' since they do not gain a voice in the legislature. What this often translates into is that the FPTP system, which boasts of the fact that it provides a majoritarian (and hence more democratic) government, is itself not able to adequately uphold majoritarianism in a multiparty system, since the winning candidate may win only about 20–30% of the votes.

Examples abound from Lok Sabha and state assembly elections, where parties enjoying significant vote shares have failed to translate them into seats. For example, the Indian National Congress won only about 49. 10% of the total vote share in the 1984 General Elections to the Lok Sabha, but had a sweeping majority of 405 out of 515 seats in the House. In the elections to the Tamil Nadu Legislative Assembly in 1996, the AIADMK polled 21. 47% votes, but could secure only four (1. 71%) seats in the state legislature.

Smaller parties, when they have a broad base across constituencies rather than a concentrated following in a few constituencies, may fail to win even a single seat even if their vote share is significant. This also means that slight swings in the vote share cause dramatic changes in the number of Parliamentary seats won or lost, causing the Indian electorate to be characterized as one that decisively swings in one direction or the other.

On the other hand, while the representativeness of political parties is not ensured in the FPTP system, it does encourage political parties themselves to have a more broad-based participation. Moreover, it ensures that there is a link between a constituency and its representative in the legislature and incentivizes representatives to serve their constituents well. Further, smaller constituencies are more likely to comprise common interests. The small size also facilitates better delineation of regional interests through increased movements at the grass-roots level. This ensures that representatives interact more closely with the constituents, at least in theory. This might, however, not hold true for constituencies with large populations.

Proportional Representation System

There has been a debate about whether India should switch from first-past-the-post system to proportional representation since the setting up of constituent assembly. Many legal luminaries and constitutionalists had argued for having a proportional representation system as it has many merits over first past the post system. In this context, it is important to understand this system as it continues to be part of various debates about the future of India electoral system.

In the proportional representation (PR) system, once the votes are counted, each party is allotted the share of seats in the Parliament in proportion to its share of votes. Each political party declares a preference list of candidates before the elections. It fills its quota of seats by picking the required number of nominees based on the number of votes won. This system of is known as the party list PR system. For example, if the Conservative party wins 36.1% of the votes, as shown in Fig 2.1, it will get a proportional number of seats, i.e., 306 seats out of a total of 850 and so on for other parties.

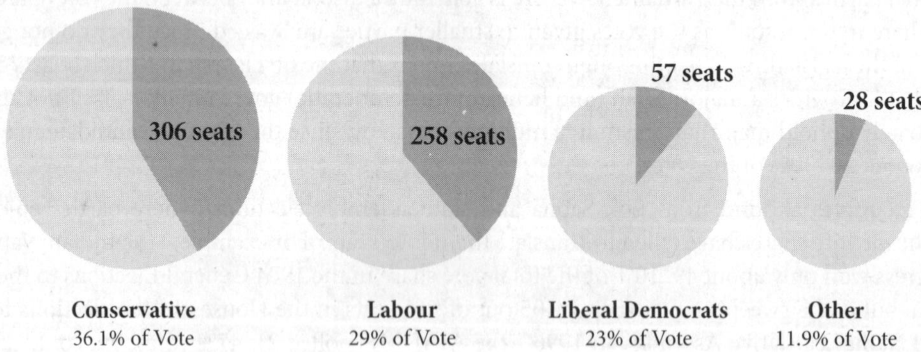

Figure 2. 1: Proportional representation electoral system

Merits and Demerits of Proportional Representation System

Simplicity

Proportional representation undoubtedly falls second in competition with the FPTP system in terms of simplicity in voting, but scores higher in terms of convenience during the campaign. Candidates can simply focus pointed attention on defined groups to appeal to, and consequently, the problems of campaign financing do not feature as prominently in the process.

Stability

As parties are granted seats in accordance with their vote share, numerous parties get seats in the legislature in the proportional representation system, reducing the scope for any party gaining a majority. This detracts from the stability of the system. A coalition government becomes inevitable, along with the challenges that accompany such governments. This is also why the Constituent Assembly decided that proportional representation would not be suited to the Parliamentary form of government that our Constitution lays down.

Representativeness

Proportional representation, as the name suggests, tries to ensure that the election results are as proportional as possible by curbing the inconsistency between the share of seats and votes. It ensures that smaller parties get representation in the legislature, particularly when they have a broad base across constituencies. It also encourages new parties to emerge and more women and minorities to contest for political power.

Proportional representation, particularly the single transferable vote variant of it, also ensures that voters do not feel encumbered by tactical voting strategies in the worry that their vote might go 'waste'. In that sense, proportional representation ensures honesty in the election process both from the side of the candidate, who can choose their ideological commitments freely, and from that of the voter who can vote freely.

One potential drawback of this system is that the relationship between a voter and the candidate may dilute, for the candidate may now be seen as representing the party and not the constituency. The other way of looking at this is that a constituent could approach any representative of their choice in case of a grievance, which plays out as an advantage of this system.

Detractors of the list system of proportional representation point out, however, that while the method ensures that more political parties are represented, it concentrates power, within a political party, in the hands of the leaders who decide on the list of candidates.

Electoral Reforms

Reforms in the election procedure are a must to ensure that muscle and money power do not manipulate this process for the benefit of malicious characters in our democracy. The Parliament and state legislatures are supreme bodies to ensure such reforms. To this end, the various constitutional provisions are as follows:

1. Articles 327 and 328 of the Constitution confer power on the Parliament and state legislature (where laws made by the Parliament are either not there or inadequate), respectively, to make rules/regulations for elections to the Parliament/state legislature.
2. Under the Constitution, Articles 102 and 191 provide the grounds for disqualification of MPs and MLAs, respectively, from elections. These grounds are:
   (a) Mental unsoundness
   (b) Being an undischarged insolvent
   (c) Citizenship under doubt
   (d) Holding an office of profit

The Parliament can make additional laws for disqualification, which it has done through the Representation of People's Act (RPA), 1951. Some provisions for disqualification under the Act are given here:

(a) If someone is convicted for an offence for 2 years or more, the person will be disqualified for the term of sentence plus 6 years
(b) If found guilty of corrupt practices
(c) If dismissed for corruption
(d) If disqualified for a contract entered into on government-related matters
(e) If someone fails to lodge expense accounts of elections
(f) A person remains disqualified as long as they are a managing agent, manager, or secretary of any government company or corporation

Dr Ambedkar on Proportional Represenation

In the Constituent Assembly debate on 4 January 1949, Dr B. R. Ambedkar noted that "Proportional representation is not suited to the form of government which this Constitution lays down...in the House where there is a Parliamentary system of government, you must necessarily have a party which is in majority and which is prepared to support the government. One of the disadvantages of proportional representation is the fragmentation of the legislature into a number of small groups. Proportional representation would not permit a stable government to remain in office, because Parliament would be so divided into so many small groups that every time anything happened which displeased certain groups in Parliament, they would, on that occasion, withdraw their support from the Government, with the result that the Government losing the support of certain groups and units, would fall to pieces. Our future government must do one thing, namely, it must maintain a stable government and maintain law and order."

Criminalization of politics

Money and muscle power lead to the criminalization of politics. To ensure clean politics and to prevent any efforts to dilute the already existing measures of disqualification, the Election Commission of India (ECI) has suggested/implemented some measures. Some of these are as follows:

1. Replacing the current FPTP system with the two-ballot electoral system.
2. Implementing 'Right to reject' for voters by making the NOTA option available.
3. Anyone convicted by an enquiry committee shall not be allowed to contest elections till acquitted in a court of law.
4. Anyone convicted for a serious offence (calling for imprisonment for more than 5 years) shall not be allowed to contest elections if the charges are framed by a judicial magistrate.
5. Increasing the duration of conviction under Article 125(4) of RPA 1951 for providing wrong information from 6 months to 2 years for the disqualification provision under RPA 1951 to take effect.
6. In 1998, the ECI directed all returning officers to pay heed to the 1997 judgment of the Supreme Court.

Immediate Disqualification

Section 8(4) of the RPA 1951 provides relief from immediate disqualification if an appeal is filed within three months after the conviction. However, in 2013, the Supreme Court, in the Lily Thomas case, 2013 (Lily Thomas v. Union of India, 2013), declared this section unconstitutional and ruled that an MP (member of Parliament)/MLA (member of legislative assembly) convicted for 2 years or more would be disqualified immediately.

Arguments against immediate disqualification

1. The first argument is that immediate disqualification could have serious ramifications for a government that has a thin majority, specifically if the member is acquitted later.
2. The right to judicial remedy, which also extends to the appeal process, is a fundamental right. In case of immediate disqualification, this right is violated. So, before being disqualified, such lawmakers should be allowed to pass all stages of appeal.

However, the proponents of immediate disqualification contend that due to the slow judicial process, Section 8(4) of the RPA has been used as a loophole and has led to the criminalization of politics.

So the core issue is speedy disposal of criminal cases against lawmakers. The Supreme Court's suggestion to set new fast-track courts (through legislation) to expedite criminal case trials against lawmakers is worth considering. This will ensure that lawmakers are given their right to appeal and, in case the sentence has been stayed, such appeals should be disposed of speedily. Thus, lawmakers should be allowed to continue until their appeals are disposed of. Apart from that, there should be greater scrutiny at the time of nomination so that the entry of criminals into politics can be prevented at an early stage.

Relevant Case Laws

- The Supreme Court, in the Lily Thomas case in 2013, while reversing one of its own judgments of 2005 where it had accepted differential treatment of legislators and candidates, invalidated Section 8(4) on the grounds that differential treatment of legislators and candidates violates the Right to Equality as envisaged under Article 14.
- In the Association for Democratic Reforms2002 case, the Supreme Court made it mandatory for candidates to provide comprehensive information, including information about any cases filed against them, at the time of filing nomination.
- In *Ramesh Dalal vs. Union of India*, 2005, the Supreme Court held that any person facing criminal charges at the time of filing their nomination shall not be allowed to contest elections.
- In 2015, the Supreme Court held that even after a returning officer (a government servant on duty who is responsible for conducting the election and declaring the result) has declared the result, the election of a candidate can be nullified if he/she has not disclosed criminal records.
- The Supreme Court has also tried to make the election process more transparent and fair by upholding NOTA (None of the Above) in *People's Union for Civil Liberties v. Union of India, 2013.*
- In *PIL Foundation v. UoI*, 2014, the SC directed all courts to fast-track the judicial process in cases involving convicted legislators.

Attempts to dilute provisions to favour legislators

a. As a fallout of the Lily Thomas case, The RPA, 1951, was amended by the Parliament to annul the Lily Thomas verdict. (Based on the Lilly Thomas case, legislators who are convicted of a crime with punishment of more than 2 years in jail should be disqualified immediately.)

b. Article 102(1)(a) of the Constitution says that a person holding an office of profit will be disqualified unless explicitly exempt by a law made by the Parliament or a state legislature. The Clause has also been challenged in multiple cases, where persons holding important political positions and an office of profit simultaneously are exempt from disqualification by passing a law that specifically protects them from disqualification.

c. In 2016, the Delhi Legislature passed a law, subsequently disallowed by the President, that said that being appointed as a Parliamentary secretary does not amount to holding an office of profit.

Model Code of Conduct

Elections in India are not just a process of electing our representatives, but also a sacred ritual of democracy and a nation-wide celebration. However, elections have also presented challenges due to the misuse of government resources by ruling parties, money power, muscle power, and so on. In this respect, the Election Commission of India has laid down a set of moral, ethical, and practical guidelines, known as the Model Code of Conduct (MCC), to be followed by all political parties and all candidates in the fray. The MCC kicks in as soon as elections are announced in either the state assemblies or the Lok Sabha. The benefits of the MCC are follows:

1. It provides a level-playing field between political parties not in power and those in power.
2. It ensures that the party in power does not misuse public assets such as cars, funds, officials, media, etc. to its own benefit during elections.
3. It helps in mitigating controversies during elections so that people can focus on core issues such as poverty, education, and infrastructure.

However, the MCC has a shortcoming. It is only a moral agreement among parties, not legally enforceable. It can be and is easily violated without consequences. So to make the MCC serve its purpose effectively, the next step in this direction must be to make the provisions of the MCC legally enforceable. Despite its shortcomings, the MCC remains an important tool and above all an ethical benchmark that promotes the vision of our Constitution and democracy.

Voter Education in India

Voter education in India became imperative for two reasons:

1. Low turnout had been the bane of our elections, raising questions on the legitimacy of elected representatives.
2. Enormous public apathy, especially among the educated urban middle class, who not only abstained from voting but also used to brag about it.

To tackle these issues, some initiatives have been taken by the ECI.

National Voters' Day

National Voters' Day (NVD) or Rashtriya Matdata Diwas is celebrated on 25 January every year. The significance of NVD is to encourage more young voters to take part in the political process. Celebrating this day has required no extra budget or national holiday. Infact, voter registration as a normal activity of the Election Commission goes on as usual on NVD also. All that has been done is convert the staggered, sporadic activity into an 'event' without stretching the normal budget.

1. NVD is the flagship event of a new programme of the EC called the Systematic Voters' Education for Electoral Participation (SVEEP).

2. The first NVD was inaugurated in 2011 by then President Pratibha Patil in the presence of 30 chief election commissioners from around the world. Some of them, including those from Pakistan and Bhutan, have since declared their own NVDs.
3. Campaigns such as 'Pappu doesn't vote, aaha' have helped achieve a remarkable increase in voter turnout.
4. A key strategy has been to have brand ambassadors—headed by no less than former President A. P. J. Abdul Kalam.
5. The youth, hitherto indifferent or contemptuous of politics, started leading from the front. Twenty-five thousand campus ambassadors were appointed in universities and colleges. School children became watchdogs of voter participation, coaxing apathetic parents to vote.
6. All elections since 2010 have seen record turnouts.
7. After just four NVDs, the 2014 election was conducted with the addition of nearly 120 million more voters than in 2009. This is like adding the entire population of South Africa and South Korea combined, or three Canadas, or four Australias, or 10 Portugals, or 20 Finlands!
8. Election 2014 broke a six-decade record with 66. 4% turnout. In some states, this crossed 80%. In half of the states, women voters outnumbered men. Many have described this as a 'participation revolution'.
9. The inked finger has since become a symbol of pride—restaurants have apparently started offering discounts, barbers giving free haircuts, etc. For example, The Election Commission has launched various campaigns for voter awareness such as SVEEP (Systematic Voters' Education and Electoral Participation) and other education programs through nukkad nataks, yuva mandalis etc. The EC took the movement to further heights by declaring a National Voters' Day and also through a grand Voter Fest (Matdata Mahotsav) held in New Delhi in January 2016 attracted nearly lakhs of citizens.
10. The best endorsement has come from Prime Minister Narendra Modi, who in his 'Mann Ki Baat' programme said, "Till a few years ago, we used to see that our Election Commission is working just as a regulator. But it has undergone a significant change in the past few years. Today, our EC is not a mere regulator anymore. It has instead become a facilitator, is more voter-friendly, and voters are now at the centre of all its plans and thoughts." What makes these remarks especially significant is that the EC has consistently differed with its advocacy of compulsory voting.

———XXXX———

Practice Question (Main Examination)

1. In the light of recent controversy regarding the use of Electronic Voting Machines (EVMs), what are the challenges before the Election Commission of India to ensure the trustworthiness of elections in India?

Answer: The Election Commission of India (ECI) is the apex body that conducts the general and legislative assembly elections in India. The challenges before the ECI are as follows:

1. **Paid news:**
   a. Paid news has been used to manipulate people's views about political parties. For example, in the state of Uttar Pradesh, almost 50–60 complaints of paid news were reported to the ECI.
   b. No concrete legislations or rules exist to address the menace of paid news at the present.
2. **Social media:**
   a. Media such as Facebook, Whatsapp, and others have become a source of major news content and communication between people.
   b. A constant monitoring of these media during election periods and swiftly addressing any misuse has emerged as a must area for the ECI.
3. **Election expenditure**
   a. A Law Commission report on election reform has also highlighted the need to curb money power in elections.
4. **VVPAT (Voter verifiable paper audit trail)**

   a. Well-functioning VVPATs could provide paper trails that could address the concerns with EVMs and also provide audit capability.
5. **Voter awareness through SVEEP (Systematic Voters' Education and Electoral Participation)**
   a. The SVEEP program of the ECI must be extended in order to educate the voters more broadly about their responsibilities.

How to study for such questions:

1. This is a current affairs question, based on recent news about EVMs and the Election Commission of India
2. Expanding on the basic points is enough here. In this question, the main matter is about the "challenges" faced by the Commission, so please focus on that, as the answer is required in only 150words worth 10 marks.
3. Use capital or bold letters to highlight the main points such as VVPAT and social media, so that the examiner can check your answers quickly.
4. Give a brief introduction, a simple one. There is no need to write an introductory statement such as "Recently, the ECI has faced criticism for EVMs… ." Just provide a background of ECI and go ahead with the challenges.

5. Conclusion is not needed in such short-format questions, as there is hardly any space for content.

2. The deadly nexus between unaccounted money and politics has led 'money power' to not only distort free and fair elections but also diminish India's democratic credibility. Discuss the repercussion of this system of government on the people.

Answer: Money power has emerged as a serious challenge that is undermining the democratic election process.

1. The ability of a rich person to just 'buy' votes seriously violates the principle of free and fair elections envisaged by the Constitution.

2. Political parties are funded under a much opaque process, which harms their public mandate.

→Political leaders are prone to becoming champions of the interests of corporates and rich people rather than those of the common people.

3. The rule of law, a critical pillar of democratic credibility, is affected negatively by money power.

4. Merit and not money should determine political leadership in a democracy. Election of individuals wielding money power leads to the promotion of the policy of nepotism and kinship, disregarding the real needs of the masses. Our Constitution envisages a welfare society but neo-capitalism has crept into aggravate the problem of inequality through money power.

Way forward

1. The Election Commission has a recommended a new section under the Representation of People Act, 1951 to effectively counter money power.
2. Political parties can voluntarily come under the ambit of RTI to help address the transparency and accountability issue.

There are over 50% Members of Parliament today with assets over INR 1 crore. Their interest must be aligned with the people's interests to ensure healthy democracy in India. Hence, appropriate action by themselves on this issue could raise the confidence of the common people in politics and help us navigate through this issue.

Overview of the Chapter

3

UPSC Syllabus Covered:

- Structure, organization and functioning of the Executive and the Judiciary, Ministries and Departments of the Government; pressure groups and formal/informal associations and their role in the Polity.
- Salient features of the Representation of People's Act.
- Appointment to various Constitutional posts, powers, functions and responsibilities of various Constitutional Bodies.
- Statutory, regulatory and various quasi-judicial bodies.

Answer Writing Tips:

- Give examples of cases and judgments passed by Supreme Court/High Courts in the past to boost your stand.
- Use various commission reports such as Sarkaria Commission, Parliamentary reports, Law Commission reports etc. to provide teeth to your argument.
- Avoid providing your personal opinions. Take objective approach, which means use examples, logic and various official studies/reports to answer the questions.

3

Judiciary and Its Issues

The Judiciary in India

The Indian Constitution has provided for a single integrated system of judiciary, i.e., the Supreme Court at the apex, followed by the high courts,and then district courts. This means that, unlike some other federal countries of the world, India does not have separate state courts. For instance, in the US,a double system of courts is in place, at state and federal levels.

This single integrated system of judiciary was adopted from the Government of India Act, 1935 and enforces both Central laws and state laws. In the US, however, federal laws are enforced by the federal judiciary and the statelaws by the state judiciary.

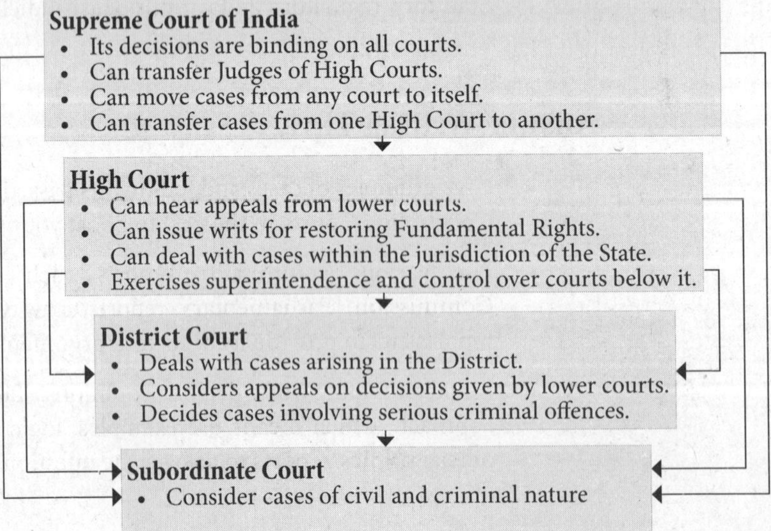

Figure 3.1: Pyramid structure of Indian Judiciary

The structure of the Judiciary in India is pyramidal, with the Supreme Court at the top, high courts below it, and district and subordinate courts at the lowest level (see Fig. 3.1). The lower courts function under the direct superintendence of the higher courts.

Features of Indian Judiciary

Some of the features of the Indian judicial system are as follows:

- Single and integrated system
- Independent by means of appointment, removal (through difficult impeachment), independent establishment, etc.
- Power of judicial review
- Guardian of fundamental rights and the Constitution
- Separation from the Executive

Supreme Court of India

Established in 1950, the Supreme Court (SC) replaced the federal court, which was established in 1935 by the Government of India Act. However, it has a larger jurisdiction than its predecessor, as the Supreme Court replaced the British Privy Council as the highest court of appeal. Before Independence, the British Privy Council was the highest body of appeal for any criminal and civil case.

The Parliament has all the powers to regulate the constitutional organization, jurisdiction, and powers of the Supreme Court. However, it is to be noted that the Parliament does not have the power to 'curtail' the jurisdiction of the SC (Article 138). It can only 'further' the jurisdiction of the courts and not limit or reduce it.

The Supreme Court consists of a maximum 31 judges, including the Chief Justice of India (CJI). The CJI has the power to appoint any retired judge of the SC or qualified judge of a high court as an ad hoc judge of the SC for a temporary period if there is a lack of quorum of permanent judges (with prior consent of the President and with permission of the concerned high court chief justice).

Jurisdiction of Supreme Court

The Supreme Court of India is one of the very powerful courts in the world. However, it functions within the limitations imposed by the Constitution. The functions and responsibilities of the Supreme Court are defined by the Constitution. The Supreme Court has specific jurisdiction or scope of powers:

1. Article 137 states that the Supreme Court shall have power to review any judgment pronounced or order made by it.
2. Article 144 state that all authorities, civil and judicial, in the territory of India shall act in aid of the Supreme Court.

3. Therefore, decisions made by the Supreme Court are binding on all other courts within the territory of India. Orders passed by it are enforceable throughout the length and breadth of the country. However, the Supreme Court itself is not bound by its decision and can review it any time. Besides, if there is a case of contempt of the Supreme Court, then the Supreme Court itself decides such a case (see Fig. 3.2).

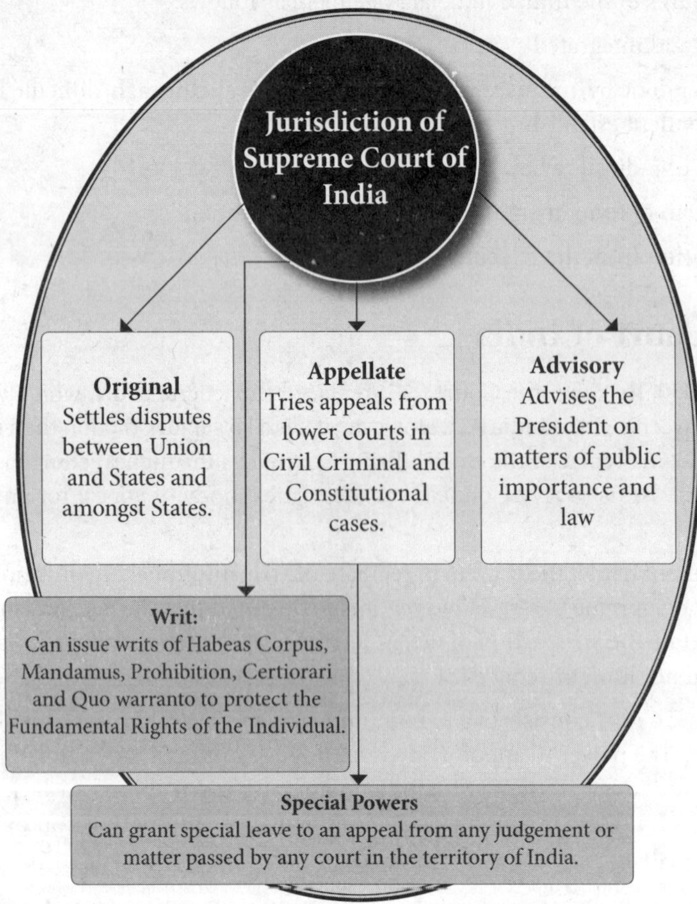

Figure 3.2: Jurisdiction of the Supreme Court of India

Independence of Judiciary

The court has been creative in considering ways and means to pass judgments and also consider various cases otherwise thought to be beyond its jurisdiction. These include, and are not limited to, judicial review of the powers of the President and the Governor.

The Supreme Court has also been involved in directing the executive branch to deliver justice to the common citizen. The Hawala case, Narasimha Rao Case, Allotment of Petrol

Pumps are some examples where the court had given directions to the Central Bureau of Investigation (CBI) to initiate investigations to bring the guilty to justice.

> "While there can be no two opinions on the need for the maintenance of judicial independence, it is also necessary to keep in view one important principle. The doctrine of independence is not to be raised to the level of a dogma so as to enable the judiciary to function as a kind of super-legislature or super-executive. The judiciary is there to interpret the Constitution or adjudicate upon the rights..."
>
> — Alladi Krishnaswami Ayyar[1]

Kesavananda Bharati Case

The controversial nature of the relationship between the Legislature and Judiciary came to a tipping point in 1973, when the Supreme Court gave a decision that has become very important in regulating the relation between the two. This case is famous as the *Kesavananda Bharati case*[2]. The following issues were at the centre of the controversy between the Parliament and the Judiciary.

1. What is the scope of Right to Private Property?
2. What is the scope of the Parliament's power to curtail, abridge, or abrogate fundamental rights?
3. What is the scope of the Parliament's power to amend the Constitution?
4. Can the Parliament make laws that abridge the fundamental rights while enforcing Directive Principles?

In this case, the Court ruled that there is a basic structure of the Constitution in place (now known as the basic structure doctrine), and no body, not even the Parliament, can violate the basic structure through an amendment or deletion of any article under the Constitution. Further, the Court also declared that the Right to Property (the disputed issue in the case) was not part of the basic structure and, therefore, could be suitably abridged. Second, the Court reserved to itself the right to decide whether the various matters are part of the basic structure of the Constitution. This case also illustrated how the Judiciary can use its power to interpret the Constitution in new creative ways.

Appointment of Judges to the Supreme Court

The Chief Justice of India and the judges of the Supreme Court are appointed by the President under Clause (2) of Article 124 of the Constitution. The convention has been that the senior-most judge of the Supreme Court is appointed as the CJI by the Government. However, there have been two instances when this did not happen:

---

[1] Constituent Assembly Debates. (1949, 23 November). Proceedings, Vol. XI, p. 837

[2] Kesavananda Bharati and Ors. v. State of Kerala and Anr. (1973) 4 SCC 225

1. In 1973, A.N. Ray was appointed as the CJI, superseding three other judges in the SC—all the three judges superseded resigned.
2. In 1977, M.U. Beg was appointed as the CJI superseding the then senior-most judge H.R. Khanna.

The Supreme Court judgement in *The Second Judge's case*[3] in 1993 curtailed this discretion and ruled that only the senior-most judge of the Supreme Court must become the CJI of India.

Whenever there is any doubt about the fitness of the senior-most judge to hold the office of the Chief Justice of India, consultation with other judges as envisaged in Article 124 (2) of the Constitution would be made for the appointment of the next Chief Justice of India.

Controversy over nomination of Supreme Court judges by the Government

Three Supreme Courts cases that highlight and give the historical background of this controversy are enlisted here.

First Judges Case (1982)

In this case, the SC held that consultation does not mean concurrence; it only implies exchange of views.

Second Judges Case (1993)[4]

In this case, the SC reversed its previous ruling and changed the meaning of the word 'consultation' to 'concurrency'. Hence it ruled that the advice tendered by the CJI to the President of India is binding in matters of the appointment of judges to the SC. However, the CJI must consult with two of his senior-most colleagues in such matters.

Road to Reform

Evolution of judicial appointments in India, through phases of executive and judicial primacy. leading up to the latest Commission that is courting controversy.

1950s- The Constitution says judges appointment should be made by the President after consultation with judges of SC and HC judges.

1960s- SC strikes down reforms like bank nationalisation. Government goes ahead by amending the Constitution.

1973 - In the Kesavananda Bharti case. SC rules that Parliament can make changes to the Constitution but cannot amend its "basic structure".

1975 - Judiciary is among the first victims of Emergency. Judges are transferred and loyalist Justice A.N. Ray is appointed as CJI over three senior judges.

1981 - Judges 1 case holds that power of appointments is still tilted towards the executive, which can

[3] Dr. B. Singh vs. Union Of India &Ors(11 March, 2004)
[4] Dr. B. Singh vs. Union Of India &Ors(11 March, 2004)

1993 - A nine-judge bench rules that "consultation" means "concurrence" or "consent". It says no appointment can be made unless it is okayed by the CJI.

1998 - After a Presidential reference, the composition and functions of the collegium are laid out.

2002 - The Justice Venkatachaliah Committee recommends a commission to decide the appointment of judges.

2008 - Law Commission after analysing the appointments made from 1993 to 2008, suggests that the judgments of 1982, 1993 and 1998 be reconsidered.

2013 - A constitutional amendment is moved suggesting a judicial commission comprising of CJI two senior-most SC judges, law minister and two eminent persons.

2014 - Parliament passes the amendment and the National Judicial Appointments Commission Bill.

The SC opined that the process of consultation involves "consultation of plurality judges" by the CJI, and the CJI's opinion alone cannot be constitutional. Hence, the CJI must consult with a collegium of four senior-most judges of the SC, and if the judges give an adverse opinion, the CJI must not send it to President as a recommendation.

The Collegium

The collegium system mandates the CJI to consult the next four senior-most judges from the Supreme Court on appointment of new judges to the SC. The views of these four judges are obtained in writing. Additionally, views of senior-most judges of the Supreme Court who hail from high courts where the persons to be recommended are functioning as judges, if not part of the collegium, must also be obtained in writing. These views are conveyed by the CJI to the Government of India. The substance of the views of the others consulted by the CJI or on his behalf, particularly those of non-judges (members of the bar) should be stated in a memorandum and be conveyed to the Government of India. The decisions should be taken on consensus only. If the CJI dissents, no one shall be appointed. If two or more members dissent, CJI shall not persist with the recommendation.

In case of non-appointment by the Government of a person nominated, the collegium shall consider whether such recommendation shall be withdrawn or reiterated. If it is unanimously reiterated, such appointment must be made.

National Judicial Appointments Commission

The National Judicial Appointments Commission was established by amending the Constitution vide the 99th Amendment passed by the Lok Sabha on 13 August 2014 and by the Rajya Sabha on 14 August 2014. Alongside, the Parliament also passed the National Judicial Appointments Commission Act, 2014 to regulate the NJAC's functions.

Both Bills were ratified by 16 of the state legislatures and the President gave his assent on 31 December 2014. The NJAC Act and the Constitutional Amendment Act came into force from 13 April 2015.

[5] Re: SC under Article 143(1)

Backdrop for NJAC

The Government proposed to come up with a bill for the appointment of judges to the higher judiciary, replacing the collegium system. For a long time now, the political executive has been of the view that the collegium system has not worked well. Hence, a Judicial Appointment Commission, in which the Executive will have a say in the appointment of judges, was necessary to achieve the objective of appointing the best people as judges in a transparent fashion.

There has been evidence that, being an opaque and closed system, the collegium system of judicial appointments has resulted in incompetent, inefficient, ethically compromised individuals being appointed as judges. Also, protests over judicial appointments have been seen in Punjab and Haryana High Court and Madras High Court.

The primary issue that bothered and engrossed the Executive was that as long as the process of judicial appointments remains opaque, the selection of judges on considerations other than merit cannot be ruled out and tackled. Too many vacancies of judges across high courts in India remaining vacant had been another issue. As of June 2013, there were 276 vacancies out of a total sanctioned strength of 904 permanent and additional judges in all the high courts of India. Not just these, most states had witnessed major canvassing on caste, community, political, and other considerations for appointment as judges.

NJAC vs. Collegium System

What is Collegium System

- Collegium system based on Three Judges Cases.
- Under it, appointment of judges are made by Chief Justice of India and four most senior Supreme Court judges.
- Has no constitutional backing.
- Constitution of India's Article 124 says appointments to be made by President in consultation with judges as President may deem necessary.
- Critics say it is a closed-door system which lacks transparency

What is NJAC

- NJAC was a body created to end the two decade old Supreme Court Collegium system of judges appointing judges.
- Was passed by Lok Sabha on August 13, 2014. Was passed by Rajya Sabha a day later.
- Will consist of six people - CJI, two senior-most Supreme Court judges, Law Minister and two 'eminent' persons.
- Critics say judges in NJAC will need support of others to push a name through. They fear judicial independence being compromised.

Criticism of NJAC

The biggest criticism of the has been that NJAC focussed not on 'how' but 'who' as the question in the appointment of judges. It laid down rules on 'who', or the committee that can nominate judges to the SC, but did not really focus on what merits those nomination decisions would be based on.

The real issue is not who appoints judges but how they are appointed. Irrespective of whether it is the Executive, the Judiciary, or a judicial commission that appoints judges, as long as the process is opaque and appointments are made on personal considerations, we will have variations of the same problems of favouritism, nepotism, and appointments on criteria other than merit and capability.

Finally, while 'who' should appoint judges can be debated endlessly, the need is to broaden the debate on the appointment of judges by focusing on other relevant issues like having jurists as judges of the Supreme Court. There has never been much debate on this issue.

Article 124(3) of the Constitution, broadly, provides for three categories of persons who are 'eligible' to be appointed to the Supreme Court—a high court judge with five years experience, an advocate in a high court with 10 years experience or a 'distinguished jurist'.

A 'distinguished jurist' refers to academic lawyers or law professors—people who have challenged and expanded the existing frontiers of legal knowledge through cutting-edge research and teaching. This requires a certain ability to theorize and conceptualize. Law professors are academically trained to theorize and conceptualize. Industrious law professors improve upon this training, through years of painstaking research and teaching in their specialized domains, often employing empirical and interdisciplinary tools. These well-developed and nuanced theorizing and conceptualizing abilities have the potential of raising the bar of legal reasoning up by several notches.

Regrettably, more than 70 long years after the Constitution was adopted; both the Judiciary and the Executive have consistently ignored this clear constitutional mandate. In the history of the Indian Republic, never ever has a distinguished jurist, i.e., a law professor, been appointed as a judge of the Supreme Court, although India has produced some outstanding law professors worthy of the 'distinguished jurist' tag. In the past 70 plus years, all appointments to the Court have been made from the first 'eligible' category, i.e., high court judges, barring four instances, where practising lawyers (the second category) were directly appointed as Supreme Court judges.

NJAC and Finalization of Memorandum of Procedure of Appointment of Supreme Court Judges

In 2015, the NJAC was declared unconstitutional by a Supreme Court bench. The NJAC was aimed at creating an updated system of appointment of judges by involving both the Executive and the Judiciary. However, it was held unconstitutional by the SC due to the fact that the Judiciary would lose its ultimate power to the Executive branch.

Subsequently, the Judiciary took upon itself the responsibility to reform the Memorandum of Procedure (MoP) of Appointment of Supreme Court and High Court Judges drafted by the

Government. The Government had drafted this MoP to bring transparency and accountability into the appointment process. However, the MoP became contentious because the Executive had introduced a clause that it can reject appointments of judges on the basis of 'national security or public interest'.

Appointing Judges: UK Process

The Judicial Appointments Commission in the UK assesses candidates against five merit criteria.

1. **Intellectual capacity:** Nominated candidates ought to demonstrate (a) a high level of expertise in chosen areas or professions with (b) the ability to quickly absorb and analyse information. They should have (c) appropriate knowledge of the law and its underlying principles, or the ability to acquire this knowledge where necessary.
2. **Personal qualities:** this range from (a) integrity and independence of mind, (b) sound judgment, (c) decisiveness, (d) objectivity, (e) ability and willingness to learn and develop professionally, and (f) ability to work constructively with others.
3. **An ability to understand and deal fairly:** This includes (a) the ability to treat everyone with respect and sensitivity whatever their background and (b) willingness to listen with patience and courtesy.
4. **Authority and communication skills:** The nominated person is expected to have (a) the ability to explain the procedure and any decisions reached clearly and succinctly to all those involved with (b) the further ability to inspire respect and confidence, and (c) maintain authority when challenged.
5. **Efficiency:** The ability to work at speed and under pressure and the ability to organize time effectively and produce clear reasoned judgments expeditiously.

Appointing Judges: US Process

The 'public' senate hearings for appointments of judges to superior courts in the US are an example of transparency. We may not find the US system implementable as it is; but nothing prevents us from incorporating the key principles of transparency, accountability, and citizen participation underlying the US system for the selection of judges.

Reforms in the Judiciary

The discussion in the previous section clearly makes a case for reforms in the way the Judiciary has been functioning.

The crucial need is to evolve objective criteria to assess a candidate, and make appointments on the basis of assessments against stated criteria. In this regard, we may usefully refer to the system adopted by the Judicial Appointments Commission in the United Kingdom to assess candidates.

Some of the other urgent reforms we need to undertake are in the following areas:

1. Speedy justice
2. Reduction in judicial costs
3. Systematic running of courts
4. Judicial transparency and accountability
5. Judiciary at the lower level—better outreach to the masses

Highlights from Law Commission Report

1. Uncle Judges—election and appointment of High Court Judges. The post of the judge of a high court has importance under our Constitution and the incumbent is supposed to be not only fair, impartial, and independent, but also intelligent and diligent. The general eligibility criterion is that a person should have put in 10 years of practice/service in the legal/judicial field. If a person has practised in a high court, say, for 20–25 years, and is appointed a judge in the same high court, overnight change is not possible. He has his colleague advocates—both senior and junior—as well as his kith and kin, who have been practising with him. This affects their impartiality and justice is the loser. Judges whose kith and kin are practising in a high court should not be posted in the same high court. This will eliminate 'uncle judges'.
2. The post of Chief Justice should not be transferable. If the Chief Justice is from the same high court, he will be in a better position not only to control the lower judiciary but also to assess the persons both from the bench and the bar for elevation to the high court. This will also curtail the unnecessary delay in filling up vacancies in high courts.
3. In our country, except for judges, the retirement age in some quasi-judicial bodies has been increased. The retirement age in different tribunals has now been increased to 70 for chairmen and 65 for members. In these circumstances, the constitutional provisions need a change for enhancing the age of retirement of high court and Supreme Court judges at least by three years.
4. The present strength of the judges should be increased manifold according to the pendency, present and probable.
5. It is necessary that the work of the high courts is decentralized, that is, more benches are established in all states.
6. Once judgments are reserved on constitutional matters by a larger bench or otherwise, the judgments should be delivered within a reasonable time. There is long and inordinate delay in delivering judgments, which should be avoided in public interest.
7. Other judicial reforms for better judiciary reforms:
   a Only some cases can be put for repeal in higher courts
   b Time allotted for oral argument (30 minutes in USA)
   c. Conduct legal audit—why do cases take so long?
   d. Repeal archaic laws

Judicial Activism

The chief instrument through which judicial activism has flourished in India is public interest litigation (PIL) or social action litigation (SAL). Public interest litigation, in simple words, means litigation filed in a court of law for the protection of 'public interest', such as pollution, terrorism, road safety, and constructional hazards. A case of this nature was filed in 1979 in India for the first time—*Hussainara Khatoon v State of Bihar*[6] on the pitiable conditions of prisoners—which led to the release of 40,000 prisoners.

Generally speaking, an individual can approach the courts only if he/she has been personally aggrieved by something. In such a case, it could be that the right of the person has been violated or some sort of dispute has taken place. This concept underwent a change around 1979. In 1979, the Court set a trend when it decided to hear a case where the case was filed not by the aggrieved persons but by others on their behalf.

A PIL is an appeal by a citizen in the court of law, requesting the court to take its cognizance and rule on it. It generally pertains to something of a larger public interest. For example, a person could appeal to the court to stop operations of an industrial complex near his/her house due to heavy pollution and file this as a PIL for larger public benefit.

As such cases involved the consideration of an issue of public interest; they came to be known as public interest litigations. Around the same time, the Supreme Court also took up the case about rights of prisoners. This opened the gates for a large number of cases in which public-spirited citizens and voluntary organizations sought judicial intervention for protection of existing rights, betterment of life conditions of the poor, protection of the environment, and many other issues in the interest of the public.

PIL has become the most important vehicle of judicial activism. The Judiciary, which is an institution that traditionally confined to responding to cases brought before it, began considering many cases merely on the basis of newspaper reports and postal complaints received by the court. Therefore, the term judicial activism became the more popular description of the role of the Judiciary.

Public interest litigation was a revolutionary concept initiated with a laudable object. In the words of the Supreme Court of India, it was aimed at "fostering and developing the laudable concept of PIL and extending its long arm of sympathy to the poor, the ignorant, the oppressed and the needy whose fundamental rights are infringed and violated and whose grievances go *unnoticed, un-represented and unheard*". However, the PIL has been misused by NGOs who are becoming "proxy litigants" or "a front for settling corporate rivalry or personal vendetta."

Abuse of PIL

While public interest litigation has made justice more accessible for the poor and resulted in many rulings that have furthered such causes as environment and human rights, it has been misused as well. Persons who describe themselves as 'public spirited persons' and others as

[6] Hussainara Khatoon v. State of Bihar, AIR 1979 SC 1369.

'social organizations' spring up overnight to canvass a multitude of causes for a variety of reasons:

- Publicity
- Private purposes
- Settling scores with rivals

The last one has a disturbing aspect in that it resorts to using proxy litigants, so the real beneficiaries and their vested interests in such litigation are not exposed.

Landmark PILs

1. *Vishaka v. State of Rajasthan*[7] or Vishaka case on guidelines regarding sexual harassment.
2. The *D.K. Basu case*[8] that shaped the D.K. Basu Guidelines for the treatment of undertrial and arrested people.
3. The *T.S.R. Subramaniam case*[9]
4. The *Prakash Singh case*[10] on police reforms
5. In 1979, the newspapers published reports about 'undertrials'. There were many prisoners in Bihar who had spent long years in jail, longer than what they would have spent if they had been punished for the offences for which they were arrested. This report prompted an advocate to file a petition. The Supreme Court heard this case. It became famous as one of the early PILs. This was the *Hussainara Khatoon vs. Bihar case.*
6. In 1980, a prison inmate of the Tihar jail managed to send a scribbled piece of paper to Justice Krishna Iyer of the Supreme Court narrating the ongoing physical torture of the prisoners. The judge got it converted into a petition. Though later on, the Court abandoned the practice of considering letters, this case, *Sunil Batra vs. Delhi Administration*[11] (1980) also became one of the pioneers of public interest litigation.

Indian Judiciary Issues

The Indian Judiciary is faced with multiple issues. Some of these are listed here.

Shortage of Staff

1. The country has a judicial strength of a mere 18,000 as against the requirement of about 50,000 judges.
2. At present, there are 434 vacancies of high court judges across all states.
3. The subordinate judiciary has 4580 vacancies across the country.
4. There is huge inadequacy of staff attached to high courts.

[7] Vishaka & Ors vs State Of Rajasthan &Ors (SC:13 August, 1997)
[8] D.K. Base v. State of W.B., (1997) 1 SCC 416 : AIR 1997 SC 610
[9] T.s.r. Subramanian & Ors. V. Union Of India &Ors. [2013] Insc 1003 (31 October 2013)
[10] Prakash Singh & Ors vs. Union Of India And Ors(22 September, 2006)
[11] Sunil Batravs Delhi Administration on (20 December, 1979)

Administrative Inefficiency

1. There are 60,260 cases pending before the Supreme Court.
2. All high courts in India, as a whole, have an incredible 38.68 lakh cases awaiting disposal.
3. The backlog of all courts, including the lower courts, is estimated to be around 3 crore cases.

Others

1. Planning and budgetary exercises are being undertaken without consulting the Judiciary.
2. Despite a ruling by the Central Information Commission (CIC), the Judiciary has kept itself out of preview of the Right to Information (RTI) Act.
3. The project of electronic conversion of all files, judgments etc. is still pending and happening at a very slow pace.

Steps Taken to Address These Issues

1. A major step has been the enactment of the Commercial Courts Act, 2015 for dedicated commercial courts at district and high court levels, and also laying down the time limits for disposal of commercial disputes/appeals.
2. The Arbitration and Conciliation Act, 1996 and the Negotiable Instruments Act, 1881 have been amended to ensure quick and cost-effective settlement of commercial disputes.
3. To improve the quality of legal education in India, setting up of the Lawyers' Academy in Kochi is a step in the right direction.

Reforms Required

Justice is an integral part of our Constitution. To achieve this objective, we need to continuously improve our legal and judicial framework so that timely and cost-effective justice is made available at the doorstep to our people. In this direction, the following measures are needed:

1. Setting up of e-courts, debt tribunals, insolvency courts, commercial courts.
2. Setting up of more fast-track courts, additional courts, and family courts.
3. Increasing the ICT (information and communications technology) capabilities of the courts.
4. Strengthening of alternative dispute resolution centres such as Lok Adalats.
5. Adopting uniform methodology to collect judicial data and streamlining of court processes.

6. Boosting the confidence of the people in the Judiciary by revealing information such as the number of pending or reserved judgments by bringing itself under the ambit of the RTI.
7. Simplifying the laws by removing old and dysfunctional elements in legislation by amending the Indian Penal Code, Civil Procedures Code, and the Indian Evidence Act.
8. Changing rules to set a uniform retirement age for judges of the Supreme Court and the high courts.
9. Preventing corruption by introducing a cooling off period for judges before taking up any new government assignment post retirement.

Apart from these, as suggested by the Law Commission in its 245th report, a 'rate of disposal' method should be adopted in which the number of judges required at each level to dispose of a particular number of cases could be computed based on analysis.

Challenges of Criminal Justice System in India

The criminal justice system in India has been painfully slow. It has resulted in a long pile-up of cases and consequent inordinate delay in delivering justice. Due to the delay and uncertainties involved, criminals are not deterred effectively. Some other issues facing the system are as follows:

1. Punishments for those convicted are ineffective.
2. Wide discretion to police and prosecution makes the system vulnerable to corruption and manipulation.
3. The system ignores the real victim, leading them to resort to extralegal methods of seeking justice.
4. The system imposes a heavy economic burden on the state without the returns.
5. The system is overburdened with nearly 30 million pending criminal cases, and 10 million being added every year.

Strategy for Reform

The Committee on the Reforms of Criminal Justice System in India (2003) suggested a threefold strategy to reform the criminal justice in India.

First, procedural and substantive law needs a change based on changes in the society and economy, with decriminalization and diversion being the guiding principles. A suggestion here is to divide the penal code into four different codes: Social Offences Code, Correctional Offences Code, Economic Offences Code, and Indian Penal Code.

1. The Social Offences Code will include matters of civil nature that can be settled without police intervention and prison terms through administrative processes.
2. The Correctional Offences Code will include offences punishable with up to three years of imprisonment, where plea bargaining can be liberally invoked.

3. The Economic Offences Code will include property offences, which affect the financial stability of the country, to be dealt with through a combination of criminal and administrative strategies.
4. The Indian Penal Code will include only major crimes warranting 10 years imprisonment or more or death.

The second is the institutional reform of police processes. This includes investigation, professionalization, rationalization of court systems through technology, and limiting appeal procedures to the minimum.

The third is to give a bigger and more responsible role to the victim in the whole procedure. It involves restoring the confidence of the victim in the system. This would include conferring rights on the victim, such as to:

1. Participate in proceedings.
2. Engage an advocate, track progress of the case, and assist the court in pursuit of the truth.
3. Seek compensation for injuries suffered irrespective of the fate of proceedings.
4. Follow a restorative means, which enjoys community support, victim satisfaction, and offender acknowledgement of obligations.

Alternative Dispute Resolution

The Indian judicial system is characterized by rampant delay in the disposition of the cases due to inadequate number of courts and judges in the country. High cost of litigation and complex legal procedure alienate the poor and uneducated from the judicial system. This situation necessitates alternative dispute redressal mechanisms (ADRs).

Alternative dispute redressal mechanisms include dispute resolution processes and techniques that act as a means for the disagreeing parties to come to an agreement without litigation. Following are the tools of ADR:

1. Arbitration is a process in which a neutral third party renders a decision based on the merits of the case.
2. Mediation aims to facilitate the development of a consensual solution by the disputing parties. Mediation is overseen by a non-partisan third party.
3. Conciliation is a process by which dispute resolution is achieved by compromise or voluntary agreement. In contrast to arbitration, the conciliator does not render a binding award.

ADR and Constitution

ADR first started as a quest to find solutions to the perplexing problem of the ever-increasing burden on the courts. It was an attempt made by the legislators and Judiciary alike to achieve the 'Constitutional goal' of achieving Complete Justice. ADR in India was founded on the Constitutional basis of Articles 14 and 21 which deal with Equality before Law and Right to Life and Personal Liberty, respectively. ADR also tries to achieve the Directive Principle of State Policy relating to Equal Justice and Free Legal Aid as laid down under Article 39A of the Constitution.

The Acts that deal with ADR are Arbitration and Conciliation Act, 1996 and the Legal Services Authorities Act, 1987. Section 89 of the CPC 1908 makes it possible for arbitration proceedings to take place in accordance with these Acts.

Advantages of ADRs

Alternative dispute resolution mechanisms have plenty of advantages:

1. These are less expensive.
2. These are less time consuming.
3. These are free from the technicalities of conducting cases in law courts.
4. The parties are free to discuss their difference of opinion without any fear of disclosure of this fact before any law court.
5. The last but not the least is the fact that the disputes are settled in a win-win manner for both. Neither party is a loser, so they have no ill will towards each other.

Lok Adalats

Based on Gandhian principles, Lok Adalat is India's contribution to the world jurisprudence of ADR. The first Lok Adalat was held in Gujarat in 1982. It is a step towards fulfilling the directives under Article 39A for equal justice and free legal aid. Lok Adalats can ensure speedy justice, as they can be conducted at convenient places and in local languages. This is the only institutionalized mechanism of dispute resolution in which the parties do not have to bear any expenses, and the fee paid in a regular court is refunded if the case is settled in a Lok Adalats. In Lok Adalats, not only are disputes settled but also cordial relations between the parties are retained, as disputes are resolved amicably.

Disputes can be directly brought before the Lok Adalats and no appeal lies against the order of the Lok Adalats; thus these help to alleviate the burden of arrears of cases. The introduction of Lok Adalats has succeeded in providing a supplementary forum to the victims for the satisfactory settlement of their disputes. This mechanism should be taken full advantage of and more Lok Adalats need to be organized to achieve 'access to justice for all.' We will discuss Lok Adalats further later in this chapter.

Increasing Tribunalization in India

The first tribunal was set up in India 25 years ago to take the load off high courts. At the last count, there are 93 specialized tribunals in India, the latest one being the 61-member Companies Appellate Tribunal. Tribunals were established with the object of providing speedy, cheap, and decentralized determination of disputes arising out of the various welfare legislations. Another important reason for this development was that while the courts were accustomed to dealing with cases primarily according to law, the exigencies of modern administration required the adjudication of disputes not necessarily on the basis of technical questions of law but also after considering the policy intentions and public interest. Besides, tribunals were also seen as bodies manned by experts who could professionally and fairly deal with the issues that, though challengeable in the courts of law, yet required technical expertise. The Railway Claims Tribunal, CESTAT, ITAT, Labour Tribunals, the Companies Tribunal, various Compensation Tribunals, Revenue Courts of various states, etc. can be cited as examples of such tribunals.

Tribunals are under the direct administrative control of ministries within the Government, which administer their day-to-day functioning and appointments, and hence are likely to be influenced by the Government's opinion, thus interfering with justice delivery. However, not all tribunals are disconnected from the mainstream Judiciary, for example Rent Control Tribunals, Motor Vehicles Tribunals, and Labour Tribunals are part of the Judiciary and are working better than the independent tribunals. Thus, despite so many concerns, the tribunals have been pivotal and effective in addressing disputes.

However, increasing tribunalization, which refers to the perception of usurping of certain judicial powers from courts by tribunals, arises from the over-interpretation of Article 50 of the Indian Constitution, which deals with the separation of the Judiciary from the Executive. It points out that State shall take steps to separate the Judiciary from the Executive in the public services of the State.

The Supreme Court in the Chandra Kumar v. UOI Case[12] (1997) suggested that the tribunals should enjoy the same constitutional protections as the courts (HC and SC). This meant that when the jurisdiction is being transferred from a court to a tribunal, the members of this tribunal should hold a rank, status, and capacity as close to those of the judges in a court as possible. However, finding retired judges and competent candidates with qualifications set out by the Parliament to be members of quasi-judicial tribunals has been a difficult task.

The recent Supreme Court judgment that struck down the National Tax Tribunals has spelt out the parameters to test the constitutionality of tribunals. Further , the Department of Legal Affairs in the Law Ministry has recently proposed an idea for the "possibility of merging the functions of tribunals with some other tribunals" to avoid "overlapping/identical functions" being discharged by them.

Legal Services Authorities Act, 1987

A legal aid scheme was first introduced by Justice P.N. Bhagwati under the Legal Aid Committee formed in 1971. Article 39A of the Constitution of India provides that the State shall secure that the operation of the legal system promotes justice on a basis of equal opportunity. Articles 14 and 22(1) also make it obligatory for the State to ensure equality before law and a legal system that promotes justice on the basis of equal opportunity to all.

The linkage between Article 21 of the Constitution of India and the right to free legal aid was forged in the decision of *Hussainara Khatoon v. State of Bihar (AIR 1979 SC 1369)*[13]. In this

[12] L. Chandra Kumar v/s U.O.I [A.I.R 1997 SC 1125]

[13] Supra note 10.

case, the SC declared that "there can be no doubt that speedy trial is an integral and essential part of the fundamental right to life and liberty enshrined in Article 21."

In 1987, the Legal Services Authorities Act was enacted by the Parliament, which came into force on 9 November 1995 to establish a nationwide uniform network for providing free and competent legal services to the weaker sections of the society. The Legal Services Authorities Act provides the provision to set up the national legal services authority (NALSA) in order to provide free legal services to the needy. It has prescribed the rules to do so as well.

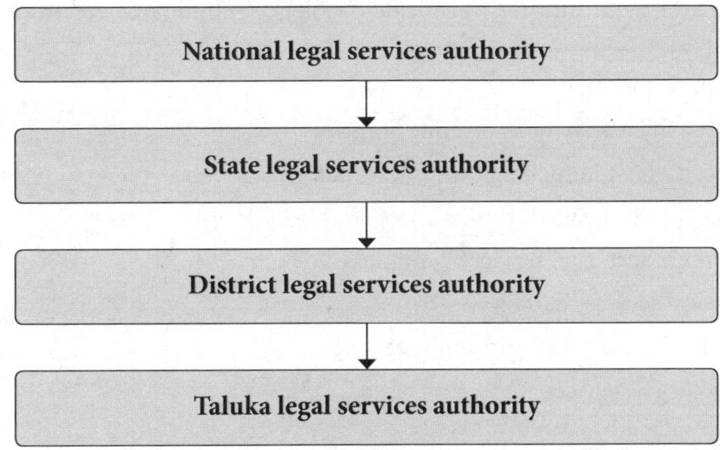

Figure 3.3: Hierarchy of bodies created under the Legal Services Authorities Act, 1987

National Legal Services Authority

The NALSA has been constituted under the Legal Services Authorities Act, 1987 to provide free legal services to the weaker sections of the society. The Chief Justice of India is the Patron-in-Chief and the senior-most Honourable Judge, Supreme Court of India, is the Executive Chairman of the authority.

The first member secretary of the authority joined in December 1997 and by January 1998 the other officers and staffs were also appointed. By February 1998 the office of the NALSA became functional for the first time. In October 1998, Justice A.S. Anand assumed the office of the Chief Justice of India and thus became the first Patron-in-Chief of the NALSA, while Justice S.P. Bharucha, the senior-most judge of the Supreme Court of India, became the first Executive Chairman of the authority.

Public awareness, equal opportunity, and deliverable justice are the cornerstones on which the edifice of the NALSA is based. The principal objective of the NALSA is to provide free and competent legal services to the weaker sections of the society, to ensure that opportunities for securing justice are not denied to any citizen by reason of economic or other disabilities, and to organize Lok Adalats for amicable settlement of disputes. Apart from these, the functions of NALSA include spreading legal literacy and awareness and undertaking social justice litigations.

In carrying out all these responsibilities, NALSA works in close coordination with the various state legal services authorities, district legal services authorities, and taluk legal services authorities (see Fig. 3.3). The persons covered under NALSA for legal aid include:

a. Schedule castes/scheduled tribes
b. Women and children
c. Victims of trafficking, or beggars
d. Mentally ill or disabled persons
e. Victims of mass disasters, genocides, violence (ethnic), caste atrocities, droughts, earthquakes, and industrial disasters
f. Industrial workmen
g. Children in custody or in juvenile homes
h. All those whose annual income is less than INR 1 lakh

The services can be availed from:

1. Supreme Court legal services committee
2. State legal services authority
3. High court legal services committee
4. District legal services authority

The Role of Lok Adalats

As discussed earlier, the Lok Adalat is a statutory forum for conciliatory settlement of legal disputes. Disputes pending in any court of law or at the pre-litigation stage can be settled here. It has been given the status of a civil court and can settle marriage disputes, land disputes, partition/property disputes, labour disputes, and also 'compoundable criminal' cases. Its awards are enforceable, binding, and final, as no appeal lies before any court against them.

Lok Adalats are held by the district authority, state authority, high court legal services committees, Supreme Court Legal Services Committee, and taluk legal services committees. These are presided over by retired judges, social activists, or members of the legal profession. Permanent and continuous Lok Adalats are being established in all the districts in the country.

NALSA has been providing and shall continue to provide funds to state legal services authorities for the implementation of the legal aid schemes and programmes, but the infrastructure has to be provided by the respective state governments.

Separate permanent and continuous Lok Adalats in various government departments are aimed at amicably settling pending cases as well as the matters at the pre-litigative stage between the departments and the general public, so that the inflow of litigation to regular courts is reduced. Such Lok Adalats have become functional in many government bodies. For example, in Delhi, permanent Lok Adalats have been established in the Delhi Vidyut Board, Delhi Development Authority, Municipal Corporation of Delhi, MTNL, and General Insurance Corporation.

These Lok Adalats are becoming popular day-by-day, and it is expected that very soon a large number of disputes between public and statutory authorities would start getting settled at the pre-litigative stage itself, thus saving the parties from unnecessary expense and litigational inconvenience.

The Role of Gram Nyayalayas

Gram Nyayalayas have been established under the Gram Nyayalayas Act, 2008.

Each gram nyayalaya is a court of judicial magistrate of the first class, and its presiding officer (nyayadhikari) is appointed by the state government in consultation with the high court. Gram Nyayalayas are established for every panchayat at the intermediate level or a group of contiguous panchayats at the intermediate level. The judges are strictly judicial officers. They draw the same salary and derive the same powers as first-class magistrates working under high courts. Gram Nyayalayas are mobile courts and exercise powers of both criminal and civil courts.

Judicial Review in India

The power of judicial review in India has been modelled on the lines of the American Constitution. The Parliament is not supreme in India, but the Constitution is. Hence, the Supreme Court has the power to preserve the Constitution through the power of judicial review.

The power to declare any law void is provided explicitly by Article 13 of the Constitution. Additionally, Article 32 also enables this provision by declaring the Supreme Court as the protector of the Constitution. The Supreme Court of India has declared the judicial review as one of the basic features of the Indian Constitution. This was declared so in *Maneka Gandhi v. Union of India*[14] in 1978 when the Court ruled that any fundamental right and law of the Parliament are subject to judicial review by the Supreme Court.

Importance of judicial review

First, judicial review enables a citizen to seek remedies from the court in case he or she has been wronged by any unjust legislation. Second, judicial review provides a check and balance against the powers of the Parliament to legislate indiscriminately. This is evidenced by the Maneka Gandhi case, ruling in which the Supreme Court has clearly opined that a law cannot only be procedurally fair but must also be naturally fair. Third, judicial review ensures that the most pertinent social, environmental, economic, political, and ethical issues are not ignored by the legislature and are duly and fairly addressed. Finally, it helps preserve the Constitution and the ideals of equality, liberty, and fraternity.

Disadvantages of Judicial Review

The judicial review provides almost unchecked power to the Judiciary to strike down anything it pleases. This can create a power struggle between the Judiciary and the Executive. The judicial

[14] Maneka Gandhi. Versus. Union of India. [1978 AIR 597, 1978 SCR (2) 621]

review can increase the instances of court cases, thereby burdening the Judiciary. It can also be misused to strike down desirable laws.

Tribal Justice System

India is home to a vibrant community of approximately 104 million tribals spread across states and falling into various distinct tribes. These tribal communities have developed their own system of social hierarchies, various personal customs, and tribal laws that govern them.

The Indian Constitution permits the north-eastern states to set up customary village councils or courts to resolve disputes between two parties belonging to a scheduled tribe. This tribal justice system involves the interpretation of uncodified customary laws by the village chiefs, assisted by elders of the village. However, questions have been raised over the conflict of such systems with the common law system provided by the Constitution. In this context, the Standing Committee on Personnel, Public Grievances, Law, and Justice submitted its report on the 'Synergy between tribal justice system and the regular justice system of the country'.

The salient observations and recommendations of the Committee include the following:

1. The Committee has noted that most tribal communities preferred the tribal justice system because of (a) their familiarity with customary laws, (b) its minimal procedure and cost effectiveness, and (c) timely delivery of justice. However, there were certain challenges:
    a. Every tribe within a state had its own customary practices of dispute resolution.
    b. Most decisions were not written down and gave the tribal chief wide discretion.
    c. As a result, punishments for the same crime varied from person to person.
2. Statutory recognition to tribal courts:
    a. The Committee recommended that the Parliament enact a law to set up a tribal justice court system.
    b. States would be permitted to modify the law as per their requirements. This would give the tribal courts an institutional framework in relation to the appointment of personnel, salary and benefits, etc.
    c. Further, this would enable the states to codify their customs, write judgments and orders, and follow laws and precedents.
    d. To facilitate this, special funds may be allocated to state judicial academies and village mobile courts.
3. Separate high courts for north-eastern states:
    a. In its earlier report, in 2008, the Committee had recommended that separate high courts be established in the north-eastern states.
    b. The Committee reiterated this recommendation, as these high courts could play a role in the codification of tribal laws.
    c. The judgements of the high courts would be treated as precedents, and their interpretations of customary law could be documented.

4. The Committee also recommended that independent judicial academies be established in every state.

Condition of Undertrials

India has over 2.78 lakh undertrials lodged in various prisons across the country. This makes about two-thirds of the total incarcerated people in jails in the country. The NHRC Report has highlighted the horrible conditions of undertrials. As per this report, many of the undertrials are languishing in jail for periods longer than their sentences.

Reasons for Huge Number of Undertrials

The primary reason for this huge number of undertrials is poverty, as these undertrials are not able to afford their legal fees. Some of the other reasons are as follows:

1. Absence of Undertrial Review Committees that function to bring these individuals to quick justice
2. Lack of adequate legal aid
3. Delays in courts due to long pendency of cases
4. Lack of effective prison management systems

Government Steps in this direction

The Government has taken some steps to mitigate this situation by amending the Code of Criminal Procedure in 2005 to introduce Section 436A to reduce overcrowding in jails. Under this Section, an undertrial must be released on their own personal bond in case they have spent more than half of the period specified for their offence in the jail already.

Recommendations for improving the Conditions of undertrials

1. Legal aid agencies must create awareness among prisoners about their rights.
2. The Government must undertake a cost-benefit analysis of the economic and social costs of keeping so many innocent people in jail, as they could even become criminals in the poor jail conditions and their mental condition may degrade.
3. Expediting the trial process is a critical point.
4. The concept of open prisons needs to be further worked on to address the overcrowding in jails, as there is disorder due to overcrowding, and only few prisoners understand the distinction between criminal conduct and good citizenship.
5. Seeking monthly reports from all the inspectors general of prisons on the number of convicts and undertrial prisoners in their jails.
6. Release of undertrial prisoners on bond if they have completed half or two-thirds of their punishment period.

7. Working out a system of holding regular special courts in prisons for early disposal of cases.
8. To offload a large number of prisoners by making the availability of bail accessible, undertaking speedy trials, and providing legal aid.
9. An institutional mechanism should be in place to protect the future of the children of the prisoners.
10. Prison conditions should be made more people-friendly, keeping in view the needs of women, aged, and mentally-ill prisoners.

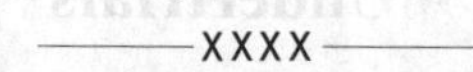

Practice Questions (Main Examination)

1. Why is judicial independence central to democracy? Do you think reforming the existing collegium system is the best way forward to select and appoint judges to ensure independence of judiciary? Critically discuss.

Answer: The Judiciary is one of the three pillars of a democracy. Its independence is central to democracy for the following reasons:

1. The Judiciary is the protector of the Constitution and the guardian of the fundamental rights of citizens. Citizens can appeal to the Judiciary in case of violation of their fundamental rights and any illegal actions against them.
2. The Judiciary, through the power of judicial review, ensures that legislations passed by the Parliament do not infringe upon the basic structure of the Constitution and against its overall principles.
3. The Judiciary ensures that the Executive and public offices carry out their duties to the citizens as envisaged.
4. The Judiciary keeps a check on the arbitrary exercise of power by the Executive and Legislature, and thus an independent judiciary is critical to the stability of democracy in India.

The collegium system has been criticized because it is an extra-constitutional authority. Dr Ambedkar held that a fine balance is to be maintained between the two organs of the Government. Appointment of judges should be an integrated, participatory process, which is not the case with the collegium system. Further, the collegium system has been held as non-transparent and has been called an island of insularity. Posts in the higher judiciary have remained vacant and about 30% of the posts of HC judges have remained vacant while this system was operational. Additionally, deep divisions were observed within the collegium system. The system of extending favours because of lack of transparency and accountability led to a decline in the quality of justice dispensation. It promoted dynasties in the Judiciary, often called the 'Uncle Judges syndrome'.

As for the NJAC, it too has its share of problems:

1. The Judiciary was under-represented in the NJAC, with only three out of the six members coming from the Judiciary.
2. The presence of the Union Law Minister in the body raised the question of fairness, as the Union of India is the largest litigant before the Judiciary.
3. The politicization of the Judiciary, as had happened prior to and post emergency, was a valid threat with the NJAC.
4. The Supreme Court, while quashing the 99th Constitutional Amendment Act as unconstitutional, held that
    a. The Judiciary cannot be caught in a "web of indebtedness" towards the Government.
    b. The independence of the Judiciary is equivalent to judicial primacy and the process of appointment of judges cannot be shared with the political executive.
    c. Organic development of civil society in India has not yet happened. Thus the burden to safeguard the rights of the citizen falls on the Judiciary, and for this the Judiciary needs to be kept completely insulated from the other organs of the Government.
    d. The tendency of the Executive has been to indulge in favouritism. Preserving the primacy of the Judiciary is a safe way of protecting it from turning into a case of spoils system. The Bench admitted that all is not well with the collegium and highlighted that the system requires a glasnost and a perestroika.
    e. A Memorandum of Procedure needs to be developed, which is transparent, mentions the eligibility criteria, establishes the secretariat, and provides for a complaint redressal mechanism. We can also imbibe the best practices from other countries, such as the UK Judicial Appointment Commission, which provides for a detailed procedure, involvement of people, and an exam and interview system for judicial appointments.

(The following answer is for illustration , therefore longer than usual word limit of 150-200 words. Please refer to end of the book for solved questions that stick to word limits.)

2. To deter the use of PILs to defame or acquire fame, a petitioner's locus standi, their direct stake in the case, should be clear. They should also be liable to punishment if the charge levelled is proved incorrect. Comment.

Answer: The public interest litigation (PIL) has emerged as a powerful tool for the public to bring their grievances to court and seek respite. However, it has also been used as 'publicity' interest litigation to further personal interests. For example, the PIL to seek planes and SUV cars for a judge in the UP district court was an attempt to gain publicity.

Fine on frivolous PILs

PILs that have no public character should be rejected outright. Fines that discourage such PIL sin the future could also be considered. This will save the court's time and maintain the integrity of purpose of PILs.

Petitioner's own interest and stake to be made clear

- The Supreme Court is free to reject PILs not filed by at least one of the affected parties in the case.
    1. Such rejection can be done at the committee level even before the PIL is brought to the bench.
    2. This would save time and resources for the courts.
- Finally, the public must itself be wary of PILs on their behalf. Bogus PILs without the participation of the actual affected party should be condemned; their cultural disapproval could lead to a decline in such cases.

Overview of the Chapter

4

UPSC Syllabus Covered:

- Development processes and the development industry- the role of NGOs, SHGs, various groups and associations, donors, charities, institutional and other stakeholders

Answer Writing Tips:

- Do not try to 'stand out'. Lot of students try to be too creative. The key is to be creative but within the accepted norms. Please remember that UPSC examiners are provided a framework within which they check the answers. They will most likely not recognize your 'creativity' if it is too difficult to relate with.
- Show a range of views in your answer. Even in questions that seem too specific, try to include various viewpoints, i.e., such as economic, constitutional, statutory, environmental, social etc. However, do not overdo this. You have to develop a sense of where to provide various viewpoints and where to be specific. This can only come with a lot of answer writing practice!

4

NGOs, SHGs

"In this life we cannot do great things, we can only do small things with great love"

- Mother Teresa

NGOs, SHGs -- The Third Sector

India has one of the most vibrant "third sector" in the world. This maybe more appropriately addressed as the "Voluntary Sector". It comprises of NGOs, SHGs, and many other civil society groups that play a critical role in the functioning of a democracy like ours.

The National Policy on Voluntary Action 2007 recognizes all formal as well as informal groups, such as, community-based organizations, non-government development organizations, charitable organizations, networks or federations of such organizations and professional membership based associations as part of the voluntary sector.

The voluntary sector has a defining role for itself in various aspects of public life in India. It can play a critical role in enabling people and people's groups, to access democratic processes and various entitlements that eventually lead to empowerment. An example of this is the Right to Information Act (RTI), which was spearheaded by a Voluntary Organization, known as Mazdoor Kisan Shakti Sangathan (MKSS).Therefore, the sector can help fill the gap between public and government interface and bring expected social, economic and political changes at a faster pace.

It is also important to have this sector for presenting a critique of public functioning and providing alternatives. Dissent is a critical feature of any democracy and only independent voluntary organizations can mobilize people to present a logical and well-represented critique of poor government policy. They can also serve as a check against use of excessive power by the State and market institutions. Thus, VOs can contribute to the organic process of a democracy.

Therefore, the sector should be viewed as an agency that can contribute to the provisions adopted from the Planning Commission Report on Voluntary Sector – (latest governmental report on the sector):

1. Strengthening democracy and governance through improved participatory representation, awareness of rights and capacity-building of local institutions
2. Advancing rural and urban development through grassroot- level innovations and human resource and talent management
3. Transforming inter-personal, familial and community spaces, through awareness generation and sensitization
4. Providing platforms for dialogue and dissent, for appreciation of and respect for differences in opinions and affiliations
5. Promoting art, culture, environment protection and other forms of public enquiry; alternatively, it may be said that the sector should cover the spaces of social defense, social security, social service and social change

Various Roles of Voluntary Sector Organisations[1]

1. Agents of rapid change and social transformation

a. Through their work among the most backward and marginalized communities, in regions with poor accessibility or with depleting physical and financial resources, VOs create knowledge hubs using ecologically, culturally and socially sensitive methodologies, that are aimed at the holistic development of communities. Simultaneously, the sector ensures equality in representation, access and control in all forms of social, political and economic relationships and through this, maintains the social fabric of the nation, rekindling the notion of self-governance at the level of society, and making it more just and egalitarian.

2. Expertise and promotion of thematic domains

a. The various thematic domains that VOs work in includes art, culture, sports, spiritual enlightenment, environment and wildlife conservation, gender equity, innovations in education, science and technology, access to justice, peace-building, conflict resolution, rural development, among various others, along with awareness of and experience in regional, cultural, community and identity specific variations. Eclectic nodal institutions help promote cross fertilization of thematic issues and in the process, empower the poorest and the most disadvantaged to make self-informed choices.

[1]Adopted from the Planning Commission's Report on Voluntary Sector (VO)

3. *Enabling inclusion of the marginalized by translating people's aspirations into policy*

a. With a vast knowledge of grassroots complexities and sensitivity to socio-cultural contexts, VOs have the expertise to ensure improved interface between the state, market and the people. VOs also enable information and feedback to flow from Gram Sabhas/ people/ communities/ identity-based groups/ individuals to district and centrally situated planners, thus, outlining the different needs and specificities of each category. Simultaneously, they build capacities of people, people's organizations, implementing agencies, planning bodies and private players, to help encourage participation of and self-initiated outreach efforts by marginalized groups. Such structured information flows also enhance participatory governance. VOs can thus be viewed as supporting agents in the development of a flourishing grassroots democracy.

4. *Scaling-up grassroots innovations*

a. VOs also contribute to policy by enabling the scaling-up of grassroot level innovations in rural development and urban poverty management. Besides contributions to the creation of local health, self-help groups for women's empowerment, preservation of water resources and livelihood generation, are particularly noteworthy.

Advantages/Importance

- Backbone of the democratic society and its continuous deliberative process.

  Evidence: Russia has only 4 lakh NGOs, Kenya some 240 and India has around 3 million, US has 2 million
- Major economic force — provide employment opportunities

  Evidence: 8% employment in US generated by NGOs
- Enhance people centricity of the government
- Contribute to inclusive wealth creation
- Help to scale up productivity and competitiveness

Civil Society as a Major Economic Force

With liberalisation of the economy and globalisation, there has been a phenomenal growth in the number of non-governmental organisations across the world in the last few decades. Experts say that India has more than two million NGOs, Russia four lakhs and in Kenya some 240 NGOs are formed each year. The United States has an estimated two million non-profit organisations which employ more than eleven million workers – about eight per cent of the nation's total workforce. They are further supported by a large number of unpaid volunteers (about six millions) who have strong individual initiative and commitment to social responsibility. The presence of NGOs ensures depth and resilience in civil society. It gives expression to citizens' voices. It enables them to take responsibility for how their society is performing and allows them to talk to their government in organised ways. In India too, this sector is emerging at a fast pace.

Funding Sources

- Individuals
- Private foundations (national as well as global)
- Business houses
- Government

Government NGO interface

- The Central Social Welfare Board (CSWB) and the National Institute of Public Cooperation and Child Development (NIPCCD) are two such prominent bodies dealing with Government – NGO interface in the social welfare sector.
- The Council for Advancement of People's Action and Rural Technology (CAPART) is an agency which finances voluntary organisations to stimulate grassroot participation and encouragement of rural technology.
- There are more than 437 such autonomous organisations, functioning under various Ministries of the Government of India, excluding those under Scientific Departments.
- Another way of support is through tax concessions.

Self-help Groups

- Self-help groups work on the ideology that, "Self-help is the best Help", "United we stand, divided we fall", "Unity is strength".
- A Gandhian idea.
- A self-help group (SHG) is a village-based financial intermediary committee, which is usually composed of 10–20 local women or men. A mixed group is generally not preferred. Most self-help groups are located in India, though SHGs can be found in other countries too, especially in South Asia and South-east Asia.
- Members make small regular savings contributions over a few months until there is enough capital in the group to begin lending. Funds may then be lent back to the members or to others in the village for any purpose. In India, many SHGs are linked to banks for the delivery of micro-credit.
- As per the recent Microfinance Report released by NABARD - as on March 2012, a total number of 79.6 lakh SHGs with active bank-linkages are operating in India, which have been able to ensure involvement of around 9.7 crore people of this nation, with an aggregate bank balance of Rs. 6,551 crores. Simultaneously, latest statistics also indicate that over 90% of SHGs in India consist exclusively of women.

Beginning

1. The first organised initiative in this direction was taken in Gujarat in 1954, when the Textile Labour Association (TLA) of Ahmedabad formed its women's wing to organise those women belonging to households of mill workers, in order to train them in primary skills, like sewing, knitting, embroidery, typesetting and stenography, etc.
2. In 1972, it was given a more systematized structure, when Self Employed Women's Association (SEWA) was formed as a Trade Union under the leadership of Ela Bhatt.
3. In the 1980s, MYRADA – a Karnataka-based non-governmental organisation, promoted several locally formed groups to enable the members to secure credit collectively and use it, along with their own savings, for activities which could provide them economically gainful employment. Eg: Kudumbshree

Functions

1. Thrift and Savings — "Savings First, Credit Later"
2. Collective planning for additional income
3. Conduit for formal banking services to reach them
4. Internal lending
5. Discussing problems
    - 7.8 million active SHGs in the country, consisting of around 780 million members, 80 per cent of which are women SHGs.
    - Contributes to financial inclusion, as overall 73% of the households do not have credit links with any financial institution.

Advantages/Benefits

(1) Financial Inclusion, (2) Income Generation and Self-Employment, (3) Social Empowerment (4) Improvement in Social Indicators

1. Reduced dependency on money lenders and exploitative institutions.
2. Enabled households to spend more on education.
3. Reduction of child mortality and maternal mortality.
4. Stop exploitation of women.
5. Group support to vulnerable individuals: An economically poor individual gains strength as part of a group.
6. Low transaction costs: Besides, financing through SHGs reduces transaction costs for both lenders and borrowers.
7. Reasonable interest rates.
8. **Accessibility:** While lenders have to handle only a single SHG account instead of a large number of small-sized individual accounts, borrowers as part of an SHG cut

down expenses on travel (to and from the branch and other places) for completing paper work and on the loss of workdays in canvassing for loans.

9. Empowering: Where successful, SHGs have significantly empowered poor people, especially women, in rural areas.
10. Promotes entrepreneurship and innovation for micro businesses by these individuals

Impact:

1. According to survey by NABARD:
   a. 58% of the households covered under SHGs reported an increase in assets
   b. the average value of assets per household increased by 72%, from Rs.6,843 to Rs.11,793;
   c. majority of the members developed savings habit against 23% earlier
   d. there was a threefold increase in savings and a doubling of borrowings per household;
   e. the share of consumption loan in the borrowing went down from 50% to 25%;
   f. 70% of the loans taken in post-SHG period went towards income generation ventures;
   g. employment expanded by 18%;
   h. the average net income per household before joining a SHG was Rs.20,177 which rose by 33% to 26,889; and about 41.5% of the household studied were below their State specific poverty line in the pre-SHG enrolment stage; it came down to 22%.

Participation in group activity significantly contributed to improvement of self-confidence among the members. In general, group members and particularly women, became more vocal and assertive on social and family issues.

E-Shakti [SHGs] — NABARD's SHG-Bank Linkage Program

1. SHG-Bank linkage programme was started as a test project in 1989, when NABARD, the apex rural development bank in the country, sanctioned Rs.10 lakhs to MYRADA as seed money assistance for forming credit management groups.
2. "By aggregating their individual savings into a single deposit, self-help groups minimize the bank's transaction costs and generate an attractive volume of deposits. Through self-help groups, the bank can serve small rural depositors while paying them a market rate of interest."
3. NABARD estimates that there are 2.2 million SHGs in India, representing 33 million members that have taken loans from banks under its linkage program to date.
4. Has resulted in increase of SHG deposits in banks, from 9000 crore to 17000 from 2013 to 2014, which is almost an 88% increase

5. e-Shakti has been implemented to improve the quality of interface between SHG members and banks for efficient and hassle-free delivery of banking services
6. A bank manager will be able to track the activities of SHGs sitting in a room, including particulars, like how much savings an SHG has or how regularly it meets and the profile of its members. This will not only help the banker, but also change the risk perception of SHGs

Features of Self Help Movement

- SHG model is the dominant vehicle for Micro Finance in India.
- 2.24 million SHGs under Bank linkage on 31.03.2006.
- Initially NGOs pioneered the SHG promotion processes.
- Government emerged as the largest SHG promoter.
- Various government subsidy programs linked to SHG.
- 9.64 lakh SHGs 6.20 lakh new and 3.44 lakh for repeat loan) got financed in 2005-06.
- Average loan size to a new SHG-Rs. 37,561 and average repeat loan per SHG - Rs. 62,918.
- Approximately 44% of the country's Bank-linked SHGs were in the southern States.

Organizations involved:

NABARD

Rashtriya Mahila Kosh

It was felt that the credit needs of poor women, especially those in the unorganized sector, were not adequately addressed by the formal financial institutions of the country.

Thus, RMK was established to provide loans in a quasi-formal credit delivery mechanism, which is client-friendly, has simple and minimal procedure, disburses quickly and repeatedly, has flexible repayment schedules, links thrifts and savings with credit and has relatively low transaction costs, both for the borrower and the lender

The Kosh lends with a unique credit delivery model known as "RMK-NGO-SHG Beneficiaries" model.

Lessons from Andhra Pradesh Experience

- Role of State Government critical - long term poverty eradicaiton strategy a must
- State wide support structure to induce social mobilisation
- Social capital critical - building institutions of the poor and best practitioners of the community

- Pro-poor orientation of service providers
- Faith in the capability of poor
- Learn from the poor
- Transfer ownership to institutions of poor as early as possible
- Role of community resource persons - critical

Success Stories

1. Andhra Pradesh
2. Tamil Nadu
3. Kudumbshree in Kerela

Impact of Self-help Groups on financial inclusion in India

- There are over 7.8 million SHGs in India with over 780 million members.
- Impact of SHGs:
    a. Enable members of the SHGs to get included in the banking system in India, thereby providing them access to bank account services, insurance, and ability to transfer money
    b. Reduced dependency on money lenders
    c. Women are empowered as they get financial control of their lives. This helps the family overall, as children get stable access to education, nutrition and better looking after by an empowered mother.
    d. Vulnerable sections of SCs and STs are benefitted.
    e. Help members to borrow and lend money to make them financially empowered. With lending money, they can earn a stable interest return and by borrowing, they can start new livelihoods or take care of education for their children.
    f. It helps members to understand the benefits of saving and investing money, thereby, making them financially savvy.
    g. Collective planning for additional income.
    h. Platform to discuss their problems, financial and non-financial and make better decisions.
- NABARD has shown that SHGs enabled 58% of the households with an increase in assets.

Bank Sakhi Program

They are members of RGMVP (Rajiv Gandhi Mahila Vikas Pariyojana) who were promoted as SHG federation members. Each Sakhi is allocated one Gram Panchayat covering 4-5 villages.

The function and responsibility of the programme is to:

1. Ensure prompt and efficient service to be provided to the customers
2. Ensure safe custody of cash and equipment which are at their disposal
3. BANK SAKHI-CSP (Customer Service Points) shall not charge any fee or commission or any charges from the customers
4. Maintain confidentiality with regard to customer information and do not share any customer information with any third party except BARTRONICS and Bank

The Banking Correspondent (BC) model forms the cornerstone of India's financial inclusion strategy to ensure delivery of banking services across the length and breadth of the country. An important milestone of having a bank agent or a CSP (Customer Service Point) in all villages with a population of more than 2,000 has been achieved. But, despite the remarkable progress in terms of geographical outreach, significant challenges remain. CSP and client dormancy (especially in the rural areas) are high.

NABARD's SHG-bank linkage program (SBLP) has supported the formation of SHG networks with extensive geographical coverage and client outreach. Convergence of BC based financial inclusion initiatives with SHG networks may hold some answers to the current challenges in financial inclusion.

A pilot project was, therefore, envisaged to explore the potential of SHG members functioning as Business Correspondents to offer banking services at the doorstep of the village residents, particularly women and poor households, with backing from the SHG supporting institutions.

GIZ (German development agency) NABARD joint collaboration RFIP (Rural Financial Institutions Program) supports the pilot program with the sole objective to understand the feasibility, coexistence and mutual fit of SHG networks within the BC ecosystem.

The Grameen Bank of Aryavart (GBA), in cooperation with the GIZ-NABARD Rural Financial Institutions Programme (RFIP), has identified a well-functioning SHG ecosystem that is being nurtured and promoted by Rajiv Gandhi Mahila Vikas Pariyojana (RGMVP) for this pilot project. Bank Sakhis – selected SHG members who have been acting as a link between the SHGs and the bank, have been trained and equipped to carry out the function of CSPs. Handholding/support, as well as quality control and supervision capabilities, have been built up at the level of the block-level SHG federation, with support from the RGMVP.

Self-Help Promoter Institutions (SHPIs)

1. Guidance and training of SHGs
2. Seed funding for very poor members
3. Eg: MYRADA — MYRADA was effective in setting up several Self-Help Groups in rural areas of Karnataka in 1989 by providing (a) sustained guidance, and (b) by granting seed money to them from the corpus of 10 lakhs, which was given to it by NABARD under a demonstration project.
4. SEWA in Ahmedabad, Nav Bharat Jagriti Kendra and Ramakrishna Mission in Jharkhand, and ADITHI in Bihar

Role of SHPI

Usually, a SHPI provides initial training and guidance to the participating members before launching them into a formal thrift and credit management group (SHG). In some cases, the members of the group may be economically too weak to contribute even the initial seed money to the group funds to start an activity. The promoter institution in such cases may have to provide financial support to the groups. MYRADA was effective in setting up several Self-Help Groups in rural areas of Karnataka in 1989 by providing (a) sustained guidance and (b) by granting seed money to them from the corpus of 10 lakhs which was given to it by NABARD under a demonstration project.

Challenges

1. **High NPAs:** The biggest challenge with SHGs currently is higher NPA percentage due to multiple financing, inadequacies in account keeping and other things. On an average, NPA of SHGs stands at around 7-8 per cent, which NABARD intends to, bring down to 2 per cent in the next five years.
2. **Regional variations**: (north and north-east vs. south India) — not present in credit deficient areas of India
3. **Issue of Sustainability**: Too much dependency on State for funds, marketing, skills, etc.
4. Present mostly in rural areas only, and not in urban areas of India and peri-urban areas due to heterogeneity of community
5. Poor skills in rural areas exacerbate situation in such SHGs
6. Members of the group, not necessarily from the poorest families
7. Social Inequities: Does not address the social inequities of poor people
8. **Lack of Staff:** there is lack of qualified resource personnel in the rural areas who could help in skill up-gradation / acquisition of new skills by group members
9. **Politicization like Cooperatives:** used as launch pads of politicians, used to fund political activities

Waqf

- Under Muslim rule in India, the concept of Waqf was more widely comprehended as aligned with the spirit of charity endorsed by the Quran.
- Waqf implies the endowment of property, moveable or immovable, tangible or intangible to God by a Muslim, under the premise that the transfer will benefit the needy.
- As a legal transaction, the Waqif (settler) appoints himself or another trustworthy person as Mutawalli (manager) in an endowment deed (Waqfnamah) to administer the Waqf (charitable Trust).

- As it implies a surrender of properties to God, a Waqf deed is irrevocable and perpetual.
- It works under the Mussalman Waqf Validating Act, 1913
- Currently, 300000 Waqfs in India are being administered under various provisions of the Waqf Act, 1995.
- At the national level, there is Central Waqf Council, which acts in an advisory capacity.

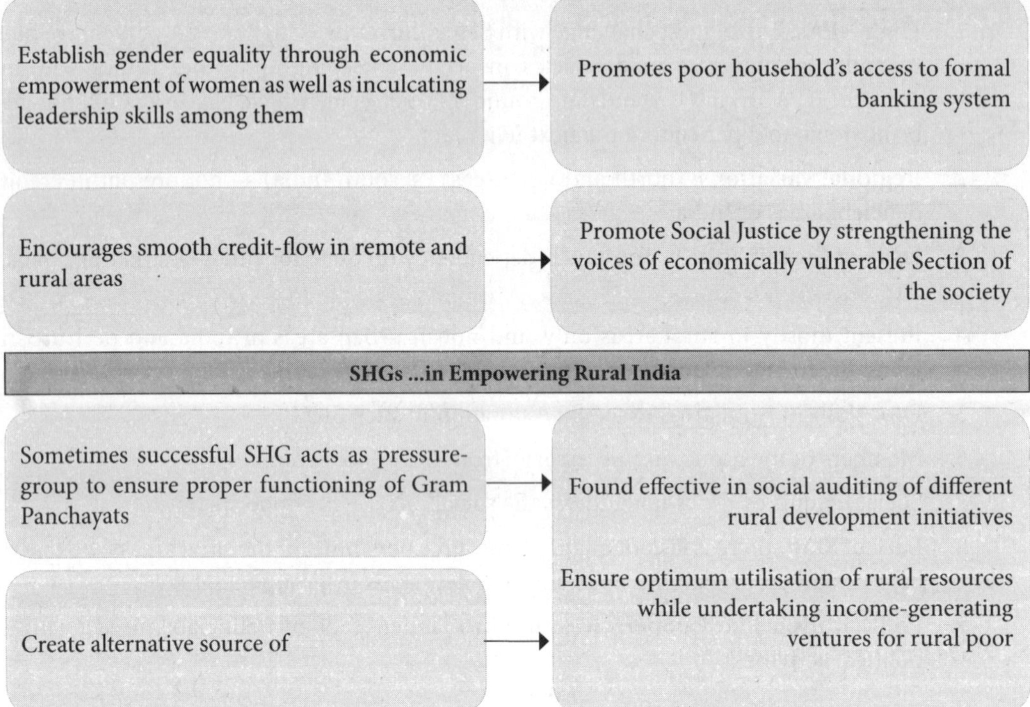

Figure 4.1. Significance of SHGs in Rural India

Charities

Any organisation that undertakes works with good intentions is said to be doing charities.

(i) The list describes the following activities as charitable :

- prevention or relief of poverty;
- advancement of education;
- advancement of religion;

- advancement of health or the saving of lives;
- advancement of citizenship or community development;
- advancement of the arts, culture, heritage or science;
- advancement of amateur sport;
- advancement of human rights, conflict resolution or reconciliation, or the promotion of religious or racial harmony or equality and diversity;
- advancement of environmental protection or improvement;
- relief of those in need by reason of youth, age, ill-health, disability, financial hardship or other disadvantage;
- advancement of animal welfare;
- other purposes that are currently recognised as charitable or are in the spirit of any purposes currently recognized as charitable.

CSR (Corporate Social Responsibility)

- The commitment of business to contribute to sustainable economic development working with employees and their families, the local community and society at large to improve their quality of life, in ways that are both good for business and good for development.
- Traditions of "trusteeship", "giving" and "welfare" have existed since long in our society.
- The concept of social good has always been part of the Indian psyche.
- From the beginning of the 20th century, business and industry in India have in different ways been paying attention to their obligation and commitment towards society and the community.
- The large number of schools, colleges, hospitals and other charitable establishments, which were set up in the 20th century in different parts of the country, are fine examples of such social commitment

Not just charity anymore:

- In recent years, CSR has shifted from the domain of charity to the domain of standard business practices.
- Together with 'profit' and 'growth', it is one of the essential parameters which define a business.
- Stakeholder awareness, increasing power of civil society, intensity of competition and environmental challenges are some of the factors, which have increased the emphasis on CSR in recent times.

Self-Regulatory Authorities

- The Self-Regulatory Authority of a profession means a select body of its members, which is responsible for growth and development of the profession, in the background of its responsibility towards society and the State.
- The functions of such a Self-regulatory body may include:
  1. Issues of professional education- development of curriculum, setting up of teaching standards, institutional infrastructure, recognition of degrees etc., and
  2. Matters connected with licensing, and ethical conduct of the practitioners
  3. A significant role as technical advisers to the government in conceptualizing, formulating, and implementing policies and standards, for providing important public services to the citizens
- Currently, there are six major professional bodies operating in India, each having been formed under a specific law.
  1. Bar Council of India (BCI) – formed under the Advocates Act, 1961
  2. Medical Council of India (MCI) – formed under the Indian Medical Council Act 1956
  3. Institute of Chartered Accountants of India (ICAI) – formed under the Chartered Accountants Act, 1949
  4. Institute of Cost and Works Accountants of India (ICWAI) – formed under the Cost and Works Accountants Act, 1959
  5. Institute of Company Secretaries of India (ICSI) – formed under the Company Secretaries Act, 1980
  6. Council of Architecture (COA) – formed under the Architects Act, 1972
- Then, there are organisations, like the Institution of Engineers which have been formed purely by voluntary action by respective members of the profession. They do not have any statutory background.
- However, their mandate to manage and regulate education for their respective professions has been challenged on the ground that it prohibits innovation
- National Knowledge Commission has recommended establishment of an Independent Regulatory Authority for Higher Education (IRAHE).
  1. The IRAHE must be at an arm's length from the government and independent of all stakeholders, including the concerned ministries of the government
  2. The IRAHE would have to be established by an Act of Parliament, and would be responsible for setting the criteria and deciding on entry.
  3. It would be the only agency that would be authorized to accord degree-granting power to higher education institutions.
  4. It would be responsible for monitoring standards and settling disputes.

5. It would apply exactly the same norms to public and private institutions, as it would, to domestic and international institutions.
6. It would be the authority for licensing accreditation agencies

- **Renewal/Revalidation of Registration**
  1. No such practice in India while this is must for professions, like doctors
- **Disciplinary Mechanism**
  1. Not well developed except a few cases
  2. Also, reporting is very low
  3. ICAI has an innovative mechanism to punish errant members and prevent unethical practices.
  4. It has a pro-active disciplinary cell, which speedily investigates complaints against its members. ICAI entertains complaints not only from stakeholders or user-groups, but also takes suo-moto action on the basis of its in-house information.
  5. The provisions contained in the code of conduct of ICAI are very stringent and the agency is equally effective in taking action against its defaulting members. Peer review is undertaken to ensure compliance with technical standards and adherence to quality control policies and procedures. Often, ICAI on its own, looks into public accounts of different organisations, including banks and financial institutions. Disciplinary action is taken if there is any deficiency in reporting. Quality control among Chartered Accountants is ensured by peer pressure and financial reporting review.
- **Accountability and Parliamentary Oversight**
  1. Self-Regulatory Authorities enjoy considerable functional autonomy.
  2. Though they have been formed under law, their accountability is currently ambiguous and incomplete.
  3. The law does not provide for an explicit mechanism which can hold them responsible for their performance. The public, Parliament, government and the professionals have a right to know how a Self-Regulatory Authority discharges its functions and to hold them accountable.
  4. Self-Regulatory Authority's primary accountability as a statutory body must be towards the Parliament, which, on behalf of the public, defines its powers and responsibilities

Social capital — SHGs and Cooperatives — a Gandhian idea of self-reliance

- During the struggle for Independence, the whole emphasis of the Gandhian movement was on self-help and cooperation.
- The cooperative movement gained momentum as a part of such self-help ethos embedded in the independence movement.

- To Gandhiji, the Swadeshi Movement was "the greatest constructive and cooperative movement in the country".
- In propagation of khadi and village industries, he found "the panacea for India's growing pauperism" and "an object lesson in cooperation".
- Gandhiji looked at cooperation as a moral movement.
- **Social capital refers to those institutions, relationships and norms that shape the quality and quantity of a society's interaction.**
  1. It consists of trust, mutual understanding, shared values and behavior, that bind together the members of a community and make cooperative action possible.
  2. The basic premise is that, such interaction enables people to build communities, to commit themselves to each other, and to knit the social fabric.
  3. A sense of belonging and the concrete experience of social networking (and the relationships of trust and tolerance that evolve) can bring great benefits to people.
- **Corporate Foundations**
  1. Towards the end of the 19th century, the corporate community in India also began setting up organisations dedicated to the welfare and development of the underprivileged.
  2. The J N Tata Endowment Trust was established in our country in 1892, much before Rockfeller and Carnegie set up their philanthropic foundations in the USA.
  3. A major contribution of this endowment was the establishment of the Indian Institute of Science at Bangalore.
  4. The JJ School of Arts, Tata Institute of Social Sciences, Tata Institute of Fundamental Research, Birla Institute of Technology, and Sri Ram College of Commerce were also established.
- **Socio-Political Movements**
  1. 1960s and 70s: Vinoba Bhave's Bhoodan and Jai Prakash Narain's Sarvodaya Movement were the two major voluntary action initiatives, which caught the attention of people across the country in the 1950s and 60s.
- **Constitutionalism**
  1. 1970s and 1980s, the growth of constitutionalism and the emergence of economic liberalisation fueled ideals of equity, human rights and expansion of economic opportunities.
  2. The environment of liberalism led to a recognition that people needed to be empowered through social action network. This supported emergence of newer categories of charities and voluntary action groups in our country.
- **Cooperatives, Societies and Waqfs**
  1. Started in the early years of the 20th century when farmers were organized into voluntary groups to secure cheap credit on collective basis, and thus, save them from usurious practices of money lenders.

2. Started in Europe.
3. Spread to India by the 1920s, as it became very well-suited for the Indian rural areas.
4. After Independence, the Union and State Governments enacted several laws with regard to Public Trusts, Waqfs, Producer Companies, other voluntary sector / civil society organisations and cooperative societies.
5. The Societies Registration Act, 1860.
6. The Waqf Act, 1954.

Constitutional Positions: (Constitutional Right to form associations and cooperatives)

- The Indian Constitution provides a distinct legal space to social capital / civil society institutions
  a. through its Article on the right to form associations or unions – Article 19 (1) (c);
  b. through Article 43, which talks of States making endeavour to promote cooperatives in rural areas; and
  c. through explicit mention in entries made in Schedule 7

As recommended by the Steering Committee of the Twelfth Five Year Plan, it is important to create an enabling environment that encourages respectful engagement between the government and the voluntary sector. Hence, the Steering Committee on Voluntary Action has envisaged the following:

1. **State Level Policies:** Introduction of state voluntary sector policies on the lines of the national policy on voluntary sector, to enable and empower an independent, creative and effective voluntary sector in each state
2. **Terms of Engagement:** Articulation of a set of terms of engagement that would be applicable to all forms of interactions (including consultative planning, program implementation and evaluation) between the voluntary sector and agencies of central and state governments
3. **Communication and Coordination:** Proper communication of schemes and grievance redressal mechanism may be evolved for beneficiaries awareness
   - Coordinated system of dialogue between the state and the voluntary sector on the central issues of poverty eradication, protection of the most marginalized and vulnerable communities (including minorities, nomadic tribes, transgender groups, differently-abled persons, primitive tribal groups, internally displaced persons) through access to justice, conflict resolution, sustainable development, gender equity, rural transformation, heritage and culture promotion, financial inclusion and capacity building/ talent management of India's human resource, particularly the youths.

4. **Institutionalization**: Institutionalized legal measures that are uniformly applicable across states, to ensure protection of all voluntary actors against any form of political, social or economic harassment, by either the state or market forces.
5. **Better skilled and equipped body of voluntary sector professionals,** which is empowered to work towards a more inclusive, equitable and harmonious social order.
6. **Empowered voluntary sector** that plays an important role of animating and establishing among others, a robust and participatory Panchayati Raj System of self-governance and encourages youth, both men and women to give some of their time to nation-building, as part of their own self development.

Therefore, it is clear that SHGs, NGOs and other VOs are critical in development, both economic and social. Their efficacy and efficiency must be improved through well-thought out policy interventions. Also, all the stakeholders must be consulted in such processes along the way.

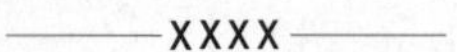

Practice Question (Main Examination)

1. While there are many successful stories about the benefits of SHGs, many are concerned about the future of the SHG movement in India. Are SHGs heading towards the right direction of women empowerment? Explain with a suitable illustration.

Answer: SHGs (self-help groups) have greatly transformed the lives of millions of households by empowering women.As on date, there over 8 crore individuals availing its benefits, and over 17,000 crore rupees have been mobilized through the SHG bank-linking programme as well (E-Shakti programme).

Are they heading in right direction?

Benefits provided:

1. Financial inclusion has been enabled by SHGs by bringing crores of householdswithin its net.
2. Women empowerment by providing them livelihood options through various small and micro loans for entrepreneurship.
   - Additionally, women are empowered as they can share information, discuss problems, and create consensus-driven solutions for the community.

Examples/Illustrations:

1. Kudumbashree in Kerala has enabled land ownership for millions of women in SHGs. Through a common land ownership program (pooling) and then cultivating it through loans from the SHG, these women have transformed their lives

2. Myrada in Karnataka has provided financial literacy for women in SHGs.

Problems:

1. Hidden default rates in SHG loans can lead to financial distress for women.
2. Forced appropriation of funds or fund misuse by the male head of the family can lead to domestic violence problems.
3. Excessive growth in SHGs can lead to financial improprieties by some ill-intentioned individuals.
4. SHGs' high interest rate can create inordinate financial burden.
5. These challenges in the growth and future of SHGs can be addressed by greater community participation and consensus-driven solutions for SHGs.

2. Over-regulation will stifle the voluntary sector, but no regulation poses a threat to democracy itself. In the light of this statement, analyse the provisions of the Lokpal and Lokayuktas Act, 2013, which necessitate it for senior management personnel working with NGOs to disclose their assets and liabilities if the NGOs receive foreign donations and funds from the Union Government.

Answer: NGOs play a central role in the Indian democracy. Some key public legislations such as RTI and Lokpal are a result of NGO work.

The Lokpal and Lokayuktas Act, 2013 addresses NGO senior management as public officials and puts them in the same category as government officials.

Additionally, the Act also requires NGO personnel to disclose all assets and liabilities.

This poses following problems:

1. Invasion of right to privacy with right to life (Article 21) of a private citizen.
2. Possible harassment by vested interest for ownership of even hereditary assets or high salary.
3. Exit from profession by capable management from NGOs to the private sector in lieu of such intervening legal provisions.
    - Over-regulation leading to problems akin to those that were caused by the License Raj in the pre-liberalization era.

Positive aspects of Lokpal provisions:

1. Monitoring of foreign funding and influence on public policy and NGO action by the government.
    - Ford Foundation has been accused of disturbing development efforts in many countries such NGOs could be monitor rise in national interest.

2. Checking corruption and money laundering and instances of black money used through NGOs.

    - A large section of laundered funds are sent/received through NGOs.

Therefore, it seems necessary from serious crisis of foreign funding and corruption that the provisions of the Lokpal Act are necessary for the overall benefit of the society.

Overview of the Chapter

5

UPSC Syllabus Covered:

- Important aspects of governance, transparency and accountability, e-governance applications, models, successes, limitations, and potential; citizens charters, transparency & accountability and institutional and other measures.
- Role of civil services in a democracy.
- Government policies and interventions for development in various sectors and issues arising out of their design and implementation.

Answer Writing Tips:

- Quote reports (such as Economic Survey, World Economic Forum etc.), data on important indicators such as IMR, MMR etc. to strengthen your answer.
- Do not overuse data, i.e. do not provide it where it is not needed. Use it only where it is clear that it will add value.
- Write at least 2-3 questions per day. You can use this book for questions or various online resources. When mains are 2-3 months away, start writing at least one practice mock paper per week.

5

Governance

Introduction

UNDP, the World Bank, and the OECD define governance as the exercise of authority or power in order to manage a country's economic, political, and administrative affairs. The 2009 Global Monitoring Report sees governance as 'power relationships,' 'formal and informal processes of formulating policies and allocating resources,' 'processes of decision-making,' and 'mechanisms for holding governments accountable.'

The word 'governance' came from the Latin verb 'gubernare,' or more originally from the Greek word 'kubernaein,' which means 'to steer.' Based on its etymology, governance refers to the manner of steering or governing or of directing and controlling a group of people or a state. Governance is commonly defined as the exercise of power or authority by political leaders for the well-being of their country's citizens or subjects.

Governance can also be defined as set and norms, strategic vision and direction, and formulating high-level goals and policies. It refers to overseeing management and organizational performance to ensure that the organization is working in the best interests of the public and, more specifically, the stakeholders who are served by the organization's mission. It is about directing and overseeing the management to ensure that the organization is achieving the desired outcomes and to ensure that the organization is acting prudently, ethically, and legally.

Transparency International Index: India features at rank 81 with a score of 40. The Transparency International Index measures the efficiency and efficacy with which governance is carried out by the country. India 'slow ranking in the international scenario shows that there is a plethora of problems that India faces in providing good governance to the people.

Good Governance

Figure 5.1: Good Governance

The concept of good governance is not new. Kautilya in his treatise Arthashastra elaborated the traits of the king of a well governed State thus "in the happiness of his subjects lies his happiness, in their welfare his welfare, whatever pleases himself, he does not consider as good, but whatever pleases his subjects he considers as good". Mahatma Gandhi had propounded the concept of 'Su-raj'. Good governance has the following eight attributes which link it to its citizens (Fig 5.1).

Four Pillars of Governance (Citizen Centric Governance)

1. Ethos (of service to the citizen)
2. Ethics (honesty, integrity, and transparency)
3. Equity (empathy for weaker sections)
4. Efficiency (speedy and effective, use of ICT—information and communication technology, and no harassment)

Governance must provide for citizen centric administration and must focus on citizen's convenience, cost, and comfort and not that of the public servants. In India institutions such as the National Human Rights Commission, National Women's Commission, National Consumer Disputes Redressal Commission, and Lokayuktas have been set up for delivering citizen centric governance.

Necessary Preconditions for Good Governance

An analysis of the barriers to good governance reveals that there are several preconditions which must be fulfilled in order to make governance citizen centric. Some of the pre-conditions are:

a. Sound legal framework.

b. Robust institutional mechanism for proper implementation of the laws and their effective functioning.

c. Competent personnel staffing these institutions, and sound personnel management policies.

d. Right policies for decentralization, delegation and accountability.

Besides, a number of tools can also be employed to make administration citizen centric. These are:

a. Re-engineering processes to make governance citizen centric.
b. Adoption of appropriate modern technology.
c. Right to information.
d. Citizens' charters.
e. Independent evaluation of services.
f. Grievance redressal mechanisms.
g. Active citizens' participation-public-private partnerships.

Features of Effective Governance

The following are the features of effective governance:

Accountability

Accountability is the basic and most important feature of effective governance. Accountability ensures answerability, i.e., questions asked of public officials have to be answered by them. There are two types of questions that can be asked of public officials.

The first type of questions is aimed at ensuring transparency. Under the Right to Information Act (RTI Act), one can merely seek information/data, though with some restrictions. This process involves one way transmission of information: from public offices to the citizen. It promotes transparency and, to a much lesser degree, accountability in government.

The second type of questions enquire not just as to what was done but also why it was done. Therefore this involves a consultative two-way flow of information, with the citizens usually providing feedback in respect of the working of government departments and service delivery of public agencies. This two-way flow of information takes the shape of citizens' charters, service delivery surveys, social audits, citizens' report cards, and outcome surveys.

Transparency

Transparency in decision-making, disclosure of standards of delivery, and openness in the everyday functioning of the administration are the hallmarks of a citizen centric approach. Since this is a reasonably new concept, which has gained acceptance after the enactment of the RTI Act, a change in approach is required at all levels of the government.

Regulation

There are many aspects of governance that call for regulation to ensure compliance in terms of the objectives of governance. However, this power to regulate needs to be limited and not overbearing. All regulation should be effective and not symbolic. While self-regulation is best form of regulation, the regulatory authorities should come out with procedures that are transparent and citizen friendly. It is necessary to involve citizen groups and professional organizations in regulation policies.

Single Window System for Delivery of Services

One of the ways in which governments across the world have approached efficient and effective service delivery to citizens (and businesses) is by adopting a 'single window system.' The driving force behind this approach is the belief that citizens need not run around different government offices for getting various services. This is achieved through a number of ways. One approach allows a service providing organization to re-engineer its processes in such a way that all the services provided by it get delivered to citizens through a single outlet/unit. Another approach is to establish an organization, which would create infrastructure through which different government organizations can provide services to citizens at a single point of delivery. Some countries such as Germany have adopted an approach where no separate organization is created—all the organizations work in tandem to establish a common service delivery infrastructure.

Bottlenecks

Common Bottlenecks in Implementation of Projects

Among the most commonly noted bottlenecks in implementation of projects are:

1. Multiplicity of laws governing same or similar set of issues.
2. Requirement of a large number of approvals/permissions.
3. Separate clearances/approvals required from different authorities on same or similar issues.
4. Too many points of contact between investor and authorities.
5. Lack of transparency in the administration of clearances and approvals.
6. Large number of returns and amount of information to be provided to many departments/agencies.
7. Little communication and information-sharing among related departments.

e-Governance

e-Governance in India owes its origins to the in-house development of applications during the 1970s and 1980s in for defence, economic planning, census, tax administration, and elections. Subsequently, massive efforts were made during the 1980s by the National Informatics Centre (NIC) to connect all the district headquarters in the country through a VSAT network. However, all these efforts were mainly government centric with the primary objective of exploiting ICTs for automating internal government functions. Citizen centricity with a focus on improving delivery of services to the citizens was not the primary goal during this period.

National e-Governance Plan

Citizen centric services spread with the coming of the Internet in the late 1990s and for most of the past one decade. The National e-Governance Plan (NeGP) was conceptualized to make use of IT for the delivery of services to citizens and also address challenges of a fragmented eGov practiced by various states in the country.

The way forward is a "Simple, Moral, Accountable, Responsive, and Transparent" (SMART) governance.

Business corporations have discovered over the last few decades that information technology can make the value chain more efficient and lead to quality improvements and cost savings. The government is responsible for providing certain services to the citizens just like an organization is responsible for managing a value chain that leads to output. Similarly, governments have discovered that information technology can make the provision of services to the citizen more efficient and transparent, can save costs, and lead to a higher level of efficiency.

Analogous to e-commerce, which allows business to transact with each other more efficiently (B2B) and brings customers closer to businesses (B2C), e-governance aims to make the interactions between the government and citizens (G2C), between the government and business enterprises (G2B), and inter-agency relationships (G2G) more friendly, convenient, transparent, and inexpensive.

e-Government is not about 'e' but about 'government'; it is not about computers and websites, but about services to citizens and businesses. e-Government is also not about translating processes; it is about transforming them. e-Government is concerned with the transformation of government, modernisation of government processes and functions and better public service delivery mechanisms through technology so that government can be put on an auto-pilot mode.

The four pillars of e-Government are:

- People
- Process
- Technology
- Resources

e-Kranti

e-Kranti aims to enhance the portfolio of citizen-centric services and ensure optimum usage of core information and communication technology. The NeGP is the most significant initiative taken in India during the last decade to mainstream ICT in governance at both central and state levels. It lays emphasis on creating the right governance and institutional framework within the country, establishing the core IT infrastructure, and implement a number of Mission Mode Projects (MMPs)at the central, state, and integrated levels.

Key principles of e-Kranti (NeGP 2.0)

1. Transformation and not translation
2. Integrated services and not individual services
3. Government process reengineering (GPR) to be mandatory in every MMP
4. ICT infrastructure on demand
5. Cloud by default
6. Mobile first
7. Fast-tracking approvals
8. Mandating standards and protocols
9. Language localization
10. National GIS (geo-spatial information system)
11. Security and electronic data preservation

Objectives of e-Kranti

The mains objectives of e-Kranti are as follows:

1. Citizen centric service delivery
2. Optimum usage of ICT
3. With ICT infrastructure on demand, the programme also seeks to ensure cloud by default, mobile first, language localization, and security and electronic data preservation.

The mission of e-Kranti is to ensure a government wide transformation by delivering all government services electronically to citizens through integrated and interoperable systems via multiple modes, while ensuring efficiency, transparency, and reliability of such services at affordable costs.

The programme management structure approved for the Digital India programme would be used for monitoring and implementation of e-Kranti and also for providing a forum to ascertain views of all stakeholders, overseeing implementation, resolving inter-ministerial issues, and ensuring speedy sanction of projects.

The thrust areas of the e-Kranti electronic delivery of services under the Digital India programme are as follows:

1. Technology for education (e-Education)
2. Health (e-Healthcare)
3. Farmers
4. Financial inclusion
5. Planning
6. Justice

7. Security
8. Cyber security

Digital India

Government of India is implementing the Digital India programme as an umbrella programme to prepare India for a knowledge based transformation into a digitally empowered society and knowledge economy.

Digital India aims to provide the much needed thrust to the nine pillars of growth areas, namely:

1. Broadband highways
2. Universal access to mobile connectivity
3. Public internet access programme
4. e-Governance: Reforming government through technology
5. e-Kranti: Electronic delivery of services
6. Information for all
7. Electronics manufacturing
8. IT for Jobs
9. Early harvest programmes

Examples of Digital India

1. G2C
   - e-courts
   - Mobile One by Karnataka Government
2. G2B
   - e-Biz
   - Taxation filings
   - e-Procurement
3. G2G
   - e-Courts
   - District level portals for administration use
   - Land records modernization
4. C2G
   - MyGov
   - Centralized Public Grievances Redress and Monitoring System (CPGRAMS)

- Citizen grievance redressal:
    a. CVC
    b. State Lokayuktas
    c. NHRC
    d. SHRC
    e. National Consumer Disputes Redressal Commission

Mobile One by Karnataka Government

This app allows users to pay utility bills, property taxes, book railway and bus tickets, file income tax returns, m-passport services, apply for driving licenses, etc. It can also be used to notify officials about grievances and ill-functioning of services. While an anganwadi worker in rural Karnataka can register her attendance through Mobile One, a software professional in Bengaluru can use it to pay electricity and water bills or book tickets.

Jaankari

Bihar's unique attempt to accept Right to Information (RTI) applications through phone calls ('Jaankari' project) has been selected for the first prize for 'outstanding performance in citizen centric service delivery' at the National Awards for e-Governance (2008-09).

e-Shakti

e-Shakti has been implemented to improve the quality of interface between self-help group (SHG) members and banks for efficient and hassle-free delivery of banking services. A bank manager will be able to track the activities of SHGs sitting in a room, including particulars such as how much savings an SHG has or how regularly it meets and the profile of its members. This will not only help the banker but also change the risk perception of SHGs. e-Shakti has resulted in increase of self-help group (SHG) deposits in banks from ₹9000 crore to ₹17000 from 2013 to 2014, almost an 88% increase.

Samanvay

Samanvay is a web portal to track the implementation of the Sansad Adarsh Gram Yojana (SAGY).

Problems in e-Governance

As with any other programme of this scale and outreach, the e-governance initiative too has its own share of problems. The primary issue is of the funding required to set up and expand the digital outreach platform. Also, with too many organizations and stakeholders, there is always an issue of interoperability. The problem is compounded when we take the linguistic diversity of India into consideration. Further, there are also issues of capacity development, resistance, digital divide, and, more importantly, security and privacy.

Consumer Protection

The welfare role of the state is of considerable importance and therefore various measures to ensure the welfare—safety, security, and well-being—of its citizens are essential. However, citizens rely on the open market for most of their purchases—particularly, goods and, also increasingly, services. The asymmetry between the consumers of goods and services and the producers of these goods and services in terms of knowledge, bargaining power, etc. necessitates State intervention. This has resulted in setting up of consumer protection mechanisms.

The Consumer Protection Act was passed in 1986 to protect the interests of the consumers. The objective of this law is to provide a simple, fast, and inexpensive mechanism to the citizens to redress their grievances in specified cases. The Act envisages a *three-tier quasi-judicial machinery at the national, state, and district levels*:

1. National Consumer Disputes Redressal Commission at the national level.
2. State Consumer Disputes Redressal Commission at the state level.
3. District Consumer Disputes Redressal Forum at the district level.

The Act also provides for establishment of Consumer Protection Councils at the union, state, and district levels, whose main objectives are to promote and protect the rights of consumers.

Financial Inclusion

Financial inclusion or inclusive financing is the delivery of financial services at affordable costs to sections of disadvantaged and low-income segments of society, in contrast to financial exclusion where those services are not available or affordable.

Nachiket Mor Committee on Financial Inclusion

Six Visions Statements		
Topic	**What will we do?**	**Vision Statement**
1. Bank Account	First, we open bank account for every adult resident, via their Aadhar card. **(mind it: "Resident" not citizen.)**	1. A Universal Electronic Bank Account
2.Access to Bank	• But if people don't have a branch office/ATM nearby then bank account is useless. • Therefore, setup "access points" to help everyone takeout/deposit money within 15 minutes of walking distance. • Setup special "Payment banks" to facilitate banking services.	2. Ubiquitous Access to Payments and Deposit Products at Reasonable Charges

Six Visions Statements		
Topic	**What will we do?**	**Vision Statement**
3. Easy loans	• Banks don't easily give loans to poor people and small businessman • Reforms in Priority sector lending (PSL), NBFC, RRB etc and also setup special "Wholesale banks" to help achieve ability for people to get easy loans.	3. Sufficient Access to Affordable, Formal Credit
4. Investment	• If you deposit money in bank, at max you can get ~6% return (on fixed deposit/FD). But today, consumer price index is 6%. The inflation is rising higher or at same rate as the money you can earn from your bank savings. • To fix this anomaly, we'll help people access variety of investment products- mutual funds, inflation indexed bonds, NPS etc. that protect your savings against inflation.	4. Universal Access to Investment Products at Reasonable Charges
5. Insurance	• Provide insurance to everyone at reasonable cost, be it life insurance, health insurance, crop insurance, livestock insurance, property/ re insurance and so on.	5. Universal Access to Insurance and Risk Management Products at Reasonable Charges
6. Consumer Rights	• Above initiatives will be meaningless, if consumers are not protected against unscrupulous agents and financial advisors. • Setup Capital a Financial Redress Agency (FRA) to protect people in banking-financial-insurance sector.	6. Consumer protection, right to suitability, grievance redressal

Important Developments

1. Pradhan Mantri Jan Dhan Yojna is a National Mission on Financial Inclusion encompassing an integrated approach to bring about comprehensive financial inclusion of all the households in the country. The plan envisages universal access to banking facilities with at least one basic banking account for every household, financial literacy, access to credit, insurance, and pension facility. In addition, the beneficiaries would get aRuPay debit card having inbuilt accident insurance cover of Rs.1 lakh. The plan also envisages channelling all government benefits (from Centre/State/Local Body) to the beneficiaries' accounts and pushing the Direct Benefits Transfer (DBT) scheme of the Union Government.
2. Vidyalakshmi.co.in is portal developed by NSDL with the help of Ministry of Finance to help students fulfil their educational aspirations.
3. **Relaxation on know-your-customer (KYC) norms:** One can now use their Aadhaar number to open an account.
4. **Engaging business correspondents (BCs):** The BC model allows banks to provide doorstep delivery of services, especially cash in-cash out transactions, thus addressing the last-mile problem. At the grass-root level, the BCs, with the help of Village Panchayat (local governing body), have set up an ecosystem of Common Service Centres (CSC). CSC is a rural electronic hub with a computer connected to the Internet, which provides e-governance or business services to rural citizens.
5. **Use of technology:** Recognizing that technology has the potential to address the issues of outreach and credit delivery in rural and remote areas in a viable manner, banks have been advised to make effective use of information and communications technology to provide doorstep banking services through the BC model where the accounts can be operated by even illiterate customers by using biometrics, thus ensuring the security of transactions and enhancing confidence in the banking system.
6. **Adoption of EBT:** Banks have been advised to implement electronic benefits transfer (EBT) by leveraging ICT-based banking through BCs to transfer social benefits electronically to the bank account of the beneficiary and deliver government benefits to the doorstep of the beneficiary, thus reducing dependence on cash and lowering transaction costs.
7. **General Credit Card Scheme:** With a view to helping the poor and the disadvantaged with access to easy credit, banks have been asked to consider introduction of a general purpose credit card facility up to ₹ 25,000 at their rural and semi-urban branches. The objective of the scheme is to provide hassle-free credit to banks' customers based on the assessment of cash flow without insistence on security, purpose or end use of the credit. This is in the nature of revolving credit and entitles the holder to withdraw up to the limit sanctioned.

8. **Opening of branches in unbanked rural centres:** To further step up the opening of branches in rural areas so as to improve banking penetration and financial inclusion rapidly, the need for the opening of more bricks and mortar branches, besides the use of BCs, has felt. Accordingly, banks have been mandated to allocate at least 25% of the total number of branches to be opened during a year to unbanked rural centres.

Citizen's Charter

A Citizens' Charter is a public statement that defines the entitlements of citizens to a specific service, the standards of the service, the conditions to be met by users, and the remedies available to the latter in case of non-compliance of standards. The Charter concept empowers the citizens in demanding committed standards of service. Thus, the basic thrust of Citizens' Charter is to make public services citizen centric by ensuring that these services are demand driven rather than supply driven. In this context, the six principles of the Citizens' Charter movement as originally framed were:

a. Quality - improving the quality of services;
b. Choice - for the users wherever possible;
c. Standards - specifying what to expect within a time frame;
d. Value - for the taxpayers' money;
e. Accountability - of the service provider (individual as well as Organization); And
f. Transparency - in rules, procedures, schemes and grievance redressal.

Recommendations for Preparing Citizen Charters

First and foremost, it is to be understood that one size does not fit all. So a charter should be prepared for each independent unit under the overall umbrella of an organisation's charter. Wide consultations with the civil society should be integrated into the process of preparing a charter. The organizational processes and structure should be reformed to meet the commitments given in the charter.Periodic evaluation of citizens' charters should be undertaken to review benchmarks in line with the end-user feedback.

Sevottam Model

Sevottam is a service delivery excellence model that provides an assessment improvement framework to bring about excellence in public service delivery.The need for a tool like Sevottam arose from the fact that citizens' charters by themselves could not achieve the desired results in improving quality of public services.

Besides, the absence of a credible grievances redressal mechanism within organizations was also becoming a major impediment in improving service delivery standards. Thus, it was felt that unless there was a mechanism to assess the outcomes of various measures, the reform initiatives would not yield the desired results. The Sevottam model works as an evaluation mechanism to assess the quality of internal processes and their impact on the quality of service delivery.

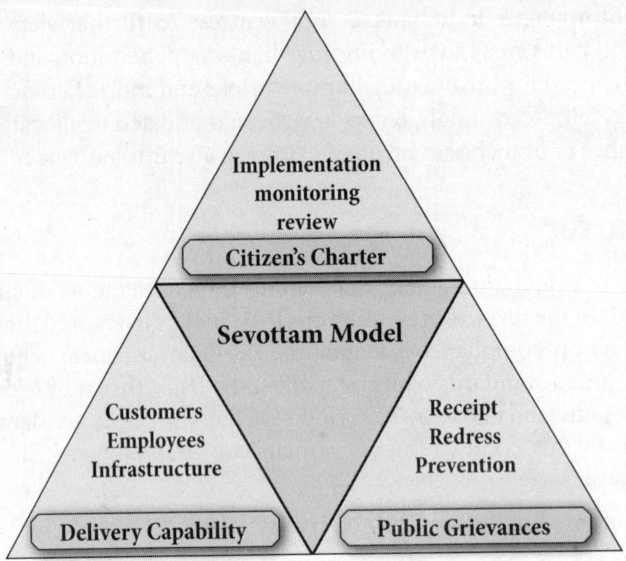

Figure 5.2 Sevottam Model

Components of Sevottam

1. Service Delivery Review
2. Grievance Redressal Review
3. Standards and Quality inspections

Citizen Participation

The mechanisms for citizens' participation in governance have been conceptualized in the following main forms:

1. **Citizens seeking information:** The RTI Act is a perfect example of how citizens' ability to access information from the government can lead to enabling greater citizen vigilance over government activities.
2. **Citizens giving suggestions:** To illustrate, the Bangalore Agenda Task Force (BATF) was set up in 1999 with the goal of transforming Bangalore into a world-class city with the participation of its leading citizens including the heads of its major IT companies, as well as prominent members of the Bangalore civic community.
3. **Citizens demanding better services:** Through citizen charters, citizens can demand better services from the government.
4. **Citizens holding service providers and other government agencies accountable:** For example, Citizen Report Cards (CRCs) on city services in Bangalore analyzed by the Public Affairs Centre—for 1994, 1999, and 2003—showed a significant improvement in the quality of services provided by city agencies.

5. **Citizens' active participation in administration and decision-making:** It is mandatory for all government organizations to develop a suitable mechanism for receipt of suggestions from citizens, which could range from the simple 'Suggestion Box' to periodic consultations with citizens' groups.

Practice Question (Main Examination)

1. **The Citizen's Charter is an ideal instrument of organizational transparency and account ability, but it has its own limitations. Identify the limitations and suggest measures for greater effectiveness of the Citizen's Charter. (250 words)**

Answer:

The Citizen's Charter is a public statement that defines the entitlements of citizens to a specific service. It covers the following as per the Administrative Reforms Commission (ARC):

1. Standards of service delivery
2. Condition to be met by users
3. Remedies available to users if they don't get the service

Hence, Citizen's Charters are effective tools to ensure citizen-centric governance to promote transparency and accountability. For example, the Income Tax Department has implemented Citizen's Charters across its offices in India.

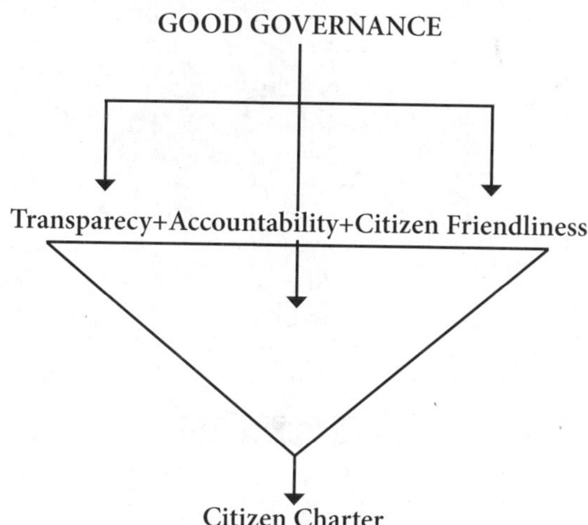

Limitations:

1. **Capacity development and training**: Lack of proper understanding among government officials leads to poor citizen interface. Bureaucratic red-tapism also leads to poor implementation.
2. **Legal enforcement**: The Citizen's Charter is not legally enforceable and, therefore, is non-justifiable. This reduces its efficacy.
3. **Awareness of citizens**: Citizens remain largely unaware of the charter and its grievance redressal mechanism, thereby making its demand-driven feature useless.
4. **Variance in standards**: There is no single standard to guide the charter formation; hence they vary across organizations, making monitoring difficult.

The Citizens' Charters initiative was introduced in India in 1997. However, implementation has faced various problems as outlined above. Measures that can be taken to solve these problems are as follows:

1. An effective awareness campaign for all the stakeholders including government officials and citizens must be undertaken at this stage.
2. Right to Service (RTS) Acts: Many states are coming up with RTS Acts to enforce the right to service for citizens. This provides the much needed legal force to Citizen's Charters.
3. Monitoring and Implementation (SEVOTTAM): Immediate adoption of the Sevottam model to address implementation, grievance redressal, and others problems.

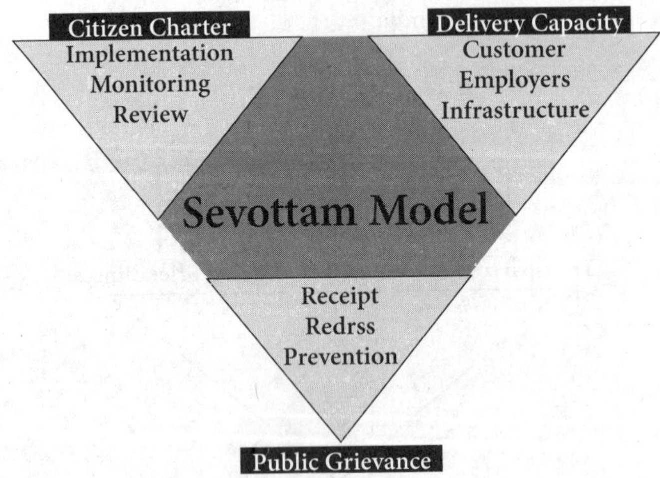

Overview of the Chapter

UPSC Syllabus Covered:

- Welfare schemes for vulnerable sections of the population by the Centre and States and the performance of these schemes; mechanisms, laws, institutions and Bodies constituted for the protection and betterment of these vulnerable sections.
- Issues relating to development and management of Social Sector/Services relating to Health, Education, Human Resources.
- Issues relating to poverty and hunger.

6

Answer Writing Tips:

- Try to limit your answers to the word limit. However, if you know the question really well, do not hesitate to go 10-20% over the word limit. If you know less, try to use general point of view to answer that question. (unless you know all 20 of them)
- Do not try to answer all the 20 questions. Target at least 18-19, out of which 10-12 are best attempts, 2-4 are average attempts and another 2-3 are general attempts. For 1-2 questions that you have left, put that time and effort in other questions you know well.

6

Social Justice

"Justice is the first virtue of social institutions"

— John Rawls, Theory of Justice, 1971

"...and to secure to all its citizens: JUSTICE, Social, Economic and Political"

— Preamble of Indian Constitution

Introduction

The United Nations' 2006 document Social Justice in an Open World: the Role of the United Nations, states that "Social justice may be broadly understood as the fair and compassionate distribution of the fruits of economic growth. . ."

In the view of former Chief Justice of India, Justice Gajendra Gadkar, the concept of social justice has dual objectives of 'removing all inequality' and affording equal opportunities for 'economic activities of all the citizens.

In D. S. Nakara v. Union of India, the Supreme Court has held that the principal aim of a socialist state is to eliminate inequality in income, status, and standards of life.

The objective of social justice is to organize the society so as to abolish the source of injustice in social relations, such as discrimination on the basis of caste, sex, religion, race, and region. Not just this, social justice may also require protective discrimination in favor of the downtrodden, underprivileged, and weaker sections of the society. Social justice leads to achievement of human rights.

Historical Underpinnings of Social Justice

The concept of social justice first surfaced in the Western thought and political language in the wake of the Industrial Revolution and the parallel development of the socialist doctrine. Social justice emerged as an expression of protest against what was perceived as the capitalist exploitation of labour and as a focal point for the development of measures to improve the human condition. It was born as a revolutionary slogan embodying the ideals of progress and fraternity. Following the revolutions that shook Europe in the mid-1800s, social justice became a rallying cry for progressive thinkers and political activists. By the mid-twentieth century, the concept of social justice had become central to the ideologies and programmes of virtually all the leftist and centrist political parties around the world. In India, social justice emerged as a major driving force after the experience of colonialism and development of India's aspirations for a just society.

Origin of the Concept of Social Justice

The concept of social justice emerged out of a process of evolution of social norms, order, law, and morality. It lays emphasis upon the just action and creates intervention in the society by enforcing the rules and regulations based on the principles in accordance with social equality.

The term 'social' as we understand it is concerned with all human beings within the society and term 'justice' is related with liberty, equality, and rights. Thus social justice ensures liberty and equality and ensures individual rights in the society.

Social Justice in Indian Political System

In India, the scheme of social justice is very well incorporated in the various provisions of the Indian Constitution. The Preamble of the Constitution includes the terms 'Socialist', 'Social and Economic Justice', 'Equality', etc., which specify that the state would extensively involve in social welfare of people and would try to establish an egalitarian society. Moreover, a distinct chapter of Directive Principles of State Policy has been dedicated towards the welfare responsibilities of the Government, which lays down the norms of ideal governance for people's welfare. The Constitution lists various fundamental rights and subsequent amendments also intended to ensure social justice to the disadvantaged citizens.

'Capabilities Approach' of Social Justice

Securing the highest possible development of the capabilities of all members of the society may be called social justice. Professor Amartya Sen. is a leading proponent of the 'rights based approach' and the 'capabilities approach'.

The capability approach is defined by its choice of focus upon the moral significance of individuals' capability of achieving the kind of lives they have reason to value. This distinguishes it from more established approaches to ethical evaluation such as utilitarianism or resourcism, which focuses exclusively on subjective well-being or the availability of means to the good life, respectively. A person's capability to live a good life is defined in terms of the set of valuable 'beings and doings' such as being in good health or having loving relationships with others, to which they have real access. It is from this that the human development index has been developed by taking various important measures such as health, education, income, etc.

Justice v. Social Justice

In dealing with the concept of social justice, it becomes essential to differentiate between the traditional idea of 'justice' and the modern idea of 'social justice' intended to establish an egalitarian society.

In modern liberal philosophy justice is defined in terms of rights not as duties. The source of such rights is the state legislation, which limits the state power non-infringing or taking away fundamental rights. In modern societies, almost all constitution's guarantee such rights and ensure their effective implementation. In this sense justice becomes a disposition to give everyone's their rights.

The notion of social justice, however, is a relatively recent phenomenon and largely a product of the modern social and economic developments. The traditional idea of justice, which is described often as a conservative approach, focused on the qualities of 'just' or virtuous man, while the modern idea of social justice assumes a just society. In ancient Greek and Hindu approaches, justice was concerned with functioning of duties, not with the notion of rights. Both Plato and Aristotle hold the state to be prior to the individual. Under the ancient Indian tradition, dharma is another name of the code of obligations and justice is nothing but virtuous conduct in line with dharma.

Constitution of India and Social Justice

Indian Constitution, the cornerstone of the nation, was intended to promote social transformation.

—Granville Austin

The Constitution of India is aimed at changing the social, political, economic, and psychological state of India. The makers of the Constitution of India were highly influenced by the feeling of social equality and social justice. For this reason, they incorporated such provisions as will ensure an equal and just society in the Constitution of India.

Social justice is the foundation stone of the Indian Constitution. That Sarkaria Commission notes, social justice is the *"defining tune of the Indian Constitution."* The makers of the Indian Constitution were well identified to use the various principles of justice. They wanted to search such form of justice that could fulfill the expectations of whole nation. Pandit Jawaharlal Nehru suggested before the Constituent Assembly: "First work of this assembly is to make India independent by a new constitution through which starving people will get complete meal and clothes, and each Indian will get best option that he can progress himself." Basically, "Wiping off every tear from every eye."

Constitutional Provisions for Social Justice

The Preamble to the Indian Constitution talks about justice—Social, Economic and Political. It says:

"WE, THE PEOPLE OF INDIA, having solemnly resolved to constitute India into a **SOVEREIGN, SOCIALIST, SECULAR, DEMOCRATIC REPUBLIC** and to secure to all its citizens:

JUSTICE, social, economic and political;

LIBERTY of thought, expression, belief, faith and worship;

EQUALITY of status and of opportunity; and to promote among them all

FRATERNITY assuring the dignity of the individual and the unity and integrity of the Nation;

IN OUR CONSTITUENT ASSEMBLY this 26th day of November, 1949, do HEREBY ADOPT, ENACT AND GIVE TO OURSELVES THIS CONSTITUTION. "

Social Justice as per the Preamble to the Indian constitution

Social justice means the absence of socially privileged classes in the society and no discrimination against any citizen on grounds of caste, creed, colour, religion, sex, or place of birth. India stands for eliminating all forms of exploitations from the society.

Provisions Relevant to Social Justice and Empowerment

Provisions Relevant to Social Justice and Emp. as a whole	
Part of the Constitution	**Article**
Preamble	"... to secure to all its citizens: **JUSTICE, social,** economic and political; **EQUALITY of status and of opportunity;** and to promote among them all **FRATERNITY assu ring the dignity of the individual and the unity and integrity of the Nation...."** are the first, third and fourth goals, respectively, mentioned in the Preamble.
III. **Fundamental Rights**	**23. Prohibition of traffic in human beings and forced labour-** (1) Traffic in human beings and begar and other similar forms of forced labour are prohibited and any contravention of this provision shall be an offence punishable in accordance with law. (2) Nothing in this article shall prevent the State from Imposing compulsory service for public purposes, and in imposing such service the State shall not make any discrimination on grounds only of religion, race, caste or class or any of them. **24. Prohibition of employment of children in factories, etc.** - No child below the age of fourteen years shall be employed to work in any factory or mine or engaged in any other hazardous employment
IV. **Directive Principles of State Policy**	**37. Application of the principles contained in this part-** The provisions contained in this part shall not be enforceable by any court, but the principles therein laid down are nevertheless fundamental in the governance of the country and it shall be the duty of the State to apply these principles in making laws.

Provisions Relevant to Social Justice and Emp. as a whole	
Part of the Constitution	**Article**
	38. State to secure a social order for the promotion of welfare of the people 1. The State shall strive to promote the welfare of the people by securing and protecting as effectively as it may a social order in which justice, social, economic and political, shall inform all the institutions of the national life. 2. The State shall, in particular, strive to minimize the inequalities in income, and endeavour to eliminate inequalities in status, facilities and opportunities, not only amongst individuals but also amongst groups of people residing in different areas or engaged in different vocations. **39. Certain principles of policy to be followed by the State - The State shall, in particular, direct its policy towards securing** - (a) that the citizens, men and women equally have the right to an adequate means of livelihood; (b) that the ownership and control of the material resources of the community are so distributed as best to subserve the common good; (c) that the operation of the economic system does not result in the concentration of wealth and means of production to the common detriment; (d) that there is equal pay for equal work for both men and women; (e) that the health and strength of workers, men and women, and the tender age of children are not abused and that citizens are not forced by economic necessity to enter avocations unsuited to their age or strength; (f) that children are given opportunities and facilities to develop in a healthy manner and in conditions of freedom and dignity and that childhood and youth are protected against exploitation and against moral and material abandonment. **39A. Equal justice and free legal aid** - The State shall secure that the operation of the legal system promotes justice, on a basis of equal opportunity, and shall, in particular, provide free legal aid, by suitable legislation or schemes or in any other way, to ensure that opportunities for securing justice are not denied to any citizen by reason of economic or other disabilities **46. Promotion of educational and economic interests of Scheduled Castes, Scheduled Tribes and other weaker sections** - The State shall promote with special care the educational and economic Interests of the weaker sections of the people, and, in particular, of the Scheduled Castes and the Scheduled Tribes, and shall protect them from social injustice and all forms of exploitation

Under The7th Schedule

Seventh Schedule (See Art 946)	List 1 - Union List
	59. Cultivation, manufacture, and sale for export, of opium
	97. Any other matter not enumerated in List Il or List Ill including any tax not mentioned in either of those Lists.
	List II - State List
	8. Intoxicating liquors, that is to say, the production, manufacture, possession, transport, purchase and sale of intoxicating liquors.
	9. Relief of the disabled and unemployable.
	List Ill - Concurrent List
	15. Vagrancy, nomadic and migratory tribes
	16. Lunacy and mental deficiency, including places for the reception or treatment of lunatics and mental deficients.
	19. Drugs and poisons, subject to the provisions of entry 59 of List I with respect to opium
	20. Economic and social planning.
	23. Social Security and social insurance employment and unemployment.

Under the 11th Schedule

There are 29 subjects under the 11th schedule. The major ones are forestry (social and farm), fisheries, agriculture including agriculture extension, land improvement, minor irrigation, minor forest produce etc. (For more exhaustive list, please refer to the internet, however a basic understanding of the broad list is sufficient).

Under the 12th Schedule

There are 18 subjects under the 12th schedule (covers urban amenities). The major ones urban and town planning, regulation of land use, construction of buildings, roads, bridges, water supply, public health, fire services etc. (For more exhaustive list, please refer to the internet, however a basic understanding of the broad list is sufficient).

In Respect of Disability and Old

Article 41: Right to work, to education and to public assistance in certain. The State shall, within the limits of its economic capacity and development, make effective provision for securing the right to work, to education and to public assistance in cases of unemployment, old age, sickness and disablement, and in other cases of undeserved want.

In Respect of Socially and Educationally Backward classes

1. Appointment of a Commission to investigate the conditions of backward classes.
2. **Article 15:** Prohibition of discrimination on grounds of religion, race, caste, sex or place of birth.
3. **Article 16:** Equality of opportunity in matters of public employment.
4. National Commission for Scheduled Castes.

Social Justice Post Liberalization

The Government of India started thinking of delivering social justice to citizens by enabling various agencies to adopt a rights-based approach.

Categorization of Social Justice Schemes

The schemes thatare being implemented by the Department of Social Justice and Empowerment are basically meant to fulfil the mandate of the Department which includes the empowerment of its target groups in the following manner.

Educational Empowerment

The schemes relating to educational empowerment of the target groups are as follows:

a. Scholarships schemes
b. Schemes relating to construction of hostels
c. Schemes relating to coaching of the students

Economic Empowerment

The following group of schemes are meant for economic empowerment of the target groups:

a. Loans at concessional rates of interest
b. Micro credit
c. Skill development

Social Empowerment

The following schemes are meant to socially empower the marginalized groups:

a. Curbing practice of untouchability, discrimination, and atrocities (Prevention of Atrocities Against SC/ST Act)

b. Support to NGOs who work for target groups

c. Recognition through national awards

B. R. Ambedkar and Social Justice

Ambedkar's life is a unique example of success despite all the odds. He struggled against the widespread social inequality, shaped by hundreds of years of exploitation and marginalization, throughout his life. Despite this inequality, he made the best of opportunities he received and made his way through the system to become one of the most intellectually inspiring figures in politics of modern India.

Ambedkar's understanding of social justice was shaped by his personal experiences of discrimination at school and later as a professor in Bombay, where despite his excellent education credentials, he was consistently treated as an 'untouchable' by fellow professors.

The epistemology of the caste system poses multiple challenges to the universal notions of liberty, equality, fraternity and justice. The discourse of power permeates the entire caste hierarchy so much so that those at the bottom of the hierarchy are almost immobilised. The sociocultural, economic and political landscape of peoples' lives is enveloped by the caste structure.

For centuries, many protest movements and social reformers have striven to undermine the caste hegemony but it was only in the twentieth century that a vigorous attack was mounted on this behemoth, both ideologically and politically. This exercise was expedited by B. R. Ambedkar, who was influenced by the ideals of the French Revolution and other western ideologues. Simultaneously, he drew upon Buddhist precepts and the works of Jotiba Phule, Narayana Guru and Periyar Ramaswamy Naickar. Coupled with this, Ambedkar's legal acumen enabled him to synthesise his knowledge in the Indian context. During the anti-colonial struggle, Indian society was in transition and Ambedkar received a fertile platform to germinate his ideas.

Views on Social Justice and Socio-cultural Rights

Ambedkar believed in complete liberty and availability of an individual to pursue every sphere of life to develop one's total personality. He understood that the Indian social system was very distinct from the western social system, and recognized that the role of the state was a must for making opportunities available for individuals of marginalized sections to be able to realize their best selves.

For this purpose (achieving social and economic rights), he believed, it was necessary to provide these sections of people with political rights that would make it possible for them and empower them to achieve these goals. This became the foundation of much of the Indian Constitution's view of social, political, and economic justice, as laid in the Preamble of the Constitution, and later with the emergence of the movement for political and economic (in public jobs) reservations in the 1980s.

For Ambedkar, social justice meant giving equal opportunity to each and every person in every sphere of life to develop one's total personality. A free social order consisted of the recognition that the individual was an end in himself/herself and that the terms of association between individuals in a society must be founded on liberty, equality and fraternity. He derived the significance of the value of equality based on the notion that the individual was inviolable. The concept of justice emphasised the right of the individual to be treated as an equal and to be respected as a member of society; irrespective of his/her caste, class, gender and other discriminations.

The attempt herein is to discuss Ambedkar's philosophy of liberalism within the broader paradigm of liberty, equality and justice. He emphasised political rights which would lead to economic and social rights. For him, rights were not merely standards but were ends as well as means, in that they provided the theoretical perspective and the necessary empowerment that was required for achieving social justice. By struggling against the state, Ambedkar used one set of rights to realise the other rights. For Western societies, state interference in realising rights is minimal. However, as the Indian society is in egalitarian, the state plays a vital role in ensuring rights. This transformative perspective is considered to be a major contribution of Ambedkar to the discourse on Indian liberalism.

As an untouchable, Ambedkar encountered social exclusion and segregation. Early in his life, he realised that a large section of his countrymen were denied their legitimate rights by the oppressive and dominant social customs and traditions. He believed that the establishment of a democratic society in India would be possible only when the untouchables and other weaker sections of society would be given an opportunity to enjoy basic human rights. The untouchables were segregated from mainstream Hindu society. The Hindu would not live in the untouchable quarter and would not allow the untouchables to live inside the Hindu quarter. This was a fundamental feature of untouchability as practiced by the Hindus. It was not a case of social separation, a mere stoppage of inter-course for a temporary period. It was a case of territorial segregation of cordon sanitaria, putting the impure inside a barbed wire, into a sort of a cage. Every Hindu village had a ghetto. The Hindus lived in the villages and untouchables in the ghetto. Therefore, Ambedkar came to the conclusion that nowhere except in India, there existed lasting separate camps and there had never been a case of a people, creating a section of their own people as permanent and hereditary slaves. Untouchability was a unique phenomenon unknown to humanity except among the Hindus. Ambedkar proved this by citing the example of the condition of the untouchables during the Peshwa rule.

Plato defined the slave as one who accepts from another the purposes which control his conduct. This could also be applicable to untouchability in India, therefore Ambedkar pointed out that the untouchables were treated as slaves because they were so socialised as never to complain of their low state; they never dreamt of improving their lot by forcing the other classes to treat them with common respect. The idea that they had been born to their lot was so ingrained in their minds that it never occurred to them to think that their fate was anything so irrevocable and nothing would ever persuade them that men are all made of the same clay, or that they have the right to insist on for better treatment than that it was meted out to them.

Ambedkar described the state of slavery of the untouchables and the denial of human rights before the Reforms Committee (Franchise), and Southborough Committee, on 27 January

1919. For Ambedkar, the exact description of the treatment was not possible. The word 'untouchable' epitomised their ills and sufferings. Not only had untouchability arrested the growth of their personality but it came in the way of their material well being. It has also deprived them of certain civil rights. For instance, in the Konkan, the untouchables were prohibited from using the public road. If some high caste man happened to cross, he had to be out of the way and stand at such a distance that his caste shadow would not fall on the former.

View on Political Rights

Ambedkar believed that the achievement of social and economic justice of the oppressed class was possible mostly through achievement of political rights for them. He advocated peaceful and constitutional means to achieve these political rights through Satyagraha, popular agitations, writings, and demand of reservations for the oppressed classes in all spheres of the government—jobs, legislative assemblies, etc. For this reason, he had demanded separate electorate for the oppressed class (STs and SCs) just like separate electorate for Muslims was granted by the British in 1909. However, this was strongly opposed by Gandhi who believed that such a step would cause further divisions of the Indian society. Finally both agreed to reservation for the oppressed class in the electorates, which would guarantee some political power as demanded by Ambedkar. He believed that democracy could not be achieved through the formation of a political democratic state. In fact, it was important for the establishment of a society that understands the value of right of each individual to personal development and freedom. Hence, there should be a social democracy to achieve a successful political democracy. As per him, democracy is not a form of government but a form of society.

Dr. Ambedkar, in 1943, argued that "A democratic form of Government presupposes a democratic form of society. The formal framework of democracy is of no value and would indeed be a misfit if there was no social democracy. " He further emphasized, "The political never realized that democracy was not a form of Government: it was essentially a form of society."

Additionally, Ambedkar believed that the oppressed class did not possess economic power; hence political power was must in achieving economic and social power for these classes. The use of pressure groups was advocated by him to lobby for the rights. It is because of these that reservation avenues opened up for the oppressed class.

Achievements of Ambedkar

Given below are some of Ambedkar's achievements:

1. Started publications, organizations, and also a Satyagraha against the caste system in 1924 in Bombay.
2. Established 'Bahiskrit Hitkarni Sabha' with social workers and people of the lower classes and untouchables.
3. Advocated 'Self-help is the best help. '
4. Stressed on education to instill confidence among the oppressed classes.

5. Organized Satyagraha at Mahad to allow oppressed classes to be able to drink water from public water tanks.
6. Organized Nasik Satyagraha for the right to temple entry.

Rights Based Approach to Social Policy

The rights based approach can be defined as the treatment of various basic minimum needs such as education, health, and social services for the citizens as essential and absolutely necessary for their development. The government must view such rights as its obligation to be provided to citizens. This approach has made governance more people centric. It allows people to demand their rights to various services and ensures that their delivery is done in an effective and efficient manner as well.

The rights based approach ensures accountability and transparency in services available to the citizens. It ensures that institutions are run for the people, and people are not harassed by institutions in demanding their entitlements. Some Example is given below.

1. The United Nations has declared the Millennium Development Goals (MDGs) and Sustainable Development Goals(SDGs) keeping in mind the basic rights of all the people to some basic services such as health, education, social safety nets, etc.
2. The Supreme Court has interpreted the Article 21, Right to Life in a variety of broad ways to include right to clean environment, right to privacy, right to life with dignity, and so on.
3. Constitutional status to panchayat raj institutions (PRIs), adoption of RTI, right to education, right to food, formulation of right to universal health coverage (UHC), social audits, etc.
4. The rights are 'basic minimum' to ensure a particular standard of living, and they are no more state patronage but they are regarded as state duties towards its citizens.

Health

As per 12th Five Year Plan, health should be viewed as not merely the absence of disease but as a state of complete physical, mental and social well being. A healthy citizenry is the very fundamental requirement for a welfare society such as India. Without a happy and healthy citizenry, growth and development are not possible. It is part of the Directive Principles of State Policy and vision of our Constitution. India is signatory to MDGs and SDGs, both of which encapsulate Universal Health coverage as a must for developmental needs. Healthy citizens increase productivity, economic growth, etc.

Social Importance of Health

A healthy citizenry is an end in itself. It is the duty of the state to ensure holistic development of people of all classes.

1. Good health is a fundamental need to achieve such goal as it ensures mental and physical ability required for citizens to be at par with each other.
2. Good health promotes freedoms of people. It enables people to achieve other freedoms such as freedom of education, secure income and so on, and hence choose their own life path.
3. The right to health is enshrined in binding international treaties and constitutions. The National Health Bill is currently under consideration (as of 2018). The Bill aims to "... provide for protection and fulfillment of rights in relation to health and well-being, health equity, and justice." Hence, it aims to make health a fundamental right just like education.
4. The quality of health has a direct relation to the quality of life.

Economic Importance of Health

Good health increases the productivity of people, hence contributes to the GDP. A large part of differences in growth rates between states in India is attributable to differences in their public health indicators. For example, if residents of Uttar Pradesh were to have life expectancy of Kerala people (nearly 15 years greater in 1995-96), the net effect on the state's output would be 60% higher than its current levels. Health problems not only account for large part of expenditure of a household but also render the household members unproductive. So poor health has a devastating impact on the poor.

Major Health Care Schemes

Almost 20% of Indian population was covered by government sponsored health insurance schemes (GSHISs) by 2010 (240 million people). This figure was projected to reach 50% or 630 million people by 2015. These schemes include Rashtriya Swasthya Bima Yojna (RSBY), Central Government Health Scheme (CGHS), Employee State Insurance (ESI) Scheme, and some others at the state level.

National Health Protection Mission (Ayushman Bharat–'Modicare')

AB-NHPM will integrate Rashtriya Swasthya Bima Yojana (RSBY) and Senior Citizen Health Insurance Scheme (SCHIS).

AB-NHPM aims to target over 10 crore families belonging to the poor and vulnerable population based on Socio-Economic and Caste Census 2011 (SECC) database. It will cover Rs. 5 lakh per family per year, taking care of almost all secondary care and tertiary care procedures. There will be no cap on family size and age in the scheme.

Benefit Cover

It includes pre and post-hospitalisation expenses. It will cover all pre-existing conditions from beginning of the policy. It will also pay defined transport allowance per hospitalization to the beneficiary.

Cashless benefits

The scheme allows the beneficiary to take cashless benefits from any public or private empanelled hospitals across the country. The payment for treatment will be done on package rate which will be defined by Government in advance basis. The package rates will include all the costs associated with treatment.

Role of state governments

They will be allowed to expand the scheme both horizontally and vertically. They will be free to choose modalities for implementation. They can implement through insurance company or directly through Trust/ Society or a mixed model.

Implementation

States/UTs will have also flexibility to modify these rates within limited bandwidth. For beneficiaries, it will be cashless and paper less transaction. States will be required to form State Health Agency (SHA) to implement scheme and at district level also, a structure for implementation of the scheme will be set up.

Entitlement

It is entitlement based scheme with entitlement decided on basis of deprivation criteria in SECC database. Different categories of families covered under scheme are Families having only one room with kucha walls and kucha roof, families having no adult member between age 16 to 59, female headed households with no adult male member between age 16 to 59, disabled member and no able bodied adult member in family, SC/ST households, landless households deriving major part of their income from manual casual labour. It will also automatically include families in rural areas having any one of the following- households without shelter, destitute, living on alms, manual scavenger families, and primitive tribal groups or legally released bonded labour. For urban areas, 11 defined occupational categories will be entitled under the scheme.

Rashtriya Swasthya Bima Yojana

RSBY has been launched by the Ministry of Labour and Employment, Government of India, to provide health insurance coverage, for secondary healthcare, for below poverty line (BPL) families. The objective of RSBY is to provide protection to BPL households from financial liabilities arising out of health shocks that involve hospitalization. Beneficiaries under RSBY are entitled to hospitalization coverage up to ₹ 30, 000 for most of the diseases that require hospitalization. The Government has fixed the package rates for the hospitals for a large number of interventions. The scheme covers pre-existing conditions from day one, and there is no age limit. Coverage extends to five members of family, which includes the head of household, spouse and up to three dependents.

Beneficiaries need to pay only INR 30/- as registration fee while Central and State Government pays the premium to the insurer selected by the State Government on the basis of a competitive bidding.

Rationale behind RSBY or BPL Health Insurance Schem es

1. Debt trap: For people living below the poverty line, illness could result in the family falling into a debt trap.
2. Preventative and early care: When the need to get the treatment arises for poor families, they often ignore it because of lack of resources, fearing wage loss, or wait till the last moment when it is too late.
3. Protection of financial and other assets of the poor: Even if the poor do decide to get the desired healthcare, it consumes their savings, thus forcing them to sell their assets and property or cut other important spending such as children's education.

Features of RSBY

1. The beneficiary can choose either a private or a public hospital.
2. Business model for many stakeholders and private players as well:
    a. Insurers
        i. The insurer is paid premium for each household enrolled for RSBY. Therefore, the insurer has the motivation to enroll as many households as possible from the BPL list. This results in better coverage of target beneficiaries.
    b. Hospitals
        i. Hospitals get refunded by the insurers, and money flows directly from the insurers to them. Hence the hospitals have an incentive to treat the patient. The insurer ensures that no unnecessary charges are charged by hospitals and business practices are ethical.
    c. Intermediaries
        i. NGOs and Micro Finance Institutions are also paid for services to reach out to beneficiaries
    d. Government
        i. By paying only a maximum sum up to INR 750/- per family per year, the Government is able to provide access to quality healthcare to the below poverty line population. It will also lead to a healthy competition between public and private health services providers, which in turn will improve the functioning of the public healthcare providers.
    e. IT intensive
        i. Every beneficiary is issued with a smart card.
    f. Safe and foolproof
        i. The use of biometric-enabled smart cards makes the system foolproof

g. Portability

i. The health insurance smart card can used at any hospital empanelled by RSBY.

h. It offers cashless and paperless transactions.

i. The scheme has a robust monitoring mechanism.

Integrated Child Development Schemes

This scheme was launched in 2nd October, 1975, to provide supplementary nutrition, preschool education, and primary healthcare to children below 6 years of age and their mothers. The scheme aims to promote proper mental, physical, and social development of children in India, as well as reduce mortality rates among children; increase nutrition levels, and reduces school dropouts. The scheme also promotes gender equality by providing equal resources to the girls as boys and benefits over 34 million children (0-6 year's age) and over seven million mothers every year. The scheme is implemented through Anaganwadi Centers by the Ministry of Health and Family welfare.

Scope of Services

1. Immunization
2. Supplementary nutrition
3. Health checkups
4. Referral services
5. Preschool non-formal education
6. Nutrition and health information

Impact

By the end of 2010, the programme had covered 80. 6 lakh expectant and lactating mothers along with 3. 93 crore children (under 6 years of age). There are 6, 719 operational projects with 1241, and 749 operational Anaganwadi centres. A study in states of Tamil Nadu, Andhra Pradesh, and Karnataka demonstrated significant improvement in the mental and social development of all children irrespective of their gender. A 1992 study of National Institute of Public Cooperation and Child Development confirmed improvements in birth weight and infant mortality of Indian children along with improved immunization and nutrition. However, the World Bank has also highlighted certain key shortcomings of the programme, including inability to target the girl child improvements, cornering of benefits by the wealthier families, and the lowest level of funding for the poorest and the most undernourished states of India.

National Rural Health Mission

This scheme was launched in 2005 as a part of the overarching National Health Mission. Its main mission is to provide effective healthcare services to rural masses in the country with a focus on states with poor public health indicators and weak healthcare infrastructure. The scheme is characterized by (1) significantly increased financing, (2) flexibility around hiring contractual staff; (3) supply chain reforms, (4) introduction of a cadre of grassroots workers paid entirely on the basis of performance, and (5) overall increased emphasis on public health expenditure

The programme under NRHM can be broadly categorized under the two:

1. Reproductive & Child Health Programmes aimed at addressing challenges of maternal and newly born health issues.
2. National Disease Control Programmes aimed at disease control.

Goals of NHM

1. Reduce MMR to 1/1000 live births
2. Reduce IMR to 25/1000 live births
3. Reduce TFR (Total Fertility Rate) to 2.1
4. Prevention and reduction of anaemia in women aged 15-49 years
5. Prevent and reduce mortality and morbidity from communicable, non communicable; Injuries and emerging diseases
6. Reduce household out-of-pocket expenditure on total health care expenditure
7. Reduce annual incidence and mortality from Tuberculosis by half
8. Reduce prevalence of Leprosy to <1/10000 population and incidence to zero in all districts
9. Annual Malaria Incidence to be <1/1000
10. Less than 1 per cent microfilaria prevalence in all districts
11. Kala-azar Elimination by 2015, <1 case per 10000 population in all blocks

Initiatives of NHM

i. Accredited Social Health Activists (ASHAs)

   1. Community health volunteers and accredited social health activists (known as ASHAs) have been engaged under the mission for establishing a link between the community and the health system.
   2. ASHA is the first port of call for any health related demand of deprived sections of the population, especially women and children, who find it difficult to access health services in rural areas.
   3. ASHA Programme is expanding across states and has particularly been successful in bringing people back to Public Health System and has increased the utilization of outpatient services, diagnostic facilities, institutional deliveries, and inpatient care.

ii. Rogi Kalyan Samiti (Patient Welfare Committee) and Hospital Management Society

    1. Manage affairs of hospitals

iii. Untied Grants to Sub-centres

    1. Untied Grants to Sub-Centres have been used to fund grass-root improvements in healthcare. For example, improved efficacy of ANMs in the field that can now undertake better antenatal care and other healthcare services.
    2. Village Health Sanitation and Nutrition Committees have used Untied Grants to increase their involvement with their local communities to address the needs of poor households and children.

iv. Healthcare Contractors

v. Janani Suraksha Yojana

    1. Janani Suraksha Yojana (JSY) aims to reduce maternal mortality among pregnant women by encouraging them to deliver at government health facilities.
    2. Under the scheme, one-time cash assistance is provided to eligible pregnant women for giving birth at a government health facility.
    3. Large-scale demand side financing under the JSY has brought poor households to the public sector health facilities on a scale never witnessed before.

vi Janani Shishu Suraksha Karyakram

    1. As part of recent initiatives and further moving in the direction of universal healthcare, Janani Shishu Suraksha Karyakarm was introduced to provide free to and fro transport, free drugs, free diagnostics, free blood, and free diet to pregnant women who come for delivery to public health institutions as well as sick infants up to one year.

vii. Rahstriya Bal Swasthya Karyakaram

    1. A Child Health Screening and Early Intervention Services has been launched in February 2013 to screen diseases specific to childhood, developmental delays, disabilities, birth defects, and deficiencies.
    2. The initiative will cover about 27 crore children between 0 and 18 years of age and also provide free treatment including surgery for health problems diagnosed under this initiative.

viii. National Iron+ Initiative

    1. The National Iron+ Initiative is an attempt to look at iron deficiency and anaemia in which beneficiaries will receive iron and folic acid supplementation irrespective of their iron/Hb status. This initiative will bring together existing programmes (IFA supplementation for pregnant and lactating women and children in the age group of 6–60 months) and introduce new age groups.

ix. National Mobile Medical Units

x. National Disease Control Programme

xi. National Vector Borne Diseases Control Programme

xii. Revised National Tuberculosis Control Programme

xiii. National AIDS Control programme

xiv. Immunization

1. Mission Indradhanush: Launched recently, the mission aims to cover all unvaccinated or partially vaccinated children by the year 2020 against seven vaccine preventable diseases. The diseases that come under the mission are diphtheria, whooping cough, tetanus, polio, tuberculosis, measles, and hepatitis B.
2. Four special vaccination campaigns were being conducted under the programme between January and June 2015.
3. About 201 districts were covered in the first phase and 297 will be targeted for the second phase.

xv. Clean Drinking Water under National Rural Drinking Water Programme (NRDWP)

1. Solar power based water supply schemes launched across rural and far-flung areas to provide clean water where electricity is a constraint

xvi. Swachh Bharat Mission (Gramin)

1. Aimed at making open defecation free India by 2019.

The Case for Universal Healthcare

a. Essential public good for the development of people's capabilities and productivity enhancement of the workforce.

b. Private healthcare is not a good substitute because of affordability.

12th FYP on Health

Problems in the Public Healthcare Domain in India

1. Low spending on public health: In India, only 1. 3% of the GDP is spent on healthcare compared to almost 4. 3% of other major developing countries such as Brazil and almost 7%–8% of the developed countries.
2. Availability: Low number of doctors, nurses and auxiliary nurses, and midwives (ANMs) and their widespread geographical variation within India.
3. Affordability: Lack of extensive coverage by the government deprives a huge population from basic health services. A lack of medicines causes the prices to be inflated artificially at private hands. A large fraction of the out-of-pocket expenditure arises from outpatient care and purchase of medicines, which are mostly not covered even by the existing insurance schemes. In any case, the percentage of population covered by health insurance is small.
4. Quality: Many practitioners in the private sector are not qualified to be doctors.

5. Total expenditure (public+private+household out of pocket) around 4.1% of the GDP, which is almost similar to other developing countries; however public expenditure is only 27% of this total expenditure, which is very low by any standard. Government must increase its expenditure drastically, which is the lowest among BRICS—Brazil and South Africa in 9% range (total expenditure).

Recommendations of High Level Expert Group on Universal Health Coverage

1. **Health Financing and Financial Protection:** Government should increase public expenditure on health from the current level of 1.2 percent of GDP to at least 2.5 percent by the end of the Twelfth Plan, and to at least 3 percent of GDP by 2022. General taxation should be used as the principal source of healthcare financing, not levying sector specific taxes. Specific purpose transfers should be introduced to equalise the levels of per capita public spending on health across different states. Expenditures on primary healthcare should account for at least 70 per cent of all healthcare expenditure. The technical and other capacities developed by the Ministry of Labour for the RSBY should be leveraged as the core of UHC operations--and transferred to the Ministry of Health and Family Welfare.
2. **Access to Medicines, Vaccines and Technology.** Price controls and price regulation, especially on essential drugs, should be enforced. The Essential Drugs List should be revised and expanded, and rational use of drugs ensured. Public sector should be strengthened to protect the capacity of domestic drug and vaccines industry to meet national needs. Safeguards provided by Indian patents law and the TRIPS Agreement against the country's ability to produce essential drugs should be protected. MoHFW should be empowered to strengthen the drug regulatory system.
3. Human Resources for Health Institutes of Family Welfare should be strengthened and Regional Faculty Development Centres should be selectively developed to enhance the availability of adequately trained faculty and faculty-sharing across institutions. District Health Knowledge Institutes, a dedicated training system for Community Health Workers, State Health Science Universities and a National Council for Human Resources in Health (NCHRH) should be established.
4. **Health Service Norms:** A National Health Package should be developed that offers, as part of the entitlement of every citizen, essential health services at different levels of the healthcare delivery system. There should be equitable access to health facilities in urban areas by rationalising services and focusing particularly on the health needs of the urban poor.
5. Management and Institutional Reforms All India and State level Public Health Service Cadres and a specialised State level Health Systems Management Cadre should be introduced in order to give greater attention to Public Health and also to strengthen the management of the UHC system. The establishment of a National Health Regulatory and Development Authority (NHRDA) a, National Drug Regulatory and Development Authority (NDRDA) and a National Health Promotion and Protection Trust (NHPPT) is also recommended.
6. Community Participation and Citizen Engagement Existing Village Health Committees should be transformed into participatory Health Councils.
7. Gender and Health There is a need to improve access to health services for women, girls and other vulnerable genders (going beyond maternal and child health).

In moving forward, there are two key questions:

1. How to combine public and private providers effectively for meeting UHC goals in a manner that avoids perverse incentives, reduces provider induced demand, and that meets the key objectives specified above
2. How to integrate different types and levels of services-public health and clinical; preventive and promotive interventions along with primary, secondary, and tertiary clinical care-so that continuum of care is assured? Inadequate prevention and inappropriate utilisation of secondary or tertiary care, when primary care should suffice, would result in much higher cost of care.

a. A mix of public and private services is the reality of most countries. In order to make this mix work, a strong regulatory framework is essential to ensure that the UHC programme is most effective in controlling cost, reducing provider induced demand, and ensuring quality.

b. Provider payment mechanisms, in themselves, are not magic bullets, and there are limits to what they can do. Capitation-based networks can reduce disincentives to continuity of care, but by themselves, they will not guarantee it. For this, there have to be, in addition, improvements in service delivery, improvements in human resources and related regulatory development and enforcement.

c. Further, there is a need to build up institutions of citizens' participation, in order to strengthen accountability and complement what the regulatory architecture seeks to do.

   i. First focus should be on public health infrastructure, which can be supplemented by PPPs and move towards the UHC system in the long run as it takes a lot of time to develop.

Illustrative List of Preventive and Public Health Interventions Funded and provided by Government

1. Full Immunisation among children under three years of age and pregnant women
2. Full antenatal, natal and postnatal care
3. Skilled birth attendance with a facility for meeting need for emergency obstetric care
4. Iron and Folic acid supplementation for children, adolescent girls and pregnant women
5. Regular treatment of intestinal worms, especially in children and reproductive age women
6. Universal use of iodine and iron fortified salt
7. Vitamin A supplementation for children aged 9 to 59 months
8. Access to a basket of contraceptives, and safe abortion services
9. Preventive and promotive health educational services, including information on hygiene, hand-washing, dental hygiene, use of potable drinking water, avoidance of tobacco, alcohol, high calorie diet and obesity, need for regular physical exercise, use of helmets on two wheelers and seat belts, advice on initiation of breastfeeding within one hour of birth and

exclusively up to six months of age, and complimentary feeding thereafter, adolescent sexual health, awareness about RTI/STI, need for screening for NCDs and common cancers for those at risk

10. Home based new born care, and encouragement for exclusive breastfeeding till six months of age
11. Community based care for sick children, with referral of cases requiring higher levels of care
12. HIV testing and counselling during antenatal care
13. Free drugs to pregnant HIV positive mothers to prevent mother to child transmission of HIV
14. Malaria prophylaxis, using Long Lasting Insecticide Treated Nets (LLIN), diagnosis using Rapid Diagnostic Kits (RDK) and appropriate treatment
15. School check-up of health and wellness, followed by advice, and treatment if necessary
16. Management of diarrhoea, especially in children, using Oral Rehydration Solution (ORS)
17. Diagnosis and treatment of Tuberculosis, Leprosy including Drug and Multi-Drug Resistant cases
18. Vaccines for hepatitis B and C for high risk groups
19. Patient transport systems including emergency response ambulance services of the dial 108 model

The present Rashtriya Swasthya Bima Yojana (RSBY) which provides 'cash less' in-patient treatment for eligible beneficiaries through an insurance based system will need to be reformed to enable access to a continuum of comprehensive primary, secondary and tertiary care. The coverage of RSBY was initially limited to the BPL population but, was subsequently expanded to other categories. It should be the objective of the Twelfth Plan to use the platform and existing mechanisms of RSBY to cover the entire population below the poverty line. In planning health care structures for the future, it is desirable to move away from a 'fee-for-service' mechanism for the reasons outlined by the HLEG (High Level Expert Group), to address the issue of fragmentation of services that works to the detriment of preventive and primary care and also to reduce the scope for fraud and induced demand.

Goals

1. Reduction of infant mortality rate
2. Reduction of maternal mortality ratio
3. Reduction of total fertility rate
4. Prevention and reduction of undernourishment
5. Prevention and reduction of anemia in women aged 15-49 years
6. Raising child sex ratio in the 0-6 years age group from 914 to 950
7. Reduction of out-of-pocket expenses of poor households

Challenges faced by current healthcare programmes

1. Anganwadi centres, where people (especially women, pregnant women, young children for vaccination, etc.) can access public health services, are located in upper class areas within the villages. This creates barriers for extremely poor and lower class individuals to access these centres, rendering the scheme less effective.
2. Disease prone and areas facing serious malnourishment must be focused on as they are too burdened.
3. High out-of-pocket spending of these individuals.
4. Workload distribution, motivation, and training of employees.
5. Reach inaccessible areas through mobile medical units. The success of Assam and Kerala's water medical units on large boats has been quite successful in reaching extremely inaccessible areas.
6. Poor infrastructure improvements.

Repositioning the AWC as a vibrant, child friendly ECD centre (Baal Vikas Kendra) which will ultimately be owned by women in the community. This will have expanded/redesigned services, extended duration 6 hours), with an additional AWW provided initially in 200 high burden districts and with piloting of crèche services in 5 percent of AWCs. These would function as the first village outpost for health, nutrition, early learning and other women and child related services. This would include the provision of adequate infrastructure, facilities such as safe drinking water, toilets, hygienic SNP arrangements, wall painting, play space and a joyful early learning environment including provision for activity corners, and anchoring of other adolescent girls through the Rajiv Gandhi Scheme for Empowerment of Adolescent Girls. Greater ownership by women and communities would also come with institutional reforms that include the establishment of Anganwadi Management Committees, which include mothers/mahila mandals/parents as members, empowered with untied funds for local action.

Re-designing and reinforcing of the package of ICDS services, including a new component of Child Care and Nutrition Counselling for mothers of children under three years. This will focus on regular and prioritised home visiting at critical contact points, improving key family care behaviours Infant and Young Child Feeding, health, hygiene, psychosocial care, early learning and care of girls and women.

Building on learnings from the positive deviance approach initiated, SNEHA SHIVIRs will be introduced for community based care of undernourished children. These include 12 day Nutrition Care and Counselling Sessions at AWCs, using positive role model mothers, whose children are growing well, for demonstrating positive care practices, cooking and feeding. (with mothers' contribution) to mothers of undernourished children in similar community environments, This improves family care and feeding behaviours (Learning By Doing) through sustainable approaches, enhancing local caregiving capacities through peer counselling, demonstrating positive care practices and enabling change, using local resources--touching the lives of young children and their communities.

Public-Private Partnerships (PPP) in Health Sector

Tertiary Care: Rajiv Gandhi Super-speciality Hospital, Raichur, Karnataka

Contracting Arrangements: Government of Karnataka and Apollo Hospitals

Type of Partnership: Joint Venture (Management Contract)

Service: Provides super speciality clinical care services and management of Hospital. Free Outpatient services for BPL patients

Rural Health Care Delivery and management of PHCS

Contracting Arrangements: Karuna Trust and Government of Arunachal Pradesh

Type of Partnership: Contracting in

Services: Manages 11 PHC provides health care facilities to the local population

Labs, Drug Supply and Diagnostic Services: Hindlabs

Contracting Arrangements: MOHFW and HLL Life Care Ltd

Type of Partnership: Contracting in

Services: A novel initiative, delivers high end diagnostic services at CGHS rates

Health Insurance: Community Health Insurance Scheme

Contracting Arrangements: Karuna Trust, National Insurance Co and Government of Karnataka

Type of Partnership: Joint Venture

Services: A community health insurance scheme to improve the access and utilisation of health services

Outreach/Health Delivery: Mobile Health Service in Sunderban, W. Bengal

Contracting Arrangements: Government of West Bengal and Non-profit NGO

Type of Partnership: Contracting in (Joint Venture)

Services: Mobile boat based health services and access to health services in remote areas

RCH Services: Merry Gold Health Network (MGHN) and SAMBHAV Voucher Scheme in UP

Contracting Arrangements: Joint endeavour of Government of India and USAID through UP SIFPSA

Type of Partnership: Social Franchising network and Voucher system

Services: Provide FP/RCH services through accredited private providers

General Issues with Healthcare in India

Low Spending

India spends only 1. 3% of GDP on healthcare. This is not only below but almost half of even countries in North Africa, Sub-Saharan Africa, and the Middle East and much below other developing and developed countries.

No Universal Healthcare

India has not achieved universal healthcare (except for recent attempts to introduce full insurance coverage through Ayushman Bharat Scheme) as compared to China, Thailand, and Mexico, all developing countries that have achieved universal health coverage for their entire populations. In China, such a programme was launched under the New Cooperative Medical Scheme and in Mexico under the Seguro Popular health insurance programme.

Poor Condition of Facilities

The healthcare infrastructure is shabby, with acute shortage of medical staff (50%–70% shortage of physicians, specialists, and lab technicians and radiographers at community health centres) and widespread leakage and corruption in government hospitals and healthcare centres.

Absence of discussions on healthcare in popular press and media

The media has not particularly focused its debates on healthcare outcomes such as maternal health, child mortality, malnutrition etc. This has led to low awareness among the general public about state of health in the country.

Underachievement in Maternal and Child Health

India has lagged miserably in maternal and child health improvement. It has recorded one of the worst performances on undernourishment and child health. It has also been unsuccessful at delinking maternal health from that of her children, which results in transmission of ill health from the mother to her children. There is abnormal regional variation with some regions lagging extremely behind others and the national average. Almost 60% children in India were undernourished in 1998-99 according to the composite index of anthropometric failure and 45. 2% stunted 15. 9% wasted, and 47. 1% underweight.

Private Healthcare Industry

The inadequacy and poor quality of the public health facilities has led to the growth of a multitude of private healthcare providers, operating either as stand-alone facilities or as well-established chains. It is no wonder then that almost 80% of outpatient and 60% of inpatient visits are to private healthcare providers (as per 12thFive Year Plan). Hence, private healthcare providers are an important part of the equation when trying to provide universal healthcare coverage in India. However, the private healthcare costs are usually high.

Problems with Private Health Insurance Based Healthcare System Efficiency Issues

Health insurance is likely to attract people who are prone to illness thus driving up premiums and leading to exclusion of low-risk customers. This is termed as adverse selection and may lead to 'screening' of patients and hence is against the principle of equity in healthcare. Another efficiency issue is called moral hazard—that both insured patients and private providers have no incentive to contain costs. At the same time, if the rates are prefixed by the government, the health providers may be forced to cut costs and minimize them regardless of the quality of healthcare provided to the patients and may even go against the interests of patients. They may indulge in 'cream skimming', i. e., focus on patients who can be treated at low cost and turn away the rest.

Distortion Issue

A commercial health insurance system is generally biased against non-hospitalized care and pre ventative care. Private health insurance tends to be aimed mostly at hospitalized care. This creates a bias against preventive health. This challenge is big especially for India since a large amount of the disease burden is that of communicable diseases. It also leads to a general overlook and reduced focus on public health systems and gives a boost to private healthcare. This is unlike the route by which countries such as China, Thailand, Brazil, and Mexico have achieved near-universal healthcare, i. e., a strong public healthcare system.

Targeting Issue

There are problems targeting any benefit to the below poverty line (BPL) people. The targeting is generally unreliable. The problem is graver in the case of health since a single ailment is enough to push an entire family below the poverty line. It is simply not possible to revise the BPL line so frequently. Further, the BPL line is based on per capita income. However a person may have sufficient income in general but the nature of disability could be so severe that he cannot finance the care on his own.

Inequity

Sources of inequity are potential screening by insurance companies, inefficient targeting, general obstacles such as low education and powerlessness in using a health insurance system.

Irreversibility Issue

A major shift to private health insurance could be irreversible as it would emerge as a very powerful lobby.

Unsustainable Model

The model is similar what is followed in the US. And the American experience is not encouraging as it has proven to be one of the most costly and ineffective models in the industrialized world. The per capita health expenditure in the US is nearly double that of Europe but the health outcomes are poorer:

1. Highly inequitable as nearly 20% population is excluded from it.
2. Reform has been difficult due to the power of the insurance industry.

On the other hand, China, Brazil, Mexico, Thailand, and Vietnam have achieved near-universal coverage with publicly funded health services.

The Nutrition Issue

The nutrition issue in the South Asia has been often referred to as the 'Asian Enigma' (made popular by Amartya Sen in his work 'The Uncertain Glory'). The nutrition situation as measured by the proportion of underweight (weight for age) children under 5 in India is poorer than sub-Saharan Africa and least developed nations. The broad patterns are the same for stunting (height for age). The oft repeated argument that Indians are genetically shorter and international anthropometric standards should not apply has been proved to be a myth by many studies. The entire Indian population also suffers severe deficiencies including of iron, vitamin A, etc. This is partly due to inadequate supplementation programmes. Actually, the numbers for nutrition are uniformly poor across South Asia even compared to many sub-Saharan African countries. Studies point to various possible reasons for this; one is the poor status and health of women. A poor nutritional status of women during pregnancy leads to low birth weights affecting the nutritional status of new borns right from their birth. The poor nutritional status of women is also a reality across South Asia.

Further, the lack of improvement over time is disconcerting. Between 1992-1993 and 2005-2006, the first National Family Health Survey (NFHS-1) and NFHS-3, nothing much had changed. However, NFHS-4 done recently by the UNICEF and Ministry of Women and Child Welfare found improvements across various parameters of mothers' and babies' health. For example, IMR has declined from 57 to 41 per 1000 live births (from NFHS-3 to NFHS-4). Institutional delivery has increased from 38. 7% in NFHS-3 to 78. 9% in NFHS-4. Total fertility rates have declined from 2. 7 to 2. 2 over the same period. Immunization rate has increased by 18% to 62% over the same period as well.

The (Successful) example of Tamil Nadu Healthcare

Tamil Nadu state has a clear commitment to free and universal healthcare covering a good range of services. Correspondingly, most of the health indicators in the state are also much better than the national averages including the infant mortality rate (IMR), maternal mortality ratio (MMR), life expectancy, proportion of underweight/stunted children, institutional deliveries, antenatal and post-natal care, breastfeeding, etc. In fact Tamil Nadu is expected to soon cover the gap with Kerala, the state with the best set of health indicators. The health policy and outcomes actually fit into a larger pattern of creative, inclusive, and comparatively active social policies.

The foundation of the Tamil Nadu's healthcare system is an extensive network of primary health centres—all well organized, supplied with essential medicines, and well staffed. The geographical density of health centres, ratio of doctors and nurses to population, and the presence of women staff are much higher in Tamil Nadu than in other states. There is timely supply of free medicines, which is handled by a pharmaceutical corporation set up by the state machinery, which is unlike other states where patients are given prescriptions and have to buy drugs from commercial pharmaceutical shops.

The Tamil Nadu healthcare programme focus on basics, i. e. , preventive healthcare, is also commendable and includes child immunization and public health (basically sanitation, hygiene, waste disposal, disease surveillance, health education, food safety regulation, etc.)

Role of Integrated Child Development Services

In Tamil Nadu, Integrated Child Development Services programme is characterized by well built infrastructure, large attendance rates even within 0–3 age group, good quality of education, and positive mothers' perception of the scheme. The state has taken initiative and ownership of the scheme and incorporated many innovations. There is a sophisticated training system for the staff and the entire programme is run by women from top to bottom. This has gone a long way in augmenting the child healthcare indicators in the state.

Suggested Focus Areas

The first and foremost suggestion is to increase public spending on health as a percentage of GDP. The need of the hour is a commitment to universal coverage through public financing without relying on the private sector. This does not mean that the private sector has no role at all. But it can only supplement and not supplant the public healthcare system. This is the route through which a large number of countries in East Asia and Latin America have transitioned to near-universal healthcare in the recent past. So the foundational role has to be played by the public sector.

We need to go back to the basics. Focus needs to shift on both preventive and curative care, making primary healthcare centres (PHCs) the foundation of our public health system, and empowering and educating village level health workers. It is necessary to consolidate the gains made by innovations such as the Janani Suraksha Yojana, role of ASHA workers in vaccination programmes, etc. While simultaneously learning and absorbing the lessons from China and Thailand, etc. and also from Tamil Nadu and Kerala.

It will be helpful to bring healthcare at the centre of attention of democratic politics and public debate. Just like the example of Tamil Nadu, the experience of Thailand also shows the importance of public involvement in health policy and issues. There is a 'Health Assembly' in Thailand that holds regular meetings where complaints and reviews on health policy are aired by the citizens.

Availability of healthcare personnel is another serious issue, more so in the rural areas. The number of doctors per lakh of population is around 45 in India, whereas the minimum number should be 85. Again there is an acute shortage of nursing and other ancillary staff.

The out-of-pocket expenses of poor are too high (almost 70% of the overall healthcare expenses). Medicines are too expensive for various communicable and no communicable diseases. Prescription drugs reforms, promotion of essential, generic medicines, and making these universally available free of cost to all patients in public facilities is required.

The private sector forms majority of the healthcare system, but it is out of reach for most of the population. Their active participation and contribution in the general health of the poor needs to be ensured.

Price controls and price regulation, especially on essential drugs, should be enforced. The Essential Drugs List should be revised and expanded, and rational use of drugs ensured. Create awareness among masses about the Jan Aushadhi Programme.

Safeguards provided by the Indian Patents law and the TRIPS Agreement against the country's ability to produce essential drugs should be protected.

Apart from these, new institutions are required to be created:

a. National Health Regulatory and Development Authority

b. A National Drug Regulatory and Development Authority

c. A National Health Promotion and Protection Trust

Steps already taken

1. Universal Health Coverage has been envisaged as the goal of new draft healthcare policy.
2. Governance reforms in healthcare.
    - Performance-linked incentives for healthcare givers.
    - Devolution of powers and functions to local healthcare institutions and making them responsible for the health of the people living in a defined geographical area.
    - NRHM's strategy of decentralization, PRI involvement, and integration of vertical programmes, inter-sectoral convergence, and health systems strengthening has been partially achieved.
    - Professional procurement agencies on the lines of Tamil Nadu.
3. National Health Mission
    - Janani Suraksha Yojana
    - Indradhanush for full immunization of children
4. Rashtriya Swasthya Suraksha Yojana
5. Focus on developing ANMs, ASHAs
6. Community involvement through
    - Jan Sunwais and Rogi Kalyan Samitis
    - Village Health Sanitation and Nutrition Committee

Universal Health Coverage Models

1. Cashless delivery of an essential health package (EHP) to all ought to be the basic deliverable in all models. Linkages of EHP with government pharmacies (for public providers) and Jan Aushadhi outlets (for all) are required.
2. An effective health information network that could be accessed by all service providers and patients (for their own records) would enable the continuum of care.
3. Targeting of people through Aadhaar.
4. Community involvement to be the focus.

5. Financing of UHC:
    - By PPP or NPPP (Not-for-profit PPP)
    - Corporate social responsibility funding can go to government hospitals, healthcare centres, etc.

Disease Control Programmes

1. National Vector Borne Disease Control Programme
    - India has 56% of world's leprosy patients and 21% of tuberculosis (TB) patients.
    - Multi-drug resistance to TB is being increasingly recognized.
2. Regulation
    - The Food Safety and Standards Act came into being in 2011 and integrated the food laws in India into one single law.
    - Various other acts such as The Transplantation of Human Organs Act and PC-PNDT Act have been amended.
    - AYUSH Ministry has been set up and the use of AYUSH medicine in place of allopathic medicine has been recommended in a phased manner in CHCs, PHCs, and district hospitals.
    - Role of ICMR (Indian Council for Medical Research] and New Health Research Division.

Food Safety

Food Safety and Standards Authority of India (FSSAI) has been established to improve transparency in its functioning and decision-making.

1. Bio-safety would be an integral part of any risk assessment being undertaken by FSSAI.
2. Standardized tests for adulteration to be introduced across the labs in India and BIS to undertake framing of guidelines as well.
3. Public information campaigns to reduce the consumption of unhealthy foods to be undertaken.
4. Food surveys would be undertaken to gather the information and their results would be published regularly.
5. Steps such as marking of vegetarian, non-vegetarian, best before dates, nutritional requirements, etc.

Early Childhood Development

According to WHO, first six months of a child's life are the most vulnerable and important days in respect to mortality as well as later growth. Some other India centric data are as follows (only two large states have been picked below for reference purpose. Other data can be seen at http://rchiips. Org):

1. IMR, MMR still high in India—MDG not achieved.
   - IMR: 44 deaths/1000
   - MMR: 140 deaths per 100, 000
2. Immunization rate in India: 51%
   - Tamil Nadu: 86%
   - Uttar Pradesh: 29% (second last)
3. Institutional Delivery Rate: 41%
   - Tamil Nadu: 90%
   - Uttar Pradesh: 22%
4. Children are stunted, wasted, and malnourished.

Education

Education forms the core of India's "tryst with destiny". Our founding fathers and freedom fighters (even spiritual torchbearers such as Vivekananda and Sri Aurobindo) had consistently written about the importance of education in a nation. Tagore once said: "the imposing tower of misery which today rests on the heart of India has its sole foundation in the absence of education."

Broad Objectives of Education

Education must develop multi-dimensional intelligence among students. This may include:

1. Cognitive intelligence covering skill development and research orientation,
2. Emotional intelligence for team spirit and risk taking attitude,
3. Moral intelligence to blend personal ambitions with national goals,
4. Social intelligence to defend civil rights and fight inequality, and
5. Spiritual intelligence for peace.

Benefits of Education

1. Improves quality of life
2. Leads to potentially productive employment
3. Enhances political voice of people

4. Creates awareness regarding health problems
5. Creates awareness about human rights
6. Creates awareness about legal rights
7. Helps empower women
8. Reduces class and caste inequalities
9. Opens up more avenues for recreation, creative engagement, and enjoyment

Relationship between education and development

Europe and USA's commitment to public education led to industrialization and economic growth. The government delivered free education in these countries led to massive social and economic improvements over the 18th and 19th centuries.

Japan's focus on education transformed the country into a global economic, military, and social power. Transformation of Japan in the late 19th century from an agrarian and feudal economy to the largest industrial power in Asia and one of the most prosperous countries was achieved by rapid advances in education after the Meiji restoration. The fundamental code of education issued in 1872 expressed a clear public mandate to achieve 100% literacy in Japan. Between 1906 and 1911, education consumed as much as 43% of the budgets of towns and villages for Japan as a whole. By 1913, Japan was fully literate. Though poorer than Britain and the US, it was publishing more books than Britain and twice as many as the US. The focus on education determined the rapid industrialization and development in Japan during this time.

Later, Taiwan, South Korea, China, Singapore, and Hong Kong embarked on similar missions to educate their masses.

Achievements

Right to Education Act 2010

Right to Education 2010 (Article 21 A) ensures free and compulsory education for children between 6 and 14 years of age.

Sarva Shiksha Abhiyan

The Sarva Shiksha Abhiyan (SSA) helped increase school enrolment ratios from 80% in 1996 to over 95% in 2006 (among children aged 6–12 years). These have caught up for children in Dalit and Muslim segments as well. By 2006, 73% schools had at least two all-weather rooms compared to only 26% schools in 1996. By 2006, 60% schools had their own toilets and 75% had drinking water facilities. Further, free textbooks were made available in nearly all schools by 2006 as compared to only 50% in 1996

To increase enrolments, mid-day meals were introduced and were functioning in 86% of the schools by 2006.

Issues with education in India

1. Rampant absenteeism among teachers and students—20% among teachers and 33% among students.
2. Missing classes by teachers who are present in schools. This leads to only 50% teaching days out of total 200 teaching days that are available to educate children.
3. Massive shortage of teachers: 12% schools in India have only one teacher.
4. Engagement of contractual teachers by school managements to cut costs jeopardizes the long-term learning process.
5. Low quality of teaching or poor standards of education.
6. High prevalence of rote learning.
7. Poor teacher training and their knowledge of basic concepts and facts: PISA Plus (conducted by Australian Council for Educational Research), an international survey conducted in 2009, placed India (states of Himachal Pradesh and Tamil Nadu) at the bottom of 74 countries in assessing the reading ability of 15 year olds. India was also ranked at lower positions in writing, science, and mathematics.

Evaluation Gap

The SSA and the Right to Education Act do not entail proper evaluation. Both guarantee automatic promotion from one class to another irrespective of what the child has learnt. This no-detention policy is harming students' learning. These do not encourage school tests as there are no repercussions to students failing the end-of-the-year class tests. So standardized tests are important to understand what kinds of help, attention, or encouragement particular children or schools need. The poor accountability mechanisms and standards to monitor teacher and student performance as well as no-detention policy lead to low performance and plunging learning outcomes.

India's no-detention policy for students up to class9 has skewed the learning system. It has resulted in students not learning appropriate skills in respective grades due to lack of accountability among government schools for children's learning outcomes.

There are no worthwhile results despite high salaries for teachers (three times the national per capita income, highest in the world). This also results in massive social gap between teachers and the families of children (these families are mostly landless labourers with low income).

Issues with private schools as an alternative

Even if affordability is resolved, informational asymmetry for first-time school goers makes them less likely to benefit the most from private schools just on the basis of their school vouchers provided by the government. School authorities may not provide the best educational experience or equal to that of other students who are actually paying fees. Lack of competition can make private schools money extracting machines (evident in the fact that private schools are not doing as well as public schools in many parts of India).

Government Schemes in Education

Sarva Shiksha Abhiyan

This scheme is aimed at the universalization of elementary education as mandated by the 86th Amendment to the Constitution of India which made free and compulsory education to children between the ages of 6 to 14 as a fundamental right. Initiatives and sub-programmes under the SSA include the following.

1. **Rashtriya Avishkar Abhiyan (RAA)**: It aims to motivate and engage children of the age group of 6-18 years, in science, mathematics, and technology by institutions of higher education such as IITs, IISERs, and NITs.
2. **Shagun Portal**: It has two components, i. e. , a repository of best practices to learn from success stories and online monitoring of the SSA implemented by states and UTs.
3. **Padhe Bharat Badhe Bharat**: To improve the reading and writing skills of children in classes I and II, along with their mathematics skills.
4. **Vidyanjali Scheme**: To enhance community and private sector involvement in government-run elementary schools across the country.
5. A new provision has been added for the reimbursement for expenditure incurred for at least 25% admissions of children belonging to disadvantaged and weaker sections in private unaided schools from the academic year 2014-15.

Shala Programmes

All School Monitoring Individual Tracing Analysis (ASMITA)

It was launched under Shala Asmita Yojana (SAY). SAY aims to track the educational journey of school students from Class I to Class XII across the 15 lakh private and government schools in the country. ASMITA will be an online database and will carry information about student attendance and enrolment, their learning outcomes, mid-day meal service, and infrastructural facilities among others.

Shala Sarathi

It is a portal launched by the Ministry of HRD. It has envisaged partnership of the State-NGO-CSR and aims to aid the collaboration among the stakeholders in sharing innovative practices across various schools.

Rashtriya Madhyamik Shiksha Abhiyan (RMSA)

It is a centrally sponsored scheme with the objective to enhance access to secondary education. Initiatives under RMSA are as follows:

1. **Shala Siddhi**: It is a web portal developed by the National University of Educational Planning and Administration to enable schools to evaluate their performance in seven key domains under the prescribed framework. It is a comprehensive evaluation system focused on well-defined quality based parameters that facilitates schools to make professional judgments for improvement.
2. **Shala Darpan**: It is an e-Governance platform, which covers all the Kendriya Vidyalayas, to improve the quality of learning, efficiency of school administration, governance of schools, and service delivery.
3. **e-Pathshala:** It is a joint initiative of Ministry of Human Resource Development (MHRD) and National Council of Educational Research and Training (NCERT) to disseminate all educational e-resources including textbooks, audio, video, and non-print materials.
4. **Kala Utsav**: To promote arts (music, theatre, dance, visual arts, and crafts) in education at the secondary stage of the education to bring art in an inclusive environment.
5. **Seema Darshan**: It is an initiative by the MHRD in collaboration with the Ministry of Defence and Ministry of Home Affairs for the students of Kendriya Vidyalayas and Navodaya Vidyalayas to provide an opportunity for the children to experience the border environment and to foster patriotism among the students.
6. **Mid-day Meal Scheme (National Programme on Nutritional Support to Primary Education).**

Some other Schemes and Initiatives

1. Skill Development Mission.
2. Scheme for setting up 6000 Model Schools at the block Level as a benchmark of excellence.
3. Scheme for providing education to Madrasas, minorities, and disabled.
4. Support for educational development including teachers' training and audit education.
5. Scholarships etc. to students of SC, ST, OBC, and religious minorities for higher education and coaching classes.
6. Maulana Abul Kalam National Scholarship for meritorious girl students.
7. **Rashtriya Uchchatar Shiksha Abhiyan:** CSS that aims at providing funding to institutions of higher education in various states.
8. **Kasturba Gandhi BalikaVidyalaya:** Educational facilities for girls belonging to SC, ST, OBC, minority communities, and families below the poverty line in educationally backward blocks.
9. **Kishore Vaihyanik Protsahan Yojana:** A scholarship programme to encourage students to take up research careers in the areas of basic science, engineering, and medicine.

Problems with Education in India

1. Primary level schooling suffers from the problem of quality—content and pedagogy.
    - Accessibility is pretty good as over 135 million children are enrolled in primary schools with gross enrolment ratio touching 100%. However, the quality of education given to them suffers due to poor course design, teacher absenteeism, and poor teaching methods.
    - Also, community participation where parents and gram panchayats can control the performance evaluation of teachers is not there.
2. Secondary level schooling suffers from the problem of choice in courses, due to which a large percentage of students drop out. The dropout rate is around 50% for students from the primary to the secondary level.
3. The tertiary and vocational level education suffers from the problem of lack of rating and certifications in public and private institutions.

New Education Policy in India

Education is the foundation of any modern society. Historically, India has had a strong tradition of promoting both scientific and religious learning. Customs such as "guru-shishya" relationship and the excellence demonstrated by Indian engineers, scientists, and management personnel on the international stage speaks volumes about the Indian mind. However, despite several measures, education has not met the evolving standards of the 21st century. An urgent policy to utilize India's massive demographic dividend is the need of the hour. In this context, TSR Subramaniam committee has submitted a new education policy for India.

Recommendations of the TSR Subramanian Committee

1. Total public spending on education must increase from current 3% to 6% of GDP with immediate effect.
2. Scrapping of the UGC.
3. Allowing foreign universities to set up campuses in India,
4. Setting up of the All India Cadre of Education Service.
5. Compulsory quality audit of schools every 3 years.
6. Position of vice chancellors in universities should be non-political.
7. Licensing or certification for teachers in government and private schools should be made mandatory, with a provision for renewal every 10 years based on independent external testing.
8. Pre-school education for the age group of 4-5 years should be declared as a right.
9. The ambit of Mid-day Meal Scheme should be expanded to cover students of secondary schools.

10. Teacher Entrance Tests (TET) should be made compulsory for recruitment of all teachers. Also for admission to the B. Ed course, the minimum marks at the graduate level should be 50%.
11. The no-detention policy must be continued for children until class V only. After class V, at the upper primary stage, the policy of detention should be restored subject to the provision of remedial coaching and at least two extra chances being offered to prove capability to move to a higher class.
12. The 25% economically weaker section quota in private schools should be extended to minority institutions because the number of schools claiming religious or linguistic minority status has increased tremendously.
13. Focus on girl-child education.
14. Inclusion of value learning and ethics in the classroom.

National Skill Development Mission

Skills and knowledge are the driving forces of economic growth and social development for any country. India currently faces a severe shortage of well-trained, skilled workers. It is estimated that only 2. 3% of the workforce in India has undergone formal skill training as compared to 68% in the UK, 75% in Germany, 52% in USA, 80% in Japan, and 96% in South Korea. Large sections of the educated workforce have little or no job skills, making them largely unemployable. Therefore, India needs to focus on scaling up-skill training efforts to meet the demands of employers and to drive economic growth.

India is one of the youngest nations in the world, with more than 54% of the total population below 25 years of age and over 62% of the population in the working age group (15–59 years). This demographic advantage is predicted to last only until 2040. India therefore has a very narrow timeframe to harness its demographic dividend and to overcome its skill shortages.

The enormity of India's skilling challenge is further aggravated by the fact that skill training efforts cut across multiple sectors and require the involvement of diverse stakeholders such as multiple government departments at the Centre and state levels, private training providers, educational and training institutions, employers, industry associations, trainees, and assessment and certification bodies.

Focus of National Skill Development Mission

1. Institutional training
2. Infrastructure
3. Convergence
4. Trainers
5. Overseas employment
6. Sustainable livelihoods
7. Leveraging public Infrastructure

National Skill Development Corporation (NSDC)

NSDC will also support the National Skill Development Mission through capacity building initiatives and by supporting private training partners. Some of the initiatives in this regard are as follows.

UDAAN

Udaan is a special industry initiative for the youth of the terrorism-afflicted state of Jammu & Kashmir in the nature of partnership between the corporates of India and the Ministry of Home Affairs. It is implemented by National Skill Development Corporation. The programme aims to provide skills training and enhance the employability of unemployed youth of J&K. The Scheme covers graduates, postgraduates, and three-year engineering diploma holders. It has two objectives:

1. To provide an exposure to the unemployed graduates to the best of Corporate India.
2. To connect Corporate India with the rich talent pool available in the state.

Pradhan Mantri Kaushal Vikas Yojana

The Pradhan Mantri Kaushal Vikas Yojana was approved by the Union Cabinet on March 20, 2015. It is a scheme for skill training of youth and will be implemented by the Ministry of Skill Development and Entrepreneurship through the National Skill Development Corporation. Skill training would be imparted based on the National Skill Qualification Framework.

The scheme will cover 24 lakh people. It will focus on first-time entrants to the labour market and will target Class 10 and 12 dropouts. A one-time monetary reward of around INR 8, 000 per trainee will be given under the scheme. The Cabinet approved a total outlay of INR 1500 crore for the scheme. Out of this, INR 1120 crore will be spent on skill training, INR 220 crore on recognition of prior learning, INR 67 crore on awareness building, mobilization, and mentorship support, and INR 150 crore for training of youth from the North-East region. Skill training would be done on the basis of demand assessed by skill gap studies, conducted by the NSDC for 2013-17. A demand aggregator platform would be launched.

The scheme would be implemented through NSDC's 187 training partners (spread across 2300 centres), in addition to government affiliated training partners. Training would include soft skills, personal grooming, good work ethics, etc. A skill development management system would be put in place to verify and record details of training centres. A grievance redressal system will also be instituted. The objective of this skill certification Scheme is to enable a large number of Indian youth to take up industry-relevant skill training to help them in securing a better livelihood.

Individuals with prior learning experience or skills will also be assessed and certified under Recognition of Prior Learning (RPL). Under this scheme, training and assessment fees are completely paid by the government. It envisages training of 10 million individuals between 2016 and 2020. The scheme envisages the as follows:

1. A national skills qualifications framework to ensure a standardized mode of training and certification across the country.
2. Skilling in a variety of fields such as manufacturing, construction, media services, etc. Through third-party partners from the private sector. This will also enable in placement of trained individuals in new jobs.
3. Quarterly review of training imparted to ensure targets are met.
4. Training people to work overseas including in Europe and Central Asia.
5. Encouraging people from the Northeast and Jammu and Kashmir and districts affected by Maoist violence to enlist for residential training
6. Spending between 10% and 15% of the budget for creating a pool of workers for jobs created under programmes such as Make in India, Swachh Bharat, and Digital India.
7. A third-party auditor will be set up to oversee the programme and to ensure that targets are met.

NSFQ

The National Skills Qualifications Framework (NSQF) is a competency-based framework that organizes all qualifications according to a series of levels of knowledge, skills, and aptitude. These levels, graded from 1to 10, are defined in terms of learning outcomes that the learner must possess regardless of whether they are obtained through formal, non-formal, or informal learning. NSQF in India was notified on 27th December 2013 and supersedes all other frameworks, including the NVEQF (National Vocational Educational Qualification Framework) released by the Ministry of HRD.

Under the NSQF, the learner can acquire the certification for competency needed at any level through formal, non-formal or informal learning. In that sense, the NSQF is a quality assurance framework. Presently, more than 100 countries have, or are in the process of developing national qualification frameworks. The NSQF is anchored at the National Skill Development Agency and is being implemented through the National Skills Qualifications Committee and comprises all key stakeholders. The NSQC's functions include approving NOSs (National Occupation Standards)/QPs (Qualification Pack), approving accreditation norms, prescribing guidelines to address the needs of disadvantages sections, reviewing inter-agency disputes, and alignment of NSQF with international qualification frameworks.

The specific outcomes expected from the implementation of NSQF are as follows:

1. Mobility between vocational and general education by alignment of degrees with NSQF.
2. Recognition of prior learning (RPL), allowing transition from non-formal to organized job market.
3. Standardized, consistent, nationally acceptable outcomes of training across the country through a national quality assurance framework.
4. Global mobility of skilled workforce from India through international equivalence of NSQF.

5. Mapping of progression pathways within sectors and cross-sectorally.
6. Approval of NOS/QPs as national standards for skill training.

Poverty Reduction

Poverty is rarely just a binary state of being poor or not. In reality, the poor may experience anything between destitution, depravation, and moderate poverty, and their condition may change from one end of the spectrum to the other over time.

The Socio Economic Caste Census (SECC), a database created by the Ministry of Rural Development, attempts to identify such diversity by measuring various parameters according to which a household is deprived. As per SECC data, nearly half of the 18 crore rural households in the country are deprived according to one or more of the seven indicators (these are: 1. Households with only one room, kucha walls and kucha roof, 2. No adult member between the ages of 16 and 59, 3. Female headed households with no adult male member between 16 and 59, 4. Households with disabled member and no able bodied adult member, 5. SC/ST household, 6. Households with no literate adult above 25 years, 7. Landless households deriving a major part of their income from manual casual labour). Staggering 75% of rural households have monthly incomes of less than INR 5000, and around 38% of rural households are landless and dependent on manual casual labour as their main source of income. The figures show that the multiple social protection and livelihood programmes implemented by successive governments, such as the Mahatma Gandhi National Rural Employment Guarantee Act and National Rural Livelihoods Mission, have been unable to reach the extreme poor.

Studies by poverty labs such as J-PAL have shown that 'ultra-poor' have little capital, minimal skills, and are usually engaged in insecure and/or low-return occupations (https://www. povertyactionlab. org). They are unable to meet basic needs, are extremely vulnerable to unexpected life events such as health emergencies, and remain trapped in a cycle of poverty.

While there is no universally accepted threshold for being 'ultra-poor', more than one-fifth of the world's population and one-third of India's rural population live on $1. 90 (purchasing power parity) or approximately INR 130 a day or less—i. e., below the World Bank and United Nations' threshold for extreme poverty.

Poverty Line Evolution in India

Poverty line can be defined as the level of income to meet the minimum living conditions. In other words, it is the minimum amount of money needed for a person to meet his/her basic needs. These basic needs are generally defined as food, education, shelter, transportation, and health.

The history of poverty estimation in India goes back to the 19th century when Dadabhai Naoroji's efforts and careful study led him to conclude subsistence-based poverty line at 1867-68 prices, though he never used the term 'poverty line'. It was based on the cost of a subsistence diet consisting of 'rice or flour, dhal, mutton, vegetables, ghee, vegetable oil and salt'.

According to him, subsistence is what is necessary for the bare wants of a human being, to keep him in ordinary good health and decency. His studies included the scale of diet, and he came to a conclusion on the subsistence-costs-based poverty line that varied from INR 16 to INR 35 per capita per year in various regions of India. At that time, the per capita income in England was INR 450. However, since necessities in India cost only about one-third as compared to that in England at that time, the real difference in terms of purchasing power parity was not fifteen times but only five times.

Post-Independence

In 1938, Congress President Subhash Chandra Bose set up the National Planning Committee with Jawaharlal Nehru as the chairman and professor K. T. Shah as its secretary for the purpose of drawing up an economic plan with the fundamental aim to ensure an adequate standard of living for the masses. The Committee regarded the irreducible minimum income between INR 15 and INR 25 per capita per month at Pre-war prices. However, this was also not tagged something as a poverty line of the country.

First Planning Commission working group

The concept of the poverty line was first introduced by a Working Group of the Planning Commission in 1962 and subsequently expanded in 1979 by a Task Force. The 1962 Working Group recommended that the national minimum for each household of five persons should be not less than INR100 per month for rural and INR 125 for urban at 1960-61 prices. These estimates excluded the expenditure on health and education, which both were expected to be provided by the State.

YK Alagh Committee

Till 1979, the approach to estimate poverty was traditional, i. e., lack of income. It was later decided to measure poverty precisely as starvation, i. e., in terms of how much people eat. This approach was first of all adopted by the YK Alagh Committee's recommendation in 1979, whereby the people consuming less than 2100 calories in the urban areas or less than 2400 calories in the rural areas were categorized as poor. The logic behind the discrimination between rural and urban areas was that the rural people do more physical work. Moreover, an implicit assumption was that the states would take care of the health and education of the people. Thus, YK Alagh Committee eventually defined the first poverty line in India.

Lakdawala Formula

Till as recently as 2011, the official poverty lines were based entirely on the recommendations of the Lakdawala Committee of 1993. This poverty line was set such that anyone above them would be able to afford 2400 and 2100 calories worth of consumption in rural and urban areas, respectively, in addition to clothing and shelter. These calorie consumptions were derived from the YK Alagh committee only. According to the Lakdawala Committee, a poor person is one who cannot meet these average energy requirements. However, the Lakdawala formula was different in the following respects in comparison to the previous models:

1. In the earlier estimates, both health and education were excluded, because these were expected to be provided by the State.
2. This committee defined the poverty line on the basis of the household per capita consumption expenditure. The committee used CPI-IL (Consumer Price Index for Industrial Labourers) and CPI- AL (Consumer Price Index for Agricultural Labourers) for the estimation of the poverty line.
3. The method of calculating poverty included first estimating the per capita household expenditure at which the average energy norm is met, and then, with that expenditure as the poverty line, defining as poor as all persons who live in households with per capita expenditures below the estimated value.

The fallout of the Lakdawala formula was that the number of people categorized as below the poverty line became almost double. The number of people below the poverty line was 16% of the population in 1993-94. Under the Lakdawala calculation, it became 36. 3%.

Suresh Tendulkar Committee

In 2005, Suresh Tendulkar Committee was constituted by the Planning Commission. The current estimations of poverty are based upon the recommendations of this committee. This committee recommended to shift away from the calorie-based model and made the poverty line somewhat broad based by considering monthly spending on education, health, electricity, and transport also.

It strongly recommended target nutritional outcomes, instead of calories; intake nutrition support should be counted. It suggested that a uniform Poverty Basket Line be used for both rural and urban regions. It recommended a change in the way prices are adjusted and demanded for an explicit provision in the Poverty Basket Line to account for private expenditure on health and education. Tendulkar adopted the cost of living as the basis for identifying poverty and stipulated a benchmark daily per capita expenditure of INR 27 and INR 33 in rural and urban areas, respectively, and arrived at a cut-off of about 22% of the population below poverty line. However, this amount was so low that it immediately faced a backlash from media and all sections of the society. Since the numbers were unrealistic and too low, the government appointed another committee under prime minister's Economic Advisory Council Chairman C. Rangarajan to review the poverty estimation methodology. Brushing aside the Tendulkar Committee, Rangarajan Committee raised these limits to INR 32 and INR 47, respectively, and worked out the poverty line at close to 30%. With estimates of the Rangarajan Committee, the percentage of the poor in India stood at around 30% in 2011-12. The number of the poor in India was estimated at 36. 3 crore in 2011-12.

Current Status

The discussions about Lakdawala Formula, Suresh Tendulkar Committee, and Rangarajan Committee make it clear that defining the poverty line in India has been a controversial issue since the 1970s. The latest poverty line defined was by the Rangarajan Formula. However, this formula also did not assuage the critics. The NDA Government turned down this report also.

To define the poverty line, the NDA Government constituted a 14-member task force under NITI Aayog's vice-chairman, Arvind Panagariya, to come out with recommendations for a realistic poverty line. After one and half years work, this task force also failed to reach a consensus on the poverty line. In September 2016, it suggested to the government that another panel of specialists should be asked to do this job (of defining the poverty line). Informally, this committee supported the poverty line as suggested by the Tendulkar Committee.

Why defining poverty line is a controversial issue

Most of the governments have mothballed the reports of committees and panels because this issue is not only politically sensitive but also has deeper fiscal ramifications. If the poverty threshold is high, it may leave out many needed people; whereas if it is low, then it would be bad for the fiscal health of the government. There is a lack of consensus among states too. We note that some states such as Odisha and West Bengal supported the Tendulkar Poverty Line while others such as Delhi, Jharkhand, Mizoram, etc. supported the Rangarajan Report. Thus, no one, including the NITI Aayog wants to bell the cat when it comes to count the number of poor in the country.

Poverty definition in other countries

In most of European countries, a family with a net income of less than 60% of the median net disposable income is counted as poor. In the United States, the poverty line represents the basic cost of food for a family multiplied by three. A family is counted as poor if its pre-tax income is below this threshold.

Social Audit

Social audit is the process of measuring the performance of various government schemes and public services as against the stated objectives. In short, the social audits help to evaluate the true ground impact of social schemes.

Benefits

1. Limits the scope of leakages and corruption.
2. Enhances local people's participation in governance and makes it more effective form of governance.
3. Increases local people's awareness about government programmes and their entitlements.
4. Increases the responsiveness of the government towards the citizens.
5. Allows for more transparency and accountability in various schemes for government.

Problems

1. Local officials are hesitant in implementing social audit principals and there is resistance against its institutionalization.
2. The redressal process of social audits is still not strong enough.
3. Stakeholders are ignored.

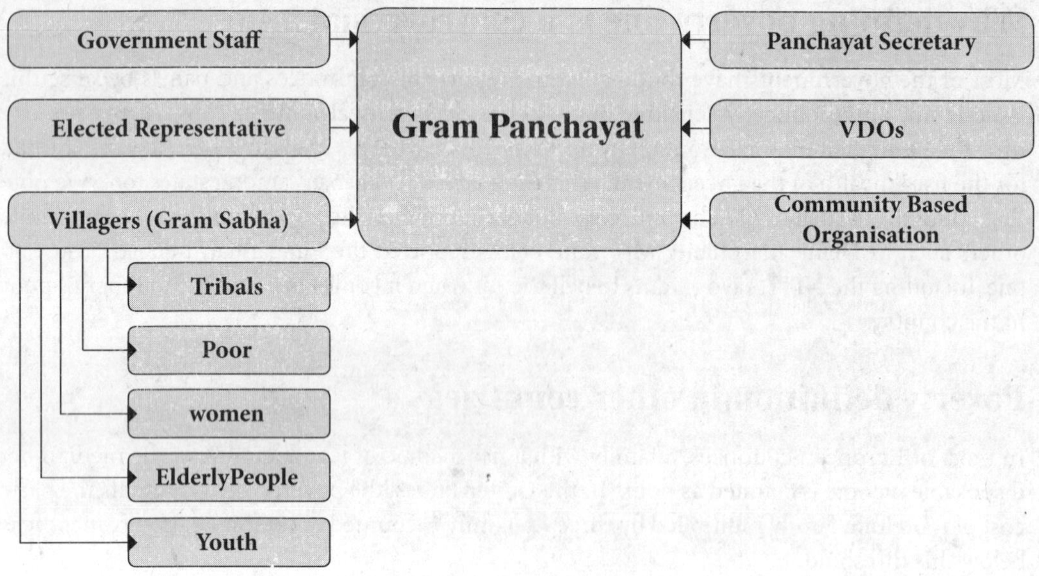

Fig. 6.1 Stakeholders of a Social Audit

XXXX

Practice Question (Main Examination)

1. Appropriate local community level healthcare intervention is a prerequisite to achieve 'Health for All' in India. Explain.

Approach:

1. Provide basic definition of 'Health for All'.
2. Provide points for the need of local community level healthcare intervention with existing provisions.
3. Conclude.

I am giving a broad overview of the answer here, not a complete answer. You can build your own answer using such points.

Answer:
Health for All is a World Health Organization (WHO) programme to ensure full primary healthcare to promote human dignity and well being.

As often said, "It takes a village to raise a child;" local community interventions are key to achieving "Health for All" in India:

1. Malnutrition starts at pregnancy, not after birth
   - If a pregnant mother has proper nutrition, the chances of a low-weight birth and other deficiencies reduce significantly. Hence, community focus on the mother's nutrition is the need of the hour.
2. Sanitation
3. Immunization
   - While some top-down led immunization programmes have been successful, communities still remain unaware of the many necessary supplemental immunizations.
4. Awareness at the local community level
   - The local community is largely unaware of basic health interventions.

Steps in India:

1. **A village-level health committee** has been set up as a part of the gram Sabha to enable local community discussions about health outcomes in the village.
2. **Anaganwadi and ASHA workers** are focused solely on the local community solutions and interventions to ailing health outcomes in India. Greater institutionalization and strengthening of these institutions will further expand Health for All.

2. Hunger and Poverty are the biggest challenges for good governance in India still today. Evaluate how far successive governments have progressed in dealing with these humongous problems. Suggest measures for improvement. (150 words)

Answer: This is a simple question that can be divided into three segments by carefully reading the question. You will most probably know the content for the answer here but its presentation is the key here. To presents it you can use a table here. This can be as follows:

Provide an introduction with the definitions of hunger and poverty through statistics.

Successive governments	*Dealing with hunger and poverty*
1950–1965 (first-third plan era/post- . independence)	Imports of grains, ICDS (Integrated Child Development Scheme), and free ration programmes

1965–1990 (era of total command economy era)	Agricultural revolution, new health schemes
1990–2004 (post-liberalization era)	Market economy, PPP, etc.
2004–2017 (recent era)	DBT(Direct Benefit Transfer)and demand-driven era

After this, provide measures for improvement. This can itself be the conclusion.

This presentation is key here, as it will enable the examiner to understand your content and give better marks.

Overview of the Chapter

UPSC Syllabus Covered:

- India and its neighborhood- relations.
- Bilateral, regional and global groupings and agreements involving India and/or affecting India's interests.
- Effect of policies and politics of developed and developing countries on India's interests, Indian Diaspora.
- Important International institutions, agencies and fora- their structure, mandate.

Answer Writing Tips:

- Draw rough maps showing important regions impacted by the issue and geo-political implications in international relations questions.
- Try to use pencil to make the diagram if you have sufficient speed. However, if you are a slow writer, just use your normal pen.
- Draw tables to answer questions where 'compare' and 'contrast' has been asked by UPSC.
- Use examples of various conventions, world groupings, recent announcements, treaties signed and visits by important dignitaries to provide depth to your IR questions.

7

7

India's International Relations

As the economic power, cultural reach, and political influence of India increase, it is assuming a more influential role in global affairs.

— US Department of Defence, Quadrennial Defence Review, 2010

Before diving into India's foreign relations with its neighbours and the rest of the world, it is important to understand the foundational principles or the Deshniti of India's foreign relations. These have remained largely unchanged over the years as India aims to occupy the role of a benevolent, socialist, and secular democracy in the world. However, with the changing dynamics of geopolitics and techno-politics across the globe, the tactics do change from time to time.

Understanding the above-mentioned concepts would be critical for being able to answer questions on international relations. One can frame one's answers from various viewpoints, including those indicated in Fig. 7.1.

In the following, we will attempt to understand India's foreign policy from a holistic perspective.

Objectives of India's Foreign Policy

India's foreign policy is fundamentally based on the principles of peaceful co-existence, friendship, and cooperation among all the countries of the world irrespective of their political systems. The foreign policy is aimed at promoting international peace and security and maintaining good and friendly relations with all the countries of the world.

Overview of India's Foreign Policy since Independence

Promotion of International Peace

Article 51 of the Constitution (DPSP) directs the Indian state to promote international peace and security, maintain just and honourable relations between nations, foster respect for international law and treaties, and settle disputes over international boundaries, etc. through arbitration. Nehru had remarked: "Peace for us is not just a fervent hope; it is an emergent necessity."

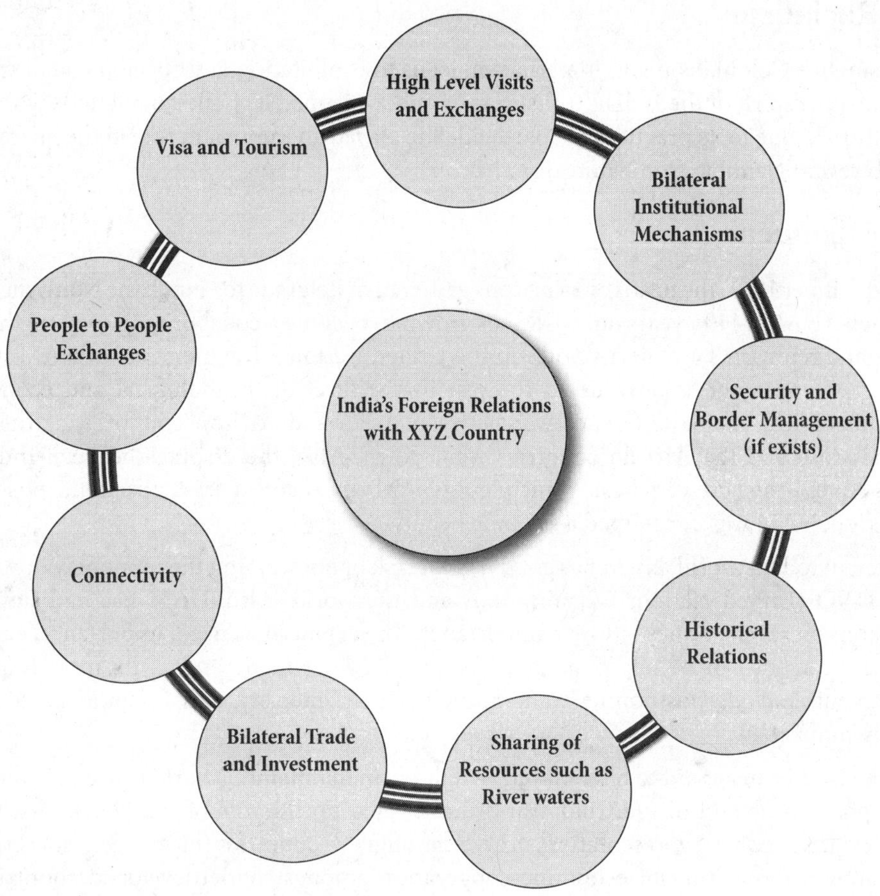

Fig. 7.1: Viewpoints in answering questions on Foreign Relation

Anti-Colonialism

Indian foreign policy opposes colonialism in any form or shape across the world, and its successive governments have used it as a policy tool across the world in matters of foreign relations. For example, Prime Minister Indira Gandhi's speech in 1972 at the United Nations Conference on Human Environment in Stockholm deployed anti-colonialism as a defence mechanism. At the meet, Mrs Gandhi argued for India's refusal of the 'environmental-friendly' standards suggested by the western powers, which would have hurt its industrial progress. She questioned the morality of western powers, who were preaching to the underdeveloped countries to respect the environment after themselves exploiting both for centuries. She reminded them about their own head start "through sheer ruthlessness, undisturbed by feelings of compassion or by abstract theories of freedom, equality or justice." Whipping up western remorse over the shameful treatment of colonized countries, she managed to avoid making environmental commitments that would have slowed down India's progress in industrialization[1].

Anti-Racialism

Racialism, like Colonialism and imperialism, leads to exploitation and social inequality, which are against the spirit of the Indian Constitution. India snapped its political relations with South Africa in 1954 due to its practices of apartheid. She played an important role in the liberation of Zimbabwe and Namibia from white domination.

Non-Alignment

On 1 September 1961, the heads of 28 nations gathered in Belgrade to launch the Non-Alignment Movement (NAM). Fifty years on, NAM has grown to become a collaboration of more than 120 nations and represents a majority voice in the United Nations. The members of NAM initially had disputes on some issues due to the gap in the level of technological and economical development. The major difference was between Asian and African countries, as the Asian countries rose and the African countries went down. Also, the disputes between India and Pakistan questioned the very basic principles of NAM—peaceful coexistence. In the post-Cold-War period, NAM was considered a sleeping beauty.

However, in today's world, NAM has got the great task of questioning the monopoly of America in the UNO (United Nations Organization) and the world. Also, NAM has had significant discussions on several issues of world importance. The extent of its need, importance, and fame of this movement can be approximated from its growing membership. Its most important achievements include postponing wars, reducing their intensity, and in some cases solving disputes completely.

The NAM can be said to have played a vital role in maintaining world peace in this nuclear age, leading to the end of the Cold War. It has beefed up the role of the UNO, in which all countries have equal representation. The non-aligned countries have been successful in establishing a foundation of economic cooperation amongst underdeveloped countries. An example of this economic cooperation among the underdeveloped countries is the South–South dialogue, which has been summoned from the non-aligned countries' front.

Another noteworthy fact is that the NAM has transformed from a political movement to an economical movement, whereby the developing and underdeveloped nations are demanding the New International Economic Order (NIEO). NIEO consists of proposals that were put forward during the 1970's by some developing countries through the United Nations Conference on Trade and Development (UNCTAD). It was meant to promote these countries' interests by improving terms of trade, increasing development assistance, tariff reductions etc. Hence, the main idea was to replace the Bretton Woods system with a new economic order led by third world countries.

[1]Patnaik, Sampad. (2017). 'Anti-Colonialism is an Old Strategic Tool of India – Shashi Tharoor Merely Repackaged it'. Scroll. in, 3 Jan. Retrieved from scroll.in/article/744066/anti-colonialism-is-an-old-strategic-tool-of-india-shashi-tharoor-merely-repackaged-it.

The characteristic features of India's policy of non-alignment are:

- Maximum participation in international affairs
- Promotion of international understanding, mutual co-operation
- Peaceful co-existence and respect for national sovereignty
- Avoidance of local, regional, and global wars
- Strengthening the cause of international peace and security
- Consideration of each international issue on its own merit
- Pursuance of an independent foreign policy without aligning itself with any power or block

Panchsheel

Panchsheel refers to the five guiding principles of peaceful coexistence that were evolved during talks between India and the People's Republic of China in 1954. These five principles, which formed the basis of the NAM, were laid down by Jawaharlal Nehru. The principles are:

1. Mutual respect for each other's territorial integrity and sovereignty
2. Mutual non-aggression against anyone
3. Mutual non-interference in each other's internal affairs
4. Equality and mutual benefit
5. Peaceful co-existence

The underlying assumption while framing the five principles was the development of the new and more principled approach to international relations by the newly independent decolonized states. China has often emphasized its close association with the five principles. It had put them forward as the five principles of peaceful co-existence at the starting of the negotiations that took place in Delhi from December 1953 to April 1954 between the delegation of the PRC (People's Republic of China) government and the delegation of the Indian government on the relations between the two countries with respect to the disputed territories of Aksai Chin and South Tibet.

The 29 April 1954 agreement was set to last for eight years. When it lapsed, the relations were already becoming sour. Hence, the provision for renewal of the agreement was not taken up, and the Sino-Indian war broke out in 1962. However, in the 1970s, the five principles again came to be seen as significant for Sino-Indian relations, more generally as norms of relations between the states.

Afro-Asian Bias

Indian foreign policy has a bias for Afro-Asian countries. This can be seen in many ways the Indian foreign policy has evolved. In 1947, the first Asian Relations Conference was held in New Delhi, right after independence. In 1949, India brought countries together on the issue of Indonesian freedom. India opened dialogues with many African countries and identified and supported them in anti-colonial movements. Then, associations such as the SAARC and Indian Ocean Rim Association for Regional Cooperation were formed, thereby strengthening the Afro-Asian bias.

Links with the Commonwealth

Immediately after independence, India continued its engagement with the colonial powers despite the negative experience of colonialism within its own borders. India quickly resolved the contradictions and resolved to participate in a new world order, where cooperation and coordination could reap the benefits of a commonwealth for everyone.

Support to the UNO

In 1945, India became a member of the United Nations Organization (UNO). In 1953; Vijaya Lakshmi Pandit was appointed the President of the UN general assembly (UNGA).India became one of the largest contributors to the UN peacekeeping missions in Korea, Congo, El Salvador, Cambodia, Angola, Somalia, Mozambique, Sierra Leone, Yugoslavia, etc. This cemented a permanent seat for India in the UN and also showcased its continuous dedication to the objective of attaining world peace.

Disarmament

India's disarmament policy is directed at achieving a world free from weapons of mass destruction, including nuclear weapons. It advocates universal, non-discriminatory disarmament in a time-bound, phased, and verifiable manner. This approach is reflected in the Rajiv Gandhi Action Plan, which India submitted at the UNGA in 1998.

While continuing to work for global disarmament, India has kept its nuclear options open. India has declined to sign the Non-Proliferation Treaty (NPT), as she considers the treaty discriminatory, an instrument that has divided the world into two parts—the P5 (USA, Russia, China, France, UK), known as legitimate nuclear powers, and the rest of the world. India has recently signed agreements such as the Wassenaar Arrangement and the Australia Group to adhere to the international requirement of developing weapons for self-defence.

Look East Policy

The Look East policy was initiated in 1991 by then Prime Minister P.V. Narasimha Rao. Based on this policy, India is one of the first countries in South Asia to extend support beyond its borders to enhance the prosperity of the East Asian region. This has been the cornerstone of India's foreign policy ever since.

The policy emphasizes on improving ties with the South East and Eastern Asian nations to a much greater extent than what exists at present. It focuses on:

- Improved connectivity
- Promotion of trade

- Investment
- Cultural exchanges

The various initiatives are implemented through the ASEAN, East Asia Summit, Bay of Bengal Initiative for Multi-Sectoral Technical and Economic Cooperation (BIMSTEC), and the Mekong-Ganga Cooperation. India has already initiated discussing ideas on these lines with Thailand, Bangladesh, Myanmar, China, and other countries of the (ASEAN).

Gujral Doctrine

The Gujral Doctrine was initiated by the Foreign Minister of India, Inder Kumar Gujral, under the Deve Gowda government in 1996. This doctrine suggests that India, being the biggest South Asian country, should extend concessions to its smaller neighbours. This means that India should exercise economic diplomacy with its smaller neighbours and adopt an accommodating approach towards these regions based on the idea of non-reciprocity.

The doctrine is a five-point roadmap to guide conduct of India's foreign relations with its immediate neighbours. These five principles are as follows:

1. With the neighbours like Bangladesh, Bhutan, Maldives, Nepal and Sri Lanka, India should not ask for reciprocity, but give to them what it can in good faith.
2. No South Asian country should allow its territory to be used against the interest of another country of the region.
3. No country should interfere in the internal affairs of another country.
4. All South Asian countries should respect each other's territorial integrity and sovereignty.
5. All South Asian countries should settle all their disputes through peaceful bilateral negotiations.

Gujral himself explained: "The logic behind the Gujral Doctrine was that since we had to face two hostile neighbours in the north and the west, we had to be at 'total peace with all other immediate neighbours in order to contain Pakistan's and China's influence in the region."

Nuclear Policy of India

India adopted its Nuclear Doctrine in 2003. The salient features of this doctrine are:

- Building and maintaining a credible minimum deterrent. That is, having a nuclear weapon for defensive purposes of deterring an aggressor.
- A posture of 'no first use'—nuclear weapons only to be used in retaliation to a nuclear attack on India.
- The retaliatory nuclear strike will be massive and designed to inflict unacceptable damage.
- Such attacks can only be authorized by civilian political leadership through the Nuclear Command Authority. (The Nuclear Command Authority comprises a political

council chaired by the PM and is the sole body that can authorize the use of nuclear weapons. An executive council chaired by the National Security Advisor provides inputs.)

- Non-use of nuclear weapons against non-nuclear nations.
- However, in case of chemical or biological warfare on India, she retains the option to use nuclear force.
- Participation in the Fissile Material Cut-off Treaty (FMCT) negotiations and strict adherence to the norms for export of such material.
- Continued commitment to the goal of a nuclear weapon free world.

India's relation with her Neighbours

India and Pakistan

India-Pakistan relations not only impact the political discourse between the two countries, but have also come to haunt the collective conscience of a billion plus of citizens of the two countries. These relations have specially impacted the peace in the sub-continent and overall cultural and economic development of the two countries.

Issues between India and Pakistan

1. Kashmir
2. Trade
3. Terrorism
4. Indus Water Sharing Treaty
5. Balochistan Issue
6. SAARC
7. Prisoners of War and instances such as Kulbhushan Jadhav

Aspects of India-Pakistan Relations[2]

Border management and security

India shares 3,323 km of its international border with Pakistan. Noting that a volatile situation exists across the border, the Committee recommended that tangible steps need to be taken to strengthen and modernize border security. The Committee expressed concerns towards the poor road conditions across the border. It recommended that the Comprehensive Integrated Border Management System be completed in a time-bound manner. It further recommended that coastal security and surveillance should be strengthened by establishing high-level

[2](Report of Parliamentary Standing Committee on External Affairs led by Shashi Tharoor)

coordination between the Indian Coast Guard and other agencies. These agencies include the Navy, Central Industrial Security Force, Customs, and Ports.

Terrorism

The Committee recommended that the Government should continue pressuring Pakistan to expedite the 26/11 Mumbai attack trial. It further recommended that the military and non-military policy options be spelt out to deal with Pakistan-sponsored terrorism. The Committee further recommended that a thorough security review of India's security establishments should be ensured.

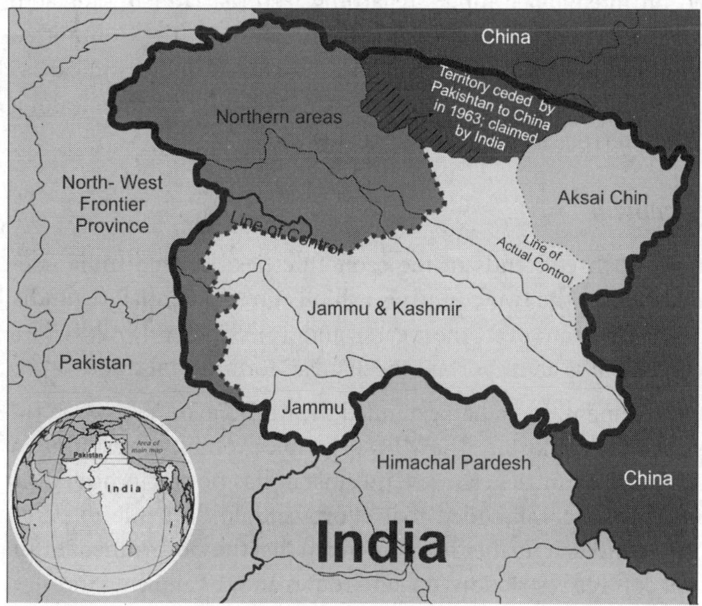

Fig. 7.2: PoK and Line of Control

Jammu and Kashmir

The Committee stated that a part of Jammu and Kashmir has been under the illegal occupation of Pakistan since 1947. It further noted that there is a growing sense of alienation in the Kashmiri youth due to radicalization and a lack of employment opportunities. It noted that efforts made by the Government, in this regard, have not given desired results. The Committee recommended that the Government should take measures such as infrastructure and economic development to prevent radicalization of the youth by Pakistan's ISI.

Nuclear and missile programme

India and Pakistan have signed an agreement on prohibition of attack against nuclear installations. The Committee noted that while both India and Pakistan are nuclear armed states, the nuclear doctrines of the two countries are contradictory. India follows the 'no first use of nuclear weapons' policy whereas Pakistan does not. Further, there is a growing cooperation between China and Pakistan in missile and nuclear programmes. In this context, the Committee recommended that the Government must aggregate its nuclear capability and enhance its deterrence capabilities.

Surgical strikes

The Committee noted that a limited counter-terrorism operation (surgical strike) was carried out by the Indian Army along the Line of Control (LoC) in September 2016. The surgical strike took place based on intelligence inputs regarding terrorist launch pads across the LoC and overall build-up of terrorist attacks, stemming from Pakistan. The Committee stated that such surgical strikes demonstrate a restrained response, and hence do not indicate a change in India's policy of 'strategic restraint'. It recommended that this policy be continued along with diplomatic outreach to highlight terrorism supported by Pakistan.

Economic engagement

The Committee noted three trends in the economic ties between India and Pakistan. These include: (a) trade between the two countries exhibits great potential, (b) India has maintained trade surplus with Pakistan over the years, and (c) SAPTA (SAARC Preferential Trade Arrangement) agreement is an important mechanism for bilateral trade.

Under the WTO agreement, India had extended the Most Favoured Nation (MFN) status to all WTO members, including Pakistan. The MFN principle prohibits discrimination among similar products from different countries. However, Pakistan has not reciprocated the MFN status to India. The Committee recommended that efforts should be made to persuade Pakistan to extend MFN status to India. It further recommended that the Government must pursue Pakistan for (a) the removal of trade restrictions on land routes and (b) allowing transit of Indian exports to Afghanistan through Pakistan.

The Committee observed that an Integrated Check Post (ICP) was opened at Attari in 2012 to handle the trade between India and Pakistan. The Committee noted several infrastructural issues regarding the ICP. These include (a) limited storage space, (b) lack of mechanized loading/unloading, and (c) inadequate cargo holding. The Committee recommended that the efficiency of the ICP be improved through technological handling.

SAARC summit

The Committee stated that by blocking major regional development projects, Pakistan has made SAARC dysfunctional. It also noted that in response to Pakistan-sponsored terrorism, Bangladesh, Afghanistan, and Nepal withdrew from the proposed SAARC summit in 2016. It recommended that the Government should undertake constructive engagements to implement the SAARC Regional Convention on 'Suppression of Terrorism'.

Case of Kulbushan Jadhav

The case of Kulbushan Jadhav, a retired Indian Naval officer, was arrested near the Iran-Pakistan border by the Pakistani establishment. He has been accused by Pakistan of espionage and spying and has been sentenced to death by a military court in Pakistan.

India, on many previous occasions, demanded consular access to Jadhav, a demand consistently rejected by Pakistan citing national security issues. India says that Jadhav was a retired Naval officer who was a businessman working in Iran and has been falsely framed by the Pakistani establishment. As there were repeated denials of the consular access, India approached the International Court of Justice (ICJ) at Hague where it put forward the argument that Vienna Convention was being violated as the consular access was denied. The ICJ has asked Pakistan to stay the execution of Jadhav and the matter is subjudice.

Review of Indus Water Treaty (1960) by India

Prime Minister Modi has famously declared that "blood and water cannot flow together". In September 2016, a meeting was held to review the Indus Water Treaty in the backdrop of the terror strikes, including the Uri attack. The Government officials have announced that the Government has decided to increase the utilization of rivers flowing through Jammu & Kashmir to fully exercise India's rights under the Treaty and to suspend all talks with Pakistan in the future in this matter.

Provisions of IWT

- The Indus Waters Treaty is a water-sharing arrangement signed by Jawaharlal Nehru, the then prime minister of India, and General Ayub Khan, the then President of Pakistan, on September 19, 1960, in Karachi.
- The treaty gave the three 'eastern rivers' of Beas, Ravi, and Sutlej to India for use of water without restriction. The three 'western rivers' of Indus, Chenab, and Jhelum were allocated exclusively to Pakistan.
- New Delhi has to share the waters of the western rivers,with Pakistan getting 80% of the entire water of the six-river Indus system. The IWT reserved for India just remaining 19.48% of the total waters.
- India can construct storage facilities on western rivers of up to 3.6 million acre feet, which it has not done so far. India is also allowed to use the waters for agriculture use of 7 lakh acres above the irrigated cropped area as on April 1, 1960. The Treaty and allowed India to use water for irrigation, transport, and power generation, while laying down precise do's and dont's for India on building projects along the way.
- The IWT permits run-of-the-river projects and requires India to provide Pakistan with prior notification, including design information, of any new project.
- Under the Treaty, in case the parties fail to resolve water disputes through bilateral means, the aggrieved party has the option to invoke the jurisdiction of the ICA or the neutral expert under the auspices of the World Bank.

- IWT is considered as the world's most generous water-sharing treaty. It is the only inter-country water agreement embodying the doctrine of restricted sovereignty, which compels the upstream nation to forego major uses of a river system for the benefit of the downstream state.
- The IWT has been a symbol of India-Pakistan cooperation and has survived the three wars of 1965, 1971, and 1999 as well as various tense standoffs between the two countries. A regular exchange of river flow data has kept away Pakistani fears and insecurities.
- There have been consistent calls in India that the Government scrap the water distribution pact to mount pressure on Pakistan in the aftermath of audacious Uri terror attack.

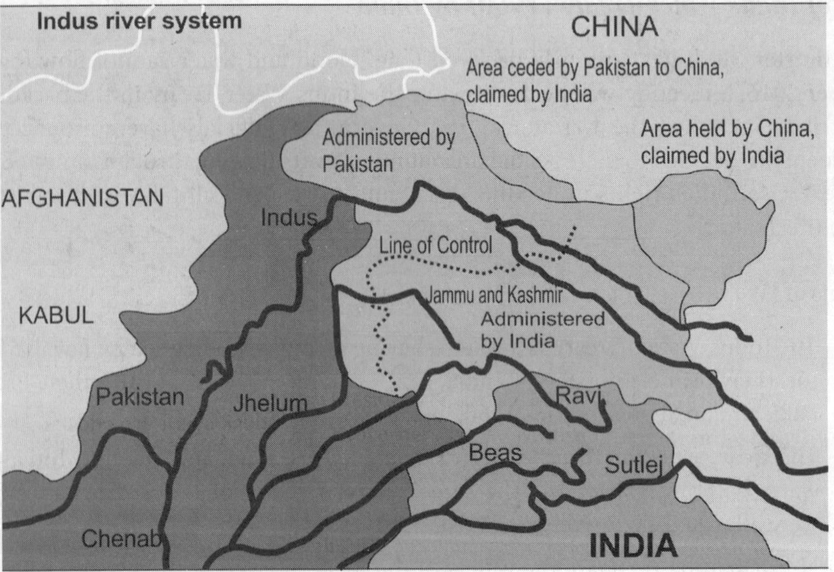

Fig. 7.3: Course of Indus & Three 'eastern rivers' of Beas, Ravi, and Sutlej were allocated to India for use of water without restriction. The three 'western rivers' of Indus, Chenab, and Jhelum went to Pakistan.

India and Bhutan

Geopolitical and Cultural Significance of Bhutan

- Bhutan is geopolitically significant to India due to its location as a buffer state across the chicken neck region connecting mainland India to its North East.
- India maintains strong economic, strategic, and military relations with Bhutan.

- Bhutan is home to Buddhism; therefore, it has a special cultural significance to India and South Asia as a whole.
- Bhutan is also a founding member of the South Asian Association for Regional Cooperation (SAARC). It is also a member of BIMSTEC, World Bank, the IMF, Group of 77, and others.

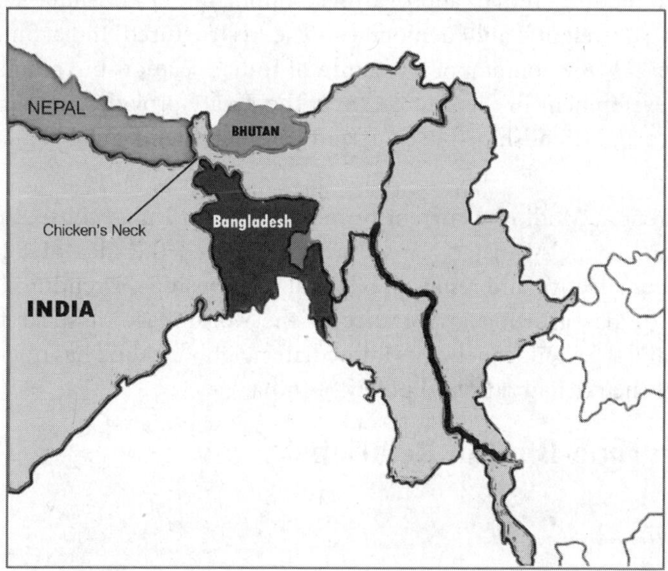

Fig. 7.4: Chicken's Neck

Bhutan's Response to India's International Position

India has been through thick and thin with Bhutan since long past. Bhutan has in return had shown enormous interest in supporting its big neighbour, India. Bhutan supports India's stand on the Non-Proliferation Treaty and Comprehensive Test Ban Treaty, which have been held as discriminatory de-nuclearization programmes. Bhutan also supports India's claim for a permanent seat in the UN Security Council. Bhutan proved to be India's trusted friend in 2003 when it launched Operation All Clear and Operation Flush out against anti-India insurgents taking shelter in its territory.

Indo-Bhutan Friendship Treaty

Bhutan is one among the few countries India has had a friendship treaty with. India and Bhutan signed the Treaty of Peace and Friendship on August 8, 1949, in Darjeeling. The treaty is termed as the continuation of the Anglo-Bhutanese Treaty of 1910. It treats the Himalayas as the sentinel of India's security. The Indo-Bhutan Treaty is dubbed as the corner stone of Bhutan's foreign policy. The Chinese annexation of Tibet in 1950 cemented bilateral relationship between India and Bhutan as the two nations consider Beijing a potential threat. With many ups and downs, the Indo-Bhutan Friendship Treaty has been a guiding document for bilateral relations since its inception.

In February 2007 the Indo-Bhutan Friendship Treaty was substantially revised, which clarifies Bhutan's status as an independent and sovereign nation. Under the revised norms, Bhutan no longer requires India's approval over importing arms. India supports Bhutan's progress towards sovereignty and democracy. The restructured India-Bhutan Friendship Treaty not only reveals the contemporary nature of India's relationship but also sets the tone for their future development in the 21st century. The Treaty provides, amongst other things, for perpetual peace and friendship, free trade and commerce, and equal justice to each other's citizens.

In 2014, Narendra Modi, the current prime minister of India, chose Bhutan as his first foreign destination. Prime Minister Narendra Modi coined the idea of B2B as 'Bharat to Bhutan' for building effective and renewed bilateral relationship. Narendra Modi has made it clear that despite India's growing importance in the world stage, it sticks to the policy of 'neighbours first' and the significance of its immediate neighbourhood has not reduced. Bhutan is a natural part of such neighbourhood policy of India.

Challenges in Indo-Bhutan Relations

Bhutan's aspirations

Bhutan is no more a subservient region to India and not guided by the 'aid and advice of India'. It is now entering the larger world by having engagements with world beyond India and by taking steps to reduce dependence on India on important matters of its notational needs and interest.

Emergence of China and border disputes

Both India and Bhutan have more engagements with China today than before. Pro-Chinese views are now up against the Article 2 of the Indo-Bhutan Friendship Treaty and accuse India of forcing a smaller neighbour into submission. Article 2 of the Treaty declares that India would not interfere in Bhutan's administrative affairs and the latter would be guided by the former's advice in its external relations. India has deep-seated concerns for the northern border with China, in the middle of which Bhutan is situated.

Connectivity

The signing of the Motor Vehicles Agreement by India in June 2015—among the BBIN countries Bangladesh, Bhutan, India, and Nepal—is likely to be of great benefit to all the countries involved.

Insurgency

Bhutan has been taken as safe haven by insurgent elements such National Democratic Front for Bodoland (NDFB), United Liberation Front of Assam (ULFA) militants, and Kamtapur Liberation Organization (KLO) that often pose threat to internal peace and security in the northeast region of India. However, Bhutan has shown enormous interest in respecting India's security concern. Operation All Clear was conducted by the Royal Bhutanese Army in 2003 after eight years of negotiations failed to convince the militants to move their camps out of Bhutan. The whole of Bhutan is dedicated to battle India's enemies and it has been a sterling example of friendship that a nation can do for its neighbour.

Trade and commerce

The economy of Bhutan depends greatly on hydropower exports. Bhutan's per capita income is the second-highest in SAARC after the Maldives. Mutually beneficial economic inter-linkages between India and Bhutan have been an important element in India's bilateral relations. India continues to be the largest trade and development partner of Bhutan. Since the launching of the First Five Year Plan of Bhutan in 1961, India has been extending financial support to Bhutan's FYPs. India has been assisting in major projects in Bhutan including the 1020 MW Tala Hydroelectric Project, 336 MW Chukha Hydroelectric Project, 60 MW Kurichhu Hydroelectric Project, Penden Cement Plant, Paro Airport, Bhutan Broadcasting Station, Major Highways, etc.

India is not only Bhutan's main development partner but also its leading trade partner. A free-trade regime exists between India and Bhutan. The India-Bhutan Trade and Transit Agreement was first signed in 1972. Year 2006 was the last time that this Agreement was renewed for a period of 10 years. This Agreement also provides for duty-free transit of Bhutanese exports to third countries. Bhutan imports above 80% of its total imports from India. Bhutan's exports to India constituted 89.38% of its total exports in 2014. Total bilateral trade grew by about 9.31% in 2014.

Chinese Engagement in Bhutan

China shares a contiguous border of 470 km with Bhutan to north and its territorial tussle with Bhutan has been a constant source of tense bilateral relationship. Further, China does not have official diplomatic relations with Bhutan. Bhutan's border with the China has never been officially recognized and demarcated, and the 1959 Tibetan Rebellion and the 14th Dalai Lama's arrival in neighbouring ally India made the security of its border with China a necessity for Bhutan.

Border disputes between Bhutan and China still persist on several areas between the two countries. In 1984, China and Bhutan began annual, direct talks over the border disputes. In 1998, China and Bhutan signed a bilateral agreement for maintaining peace on the border. In the agreement, China affirmed its respect for Bhutan's sovereignty and territorial integrity, and both sides sought to build ties based on the Five Principles of Peaceful Co-existence.

Efforts of China to build roads on alleged Bhutanese territory have been opposed by Bhutan. In 2002 an interim agreement was reached between the two countries to this effect. China's aggression in Tibet, provocation against Bhutan, and lack of economic opportunities from China ensure that Sino-Bhutan relationship is yet to take off. However, China's soft power diplomacy, increasing Chinese tourists in Bhutan, massive Chinese investment in Tibet during recent times which is likely to make Tibet a possible access point for the nascent Bhutanese traders, and the visits of Chinese official to Bhutan can be seen as measures for opening up of bilateral engagements between the two countries.

Hydroelectricity

Hydro-electric power generated by Bhutan's run-of-the river dams is the economic bedrock of the India-Bhutan relationship. India has sponsored financing the dams through a combination of aid and loans and buys the excess electricity at very low prices. It is the best example of a win-win in economic diplomacy that India has.

During Indian Prime Minister's visit in October 2015, the foundation stone for the 600 MW Kholongchu Hydro-electric project was laid. However, Bhutan fears a possible slump in the sale of electricity due to downward demand in India and low local industrial demand and also the problem of electricity loss because of poor transmission. India should leave no stone unturned to see the hydroelectricity projects in Bhutan continue to provide it the much-needed energy.

India-Bhutan Foundation

Established in 2003, the India-Bhutan Foundation (IBF) focuses on education, cultural exchanges, and environment preservation initiatives by India and Bhutan for effective bilateral cultural relationship. India also helps Bhutan form its election laws, Parliamentary traditions, and administrative culture by sending experts and high-profile officials to Bhutan. Parliamentary Friendship Groups have been formed in the Parliaments of both countries. An MOU between the two Parliaments has been signed between the two sides during the visit of Bhutanese Speaker to India in 2011.

Concept of Gross National Happiness

Bhutan has introduced the concept of Gross National Happiness instead of Gross Domestic Product, which other countries use to measure the quality of life of people of a country. This model has been highly praised by more than 60 countries as well as United Nations. Bhutan is the only country in the world which is fully organic. No chemical fertilizers, pesticides, and plastics are used in the country.

India and SAARC

The South Asian Association for Regional Cooperation (SAARC) is the regional intergovernmental organization and geopolitical union of nations in South Asia, namely:

1. Afghanistan
2. Bangladesh
3. Bhutan
4. India
5. Nepal
6. The Maldives
7. Pakistan
8. Sri Lanka

SAARC comprises 3% of the world's area, 21% of the world's population, and 3.8% (US$2.9 trillion) of the global economy (as of 2015).

SAARC was founded in Dhaka on 8 December 1985. Its secretariat is based in Kathmandu, Nepal. The organization promotes development of economic and regional integration. It launched the South Asian Free Trade Area (SAFTA) in 2006. SAARC maintains permanent diplomatic relations at the United Nations as an observer and has developed links with multilateral entities, including the European Union.

Why SAARC?[3]

The idea of cooperation in South Asia is older than the emergence of new sovereign countries in the region and that of Republic of India. There were many early attempts to form such an association in the 1940s and 1950s. However,it was not possible due to the trust deficit among the countries in the region. While there was a fear among the other six nations about the use of such organization by India in its favour and the possibility of India behaving in typical big brotherly attitude to browbeat them, India's apprehension was that such an organization might be used by her smaller neighbours to extract undue concessions by expressing their fear of being bullied by India. Pakistan was also sceptical about the formation of such an organization which might be used by India to enhance her propaganda against Pakistan.

In the late1970s, Bangladesh, Bhutan, India, Maldives, Nepal, Pakistan, and Sri Lanka agreed, in principle, upon the creation of a trade bloc and to provide a platform for the peoples of South Asia to work together in a spirit of friendship, trust, and understanding. Bangladesh President, ZiaurRahman, took the initiative by formally writing to his counterparts in the region and gave his vision for the region and compelling arguments for the need of such a regional organization. King Birendra of Nepal also urged for closer regional cooperation among South Asian countries in sharing river waters. After the erstwhile USSR's intervention in Afghanistan resulting in rapid deterioration of the South Asian security situation, the efforts to establish such an organization in the region gained momentum in 1979. Responding to Rahman and Birendra's convention, the officials of the foreign ministries of the seven countries met for the first time in Colombo in April 1981. In 1983, aninternational conference held by Indian Minister of External Affairs, P.V. Narasimha Rao, in New Delhi, the foreign ministers of the inner seven

[3]www.mea.gov.in/distinguished-lectures-detail.htm?577

countries adopted the Declaration on SAARC and formally launched the Integrated Programme of Action (IPA) initially in five agreed areas of cooperation, namely, agriculture; rural development; telecommunications; meteorology; and health and population activities.

SAARC's achievements

SAFTA

a. SAFTA was envisaged primarily as the first step towards the transition to a customs union, common market, and economic union. The SAFTA Agreement was signed on 6 January 2004 during the Twelfth SAARC Summit held in Islamabad, Pakistan.

b. Under this agreement, SAARC members were to bring their duties down to 20% by 2009. Following the Agreement coming into force, the SAFTA Ministerial Council (SMC) has been established and comprises the Commerce Ministers of the Member States. In 2012 the SAARC exports increased substantially to US$354.6 billion from US$206.7 billion in 2009. Imports too increased from US$330 billion to US$602 billion over the same period. But the intra-SAARC trade amounts to just a little over 1% of SAARC's GDP. In contrast, in The Association of Southeast Asian Nations(ASEAN) (which is actually smaller than SAARC in terms of the size of economy) the intra-bloc trade stands at 10% of its GDP .However, SAFTA is yet to be implemented.

SAARC Visa Exemption Scheme

a. The SAARC Visa Exemption Scheme was launched in 1992. The leaders at the Fourth Summit (Islamabad, 29–31 December 1988), while realizing the importance of having people to people contacts, among the peoples of SAARC countries, decided that certain categories of dignitaries should be entitled to a special travel document, which would exempt them from visas within the region.

South Asian University

a. The South Asian University opened its doors to students in August 2010.

b. It is located in New Delhi and its primary focus is to develop academic exchanges between SAARC countries.

Where SAARC failed

1. SAARC almost failed to accomplish its ambitious objectives during the last 25 years due to the political differences, conflicts, and poor economic state of the member countries.
2. Most of the programmes and achievements exist only in official documents. During the Bangladesh Cyclone of1991, Pakistan Earthquake of 2005, and Pakistan Floods of 2010, the food security reserve of SAARC could not be used to satisfy the demands of the affected people.

3. The intra-regional trade of SAARC amounted to $40.5 billion in 2011, which constitutes just 5% of member countries' trade, a figure too negligible as compared with the volume of trilateral trade between member countries of NAFTA, the North American Free Trade Agreement, (the US, Canada, and Mexico) which hit $1 trillion in 2011. While various regions of the world have progressed even to monetary union, SAARC has failed to even come up with a free trade agreement.
4. Even in the Kathmandu Summit 2014, there were three connectivity agreements on road, rail, and energy to be endorsed by the eight SAARC leaders. Only one of these—on energy—has been signed.
5. Despite promises, many SAARC level infrastructure projects continue to be a distant dream.

Reasons for failure

1. **Weak cultural identities**—Pakistan wants to assert itself as an Islamic state and calls India a Hindu state. Likewise, debates regarding identity are similarly going on in Sri Lanka and Bangladesh. The pursuit of maintaining a distinct cultural identity by every country has not allowed the region to come together.
2. **Rivalry**—The rivalry between India and Pakistan, the two largest members of SAARC, has cast its shadow on SAARC. This was evident in the boycott of the summit held in Islamabad (19th SAARC summit in 2016) by five out of the eight members.
3. The region still faces many unresolved border and maritime issues. These unresolved issue shave led to problems of terrorism, refugee crisis, smuggling, and narco trade. The unresolved issues continue to restrict cooperative relations.
4. SAARC Charter Article X(2) of the SAARC Charter mandates that decisions, at all levels in SAARC, shall be on the basis of unanimity. The SAARC platform thus cannot be used to resolve bilateral issues; this has undermined the scope and potential of SAARC.

Suggestions for the future

1. India has already taken the leadership on the agreements for bettering intra-regional connectivity.
2. India can further deepen relations through 'space diplomacy'. India has already launched the SAARC satellite in 2017 to boost such relations.
3. India's internal politics has sometimes played a negative role to the detriment of India's aspirations vis-à-vis SAARC. The Central Government's policy on Tamil Issue in Sri Lanka has not been accepted by the Tamil Nadu Government. India has to forcefully articulate South Asian Vision so as to avoid these internal domestic disruptions. The objectives and targets of SAFTA should be fulfilled.

India and ASEAN[4]

India and the 10-member Association of South East Asian Nations (ASEAN) are currently celebrating 25 years of their rapidly expanding partnership. They are also marking 15 years of their summit engagement and five years of their strategic partnership.

To mark the 25th anniversary of the partnership, all 10 heads of states/governments of ASEAN states will participate as chief guests in the Republic Day celebrations on 26 January 2018. This is for the first time that more than one head of state/government has been invited as chief guest on India's national day. It is also a measure of India's growing international profile and prestige that leaders of all 10 ASEAN countries have readily acquiesced to participate in this event.

Act East Policy

The Act East Policy (AEP) is the successor to the Look East Policy (LEP) that was put in place by then Prime Minister Narasimha Rao in 1992 under radically different geo-political and economic circumstances. LEP was primarily focused on strengthening economic ties between India and ASEAN states. The end of the cold war and the disintegration of the Soviet Union in 1991 provided a welcome opportunity for India to reach out to South-East Asia to capitalize upon its historical, cultural, and civilizational linkages with the region. As External Affairs Minister Sushma Swaraj said at the recently held ninth edition of the Delhi Dialogue, India's age old ties with South-East Asia have been established through culture, trade, and religion and not through "conquest and colonization."

India is also a part of the ASEAN-led Regional Comprehensive Economic Partnership (RCEP), which, when concluded and implemented, will cover almost 40% of the world's population, 33% of global GDP, and 40% of world trade.

India and ASEAN are natural partners in their desire to create a free, open, and inclusive regional architecture. They are active participants in the East Asia Summit (EAS), ASEAN Regional Forum (ARF), ASEAN Defence Ministers Meeting Plus (ADMM-Plus), and the Expanded ASEAN Maritime Forum (EAMF).

Currently, there exist 30 different dialogue mechanisms between India and the ASEAN states focusing on a range of sectors. These comprise an annual summit and seven ministerial meetings focused on a variety of areas that include foreign affairs, economy, environment, tourism, etc. The ASEAN-India Centre (AIC), established in 2013, has enhanced the strategic partnership by concentrating on policy research and recommendations as well as organizing meetings between think-tanks and similar institutions in India and ASEAN countries. AIC seeks to bridge the existing information divide amongst the people of the two regions. Exchange programmes have been put in place for frequent interaction between students, senior officials, diplomats, academics, media professionals, etc.

[4]Sajjanhar, Ashok. "The India-ASEAN Partnership at 25." The Economic Consequences of Military Rule in Myanmar |Institute for Defence Studies and Analyses, 2018, idsa.in/idsacomments/india-asean-partnership-at-25_asajjanhar_040118.7

Challenges and Opportunities

Connectivity between India and ASEAN, particularly Myanmar and Thailand, has emerged as a significant element in cementing bonds between the two regions. Better infrastructure connecting Northeast India and ASEAN has become the sine qua non for stronger economic and trade partnership and a vital contributor to prosperity and economic development of the region.

Two major connectivity projects, namely, the Trilateral Highway between North-East India and Myanmar and onwards to Thailand (and Laos and Vietnam) and the Kaladan Multi-modal Transit and Transport Project, have been under implementation for several years. The present government has taken it up seriously. It is highly likely that both will soon become operational. The allocation of USD 1 billion by the Government in September 2015 to support connectivity projects is testimony to the importance that the Government attaches to rapidly developing infrastructure and bring the regions closer.

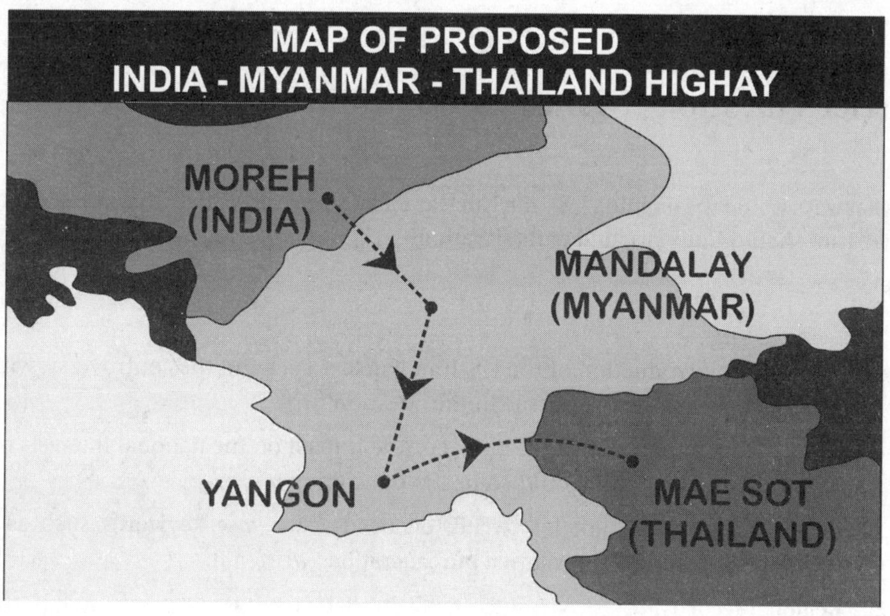

Fig. 7.5: India- Myanmar-Thailand Highway

Stronger relations between India and Myanmar have also helped to quell insurgency and extremism in the north-eastern states of India. Peace, stability, and security of north-east India will be further preserved and promoted with more robust ties and understanding with Myanmar. India has recognized that the success of the AEP will be determined by its contribution to security and economic development of north-east India.

Relations with ASEAN have become multi-faceted to encompass security, connectivity, strategic, political, space technology, counter-terrorism and anti-insurgency operations, anti-radicalization, trade and investment, maritime security and defence collaboration, in addition to economic ties. Cooperation to curb terrorism especially in the face of the rising influence of the Islamic State has assumed priority. Defence partnerships with several ASEAN states are advancing rapidly.

The large Indian diasporas in many Southeast Asian countries help strengthen diplomatic, economic, and security relations between India and ASEAN as they contribute to expand and intensify bonds. The Indian Diaspora comprises an important instrument of India's soft power.

ASEAN continues to form the central pillar of India's Act East Policy. This is evident from the very active exchange of visits that has taken place between India and the region. Prime Minister Modi has travelled to all the ASEAN countries multiple times and also visits from India have been reciprocated by high-level visits from ASEAN states to India. Relations, which were earlier seen as lackadaisical, are again assuming renewed vigour.

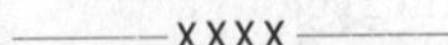

Practice Question (Main Examination)

1. In what ways would the ongoing US-Iran Nuclear Pact Controversy affect the national interest of India? How should India respond to its situation?

Answer:

Approach:

First, provide a short introduction of the US-Iran Nuclear Pact and the controversy, within 30-40 words. Basically, define the main issue in the question first.

Second, handle the main part of the question, i.e., the impact on the national interests of India. Here, the following quick points should come to your mind:

1. **Energy security**—do not just write "oil needs," etc.; use keywords such as energy security; draft your answer as if a bureaucrat has written it.
2. **Regional security.**
3. **Strategic ties with US could be impacted**—Increasing defence, communications, energy, technology exchange, and trade ties.
4. **India's image might get impacted on an international level.**
5. **Trade relations**—India's exports of rice, processed food products, raw materials, diamonds, and machineries.
6. **Impact on proposed strategic projects such as Chahbahar Port to counter China's influence will be impacted**—Also draw a rough sketch of the port connecting India with Iran to Central Asia.

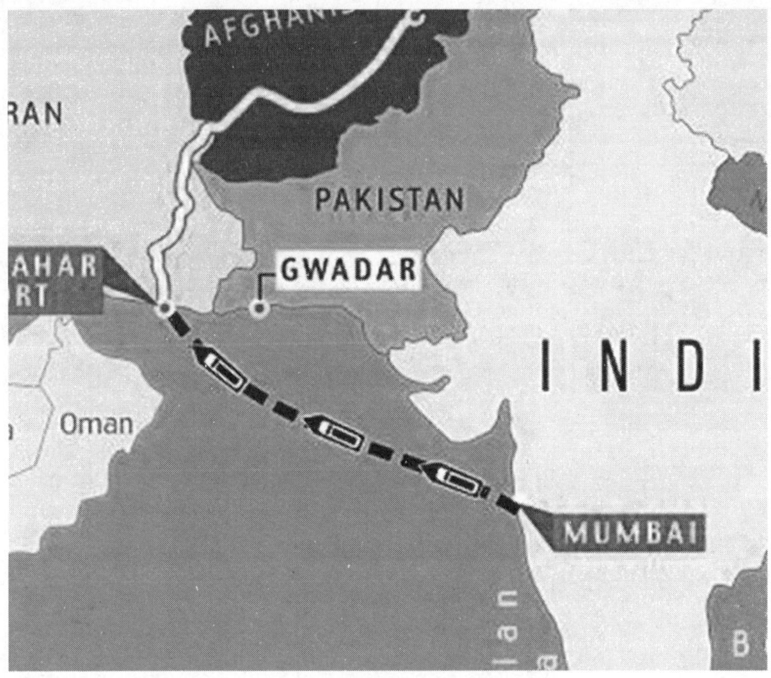

7. **Historical and Cultural Ties**

Third, move on to the next part, i.e., “What should be India’s response…” Here you can start with something like “With deepening strategic ties with the US, India finds itself in a catch 22 situation…”

India’s response (think of a maximum of three to four points):

1. A comprehensive bilateral dialogue with the US to resolve the issue. Possible multiple-partite talks with Iran and other stakeholders such as Russia and USA.
2. A continuation of all possible historical ties and exchanges with Iran in order to maintain continuity in relations.
3. Urgent delegations to both US and Iran and associated countries to resolve these matters and reaffirm India’s efforts to achieve a neutral and win-win situation for all parties.

(You may notice that I have not focused on the Conclusion much. It is something that is not strictly needed, but can be used where the need is felt. Here, both the answers already require a solution to the given problem; hence, a conclusion is not needed.)

Appendix A

Important Supreme Court Judgements

1. *Supreme Court Advocates on Record Association* vs. *Union of India, 2015:*

NJAC Act 2014 (National Judicial Appointment Commission Act, 2014) held unconstitutional by the Supreme Court.

2. *National Legal Services Authority (NALSA) vs. Union of India, 2014:*

The Supreme Court recognized transgender persons as a third gender in India and ordered the government to treat them as minorities and extend reservations.

3. *B.P. Singhal vs. Union of India, 2010:*

The Supreme Court provided various directions that should guide the removal of governors.

4. *S.R. Bommai vs. Union of India, 1994:*

- Federalism is a basic feature; rules for imposing Article 356.
- This ruling had a major implication for state-centre relations, as SC clearly curtailed the powers of Article 356 by detailing how and in what circumstances can President's Rule be imposed.

5. *Kedar Nath Singh vs. State of Bihar, 1962:*

- Section 124A of IPC (sedition) is valid.
- However, strong criticism of the government cannot be covered under this section.
- Unless criticism causes public disorder or disturbance of public peace, it cannot be termed sedition.
- The NGO Common Cause was involved in this case.

6. L. Chandra Kumar Case, 1997: Tribunalization of the Judiciary.

- Tribunalization of the Judiciary, i.e., the case enabled functioning of tribunals. It upheld the view that powers of judicial review cannot be only exercised by courts but also by alternative mechanisms that are equally efficacious.

7. Harbans Singh Jalal Case, 2001:

- Opined on legalizing the model code of conduct (MCC), but suggested against it. However, the court provided teeth to the Election Commission by ruling that MCC would come into force as soon as the Commission issues a press release of conducting elections.

8. Shreya Singhal vs. Union of India, 2015:

SC held Section 66A of IT Act as .unconstitutional: Section 66A was arbitrary, excessive, and disproportionately invades the right of free speech and upsets the balance between such right and the reasonable restrictions that may be imposed on it.

9. Novartis vs. Union of India, 2013:

- The Glivec drug by Novartis was not provided patent protection by the Supreme Court ruling.
- The Glivec drug by Novartis was not provided patent protection by the Supreme Court ruling. The Supreme Court ruling ensured that 'ever-greening' of drugs will not be allowed in India.

10. D.C. Wadhwa Case, 1987:

- Supreme Court pointed out that between 1967 and 1981; the Governor of Bihar promulgated 256 ordinances with the same text.
- The Court ruled that such repromulgation of ordinances would amount to violation of the Constitution and is liable to be struck down.

11. Naz Foundation Case:

In 2009, Section 377 was declared unconstitutional, but again in 2013 this judgment was overturned.

12. Om Prakash vs. Dil Bahar Case, 2006:

Supreme Court declared that a rape accused could be convicted on the sole evidence of the victim in spite of medical evidence not proving rape.

13. Golaknath vs. State of Punjab, 1967:

Fundamental rights are inalienable and cannot be curtailed by the Parliament.

14. Kesavananda Bharati Case, 1970:

Basic Structure doctrine(given elsewhere in chapter 1 of the book)

15. *Maneka Gandhi Case, 1978:*

- Established that fundamental rights and other laws can be subject to judicial review under the assumptions of natural law and the "due process of law," not merely by the procedure established by law (judicial review).
- The Supreme Court in this case reiterated the proposition that the fundamental rights under the Constitution of India are not mutually exclusive but interrelated.
- According to Justice K. Iyer, "a fundamental right is not an island in itself." The expression "personal liberty" in Article 21 was interpreted broadly to engulf a variety of rights within itself.
- The court further observed that the fundamental rights should be interpreted in such a manner so as to expand its reach and ambit rather than to concentrate its meaning and content by judicial construction.
- Article 21 provides that no person shall be deprived of his life or personal liberty except in accordance with procedure established by law, but that does not mean that a mere semblance of procedure provided by law will satisfy the Article; the procedure should be just, fair, and reasonable.
- The principles of natural justice are implicit in Article 21 and hence the statutory law must not condemn anyone unheard.
- A reasonable opportunity of defence or hearing should be given to the person before affecting him, in the absence of which the law will be an arbitrary one.

16. *Minerva Mills Case, 1980:*

Strengthened the Basic Structure doctrine

17. *Vishaka Case, 1997:*

- Every case of sexual harassment is a violation of fundamental rights.
- Foundation laid for enabling a protected and secure female workforce in India.
- A set of guidelines was passed by the Supreme Court for reporting and addressing instances of sexual abuse at the workplace. This has to be followed mandatorily in all workplaces in the country.

18. *R. Rajagopal Case, 1994:*

Petitioners include the editor, associate editor, printer and publisher of a Tamil magazine, Nakkheeran. The respondents include the State of Tamil Nadu, the Inspector General of Prisons, and the Superintendent of Prisons. The petitioners sought to prohibit the respondents from interfering with the publication of an autobiography of a prisoner, Auto Shanker, in Nakkheeran. Shanker was convicted of six murders and sentenced to death. While in jail, Shanker wrote his auto-biography and expressed his wish that this be published in the petitioners' magazine. Before publishing the autobiography, Nakkheeran announced the publication. Prison officials then forced Shanker to write to the magazine requesting that the auto-biography not be published. Petitioners then brought this action to prevent the respondents from violating the magazine's and the prisoner's Freedom of Expression (and the Freedom of Press).

The court ruled that Right to Privacy was a fundamental right, however, not absolute. The Court maintained that a balance should exist between the freedom of the press and the right to privacy. The Court found that the state and its officials do not have the right to impose prior restraints on the publication of materials that may be defamatory of the state. Therefore, "no such prior restraint or prohibition of publication can be imposed by the respondents upon the proposed publication of the alleged autobiography." The Court noted that this ruling does not mean that the state cannot sue for defamation after the article is published, only that they cannot place a prior restraint on the publication of the article.

19. Shah Bano Case:

Shah Bano won the alimony right (1985). The All-India Muslim Personal Law Board was formed in 1973.

20. M.C. Mehta vs. Union of India, 1986:

PIL filed by M.C. Mehta in 1986 that enlarged the concept of Articles 21 and 32 to include the right to a healthy and pollution-free environment.

21. Indra Sawhney vs. UOI, 1992:

The Supreme Court held that caste could be a factor for identifying backward classes.

22. Lily Thomas Case, 2013:

- Disqualified convicted members of Parliament or legislatures (with punishment >2 years) from membership of the house with immediate effect.
- Earlier, a stay could be taken against such an order, and until the convict exhausts all the possible measures, membership could be retained.
- According to the Association of Democratic Reforms, as many as 72 sitting MPs face criminal charges and could be disqualified if convicted for over two years. If that is the case, one can hope that the dream of "Clean Politics" might not be that far-fetched, after all?

23. Shatrughan Singh Case, 2014:

Commuted the sentence of 15 death row convicts on the basis of fundamental right to life. The court held that 'justice delayed is justice denied' and hence the convicts could not be sent to death row after delay in justice delivery for so many years.

24. Representation of the People (Amendment) Act, 2002:

The judgment of a three-member bench ordered candidates contesting elections to declare their assets and all criminal cases pending against them at the time of filing nominations.

25. NOTA, 2013 (Right to a Negative Vote):

"Negative voting will lead to systemic change in polls and political parties will be forced to project clean candidates. If the right to vote is a statutory right, then the right to reject candidate is a fundamental right of speech and expression under Constitution" — Supreme Court

26. Cheaper Cancer Drug Judgment in 2013:

- Novartis AG filed case in SC for cancer drug Glivec.
- "We certainly do not wish the law of patent in this country to develop on the lines where there may be a vast gap between the coverage and the disclosure under the patent, where the scope of the patent is determined not on the intrinsic worth of the invention but by the artful drafting of its claims by skilful lawyers, and where patents are traded as a commodity not for production and marketing of the patented products but to search for someone who may be sued for infringement of the patent."
- A one-month dose of Glivec costs around INR 1.2 lakh, while generic drugs, manufactured by Indian companies, cost INR 8,000. A patent would have given Novartis a 20-year monopoly on the drug, meaning that it would have been impossible for the average Indian to find an affordable cancer drug in that period.

27. Bachan Singh Case, 1980

- Rarest of rare doctrine for pronouncing capital punishment.
- Ignored in real application.

28. Uddar Gagan Case, 2016: Case of Land Acquisition in Haryana)

- SC cancelled the allocation of land by HUDA to private builders.
- SC declared land as a "scarce natural resource" which should be acquired from the poor only for a compelling public purpose.

Other Cases in Detail

(Just read and remember the names and important outcomes)

1. C.B. Muthamma vs. Union of India (Right to Equality)

Facts:

The petitioner was a senior member of the Indian Foreign Service. She brought this petition against the Government on the grounds that she has been overlooked for promotion because she was a woman and because some rules governing the employment of women in the Service are discriminatory in nature and therefore contrary to Articles 14 and 16 of the Constitution.

Decision:

The three appeal judges presented unanimous findings. Justice Krishna Iyer delivered the decision, first commenting that "... sex prejudice against the Indian womanhood pervades the service rules even a third of a century after Freedom. There is some basis for the charge of bias in the rules and this makes the ominous indifference of the executive to bring about the banishment of discrimination in the heritage of service rules. If high officials lose hopes of equal justice under the rules, the legal lot of the little Indian, already priced out of the expensive judicial market, is best left to guess." The Court then analysed the individual rules, finding that:

"If a woman member shall obtain the permission of Government before the marriage, the same risk is run by Government if a male member contracts a marriage. If the family and domestic commitments of a woman member of the service is likely to come in the way of efficient discharge of duties, a similar situation may well arise in the case of a male member ... If a married man has a right, a married woman, other things being equal, stands on no worse footing. Freedom is indivisible, so is justice." The Court found that since the rules in question had been or were in the process of deletion, there was no need to address or attack them. In addition, the petitioner had been promoted subsequent to her complaint, so further examination of it was pointless. The Court also noted that: "The Central Government states that although the petitioner was not found meritorious enough for promotion some months ago, she has been found to be good now, has been upgraded and appointed as Ambassador of India to The Hague, for what that is worth." The Court dismissed the petition but directed the Government to review the petitioner's case in light of the only remaining element of her complaint—that relating to the promotion of people junior to her. The Court emphasized the need to overhaul all service rules to remove discrimination.

2. *Air India vs. Nargesh Meerza (Right to Equality)*

Facts:

The case involved a challenge of Regulations 46 and 47 of the Air India Employees Service Regulations. The challenge was posited on the grounds that the aforesaid regulation created a substantial degree of disparity between male flight attendants (referred to as air flight pursers) and female flight attendants (air hostesses) (and among air hostesses, different operational standards dependent on whether one is working for Air India International on the international circuit or Indian Airlines on the domestic circuit) on multitude of grounds such as promotional avenues, differential retirement ages, conditions pertaining to termination of the air hostess' services in cases of pregnancy or marriage (the retirement age for women was 35 years as opposed to58 for their male counterparts according to Regulation 46). Furthermore, a more prosaic question was regarding the discretionary powers of the Managing Director, who, under Regulation 47,could increase the age of retirement as per his own behest—an aspect that was contested by the petitioners as being arbitrary.

Issues:

i. Whether Regulations 46 and 47 were violative of Articles 14, 15, and 16 of the Constitution of India and thus ultra vires in whole or part?

ii. Whether the discretionary powers enumerated under Regulation 47 could be deemed as being excessive delegation?

Decision:

i. The court held the clauses regarding retirement and pregnancy as unconstitutional and thus ordered for them to be struck down. Furthermore, Regulation 47 experienced a similar fate, for it was found that the said regulation suffered from excessive delegation of powers without any reasonable guidelines.

3. Shayara Bano vs. Union of India and Ors (Triple Talaq Case)

a. Recently, the Supreme Court by a 3:2 majority held that the practice of instantaneous triple talaq (talaq-ul-biddat), which authorised a Muslim man to divorce his wife by pronouncing the word 'talaq' thrice, was legally impermissible and invalid.

b. On the outcome, the Court split three to two: Justices Nariman, Lalit, and Joseph in the majority, with the Chief Justice and Justice Nazeer dissenting. However, Justice Nariman (writing for himself and Justice Lalit) and Justice Joseph used different a reasoning to arrive at the conclusion.

c. Justice Rohinton F. Nariman, writing for himself and Justice U.U. Lalit, held that the Muslim Personal Law (Shariat) Application Act, 1937 had codified all Muslim personal laws, including the practice of triple talaq. This brought it within the bounds of the Constitution. He then held that because talaq-e-biddat allowed unchecked power to Muslim husbands to divorce their wives, without any scope for reconciliation, it was "arbitrary", and failed the test of Article 14 (equality before law) of the Constitution. The practice, therefore, was unconstitutional.

d. Justice Kurian Joseph held that talaq-e-biddat found no mention in the Koran, and was not a part of Muslim personal law. Effectively, he decided the case on these grounds that talaq-e-biddat was un-Islamic, instead of unconstitutional.

e. Hence, the Supreme Court has observed in a catena of cases that all persons similarly circumstanced must be treated equally with respect to both the privileges conferred and the liabilities imposed by the law.

f. To quote the words of the former Chief Justice of India P.B. Gajendragadkar: "Wherever social inequality exists or economic injustice is found, a democratic State enters the arena, and with the aid of law, establishes social equality and removes economic injustice."

2. A.K. Gopalan vs. State of Madras (Preventive Detention Case)

a. The apex court interpreted that the words "procedure established by law" in Article 21 are to be given a wide and fluid meaning of the expression "due process of law" as given under the US Constitution but it refers only to state-made statutes and laws. If any statutory law prescribes a procedure for depriving a person of his rights or personal liberty, it should meet the requirements of Article 21.

3. Kharak Singh v.s State of UP (Right to a Dignified Life)

a. The Supreme Court relied on the US Court judgment in Munn v. Illinois (1877) 94 US Page 113 and held that the term 'Life' as used in Article 21 is something more than mere animal existence and, in other words, it means the right to live with human dignity.

4. ADM Jabalpur vs. Shivkant Shukla (1976)

a. The issue before the Court in this case was whether an order issued by the President to suspend the right of every citizen to move any Court, for the enforcement of their fundamental right to personal liberty under Article 21 upon being detained under a law providing for preventive detention, was unconstitutional.

b. The majority upheld the decision of the government/President.

c. However, Justice HR Khanna dissented. In his dissenting judgement, Justice Khanna emphatically held that the suspension of the right to move any Court for the enforcement of the rights under Article 21, upon a proclamation of emergency, would not affect the enforcement of the basic right to life and liberty. Even in the absence of Article 21, it would not have been permissible for the State to deprive a person of his life and liberty without the authority of the law. The remedy for the enforcement of the right to life or liberty would not stand suspended even if the right to enforce Article 21 is suspended.

d. In 2017, the ADM Jabalpur Case was overruled by a Supreme Court bench. In, Justice K.S. Puttaswamy (Retd.) v. Union of India (also known as the Privacy Case), ADM Jabalpur ruling was termed as 'seriously flawed'. It was D.Y. Chandrachud held, in the Privacy case, that privacy is a constitutionally protected right which emerges from judgments rendered by all the four judges (including his father) constituting the guarantee of life and personal liberty in Article 21. In addition, this right also arises from various other facets of freedom and dignity recognized and guaranteed by the fundamental rights contained in Part III of the Indian constitution. are inalienable to human existence.

5. *Maneka Gandhi vs. Union of India(Passport Case)*

a. Justice P.N. Bhagwati held that the expression "personal liberty" in Article 21 is of the widest amplitude and covers a variety of rights that go to constitute the personal liberty of humans and some of them have been raised to the status of distinct fundamental rights and given additional protection under Article 19.

b. A law that provides for deprivation of life or personal liberty under Article 21 must lay down not just any procedure but a procedure that is fair, just, and reasonable.

6. *People's Union for Democratic Right vs. UOI (Right to Minimum Wages)*

a. Extending the width of Article 21, the Supreme Court held that non-payment of minimum wages to the workers employed in the various Asiad projects in Delhi was denial to them of their right to live with basic human dignity and in violation of Article 21 of the Constitution.

7. *Olga Tellis vs. Bombay Municipal Corporation (Right to Livelihood/ Pavement Dwellers Case)*

a. The petitioners had challenged the validity of Sections 313, 313-A, 314, and 497 of the Bombay Municipal Corporation Act, 1888, which empowered the municipal authorities to remove pavement dwellers' 'huts from pavements and other public places.

b. While agreeing that the right to livelihood is included in Article 21, the Court held that it can be curbed or curtailed by following just and fair procedure. It was held that the above-mentioned sections of the Bombay Municipal Corporation Act were constitutional since they imposed reasonable restrictions on the right of livelihood of pavement and slum-dwellers in the interest of the general public.

c. The SC held that it is an obligation on the State to serve the citizens with adequate means of livelihood and the right to work, which is protected under Article 21 of the Constitution.

8. *Chairman, Railway Board vs. Chandrima Das (Bangladeshi Woman Gang Rape Case)*

a. The SC observed that rape is a crime not only against the person of a woman; it is a crime against the entire society. It destroys the entire physiology of a women and pushes her into deep emotional crisis. Rape is, therefore, the most hated crime. It is crime against human rights and a violation of the victim's most cherished right, namely, the right to life, which involves the right to live with human dignity.

9. *Justice K.S. Puttaswamy (Retd) and Anrv. UOI (Right to Privacy)*

a. The nine-judge bench of the Supreme Court unanimously delivered its judgment by holding that privacy is a constitutionally protected right that not only emerges from the guarantee of life and personal liberty in Article 21 of the Constitution but also arises in varying contexts from the other facets of freedom and dignity recognized and guaranteed by the fundamental rights contained in Part III of the Constitution. The bench overturned an earlier decision in M.P. Sharma (1954) rendered by a bench of eight judges and in Kharak Singh (1962) by a bench of six judges, which contained observations that the Indian Constitution does not specially protect the right to privacy. The judgment also overturned the ADM Jabalpur Case and upheld the minority dissent given by Justice H.R. Khanna. The judgment given in Naz Foundation related to LGBT was also criticized by the bench.

B
Appendix

Approach & Framework for Answer Writing

General Studies Paper 2, (CSE Mains 2017)

Q1. "The local self-government system in India has not proved to be effective instrument of governance." Critically examine the statement and give your views to improve the situation. (150 words)

Approach:

Understand the keywords and what the question is asking. Here, the question is about the effectiveness of the local self-government system. The question is asking for 'critical examination', so we have to view both sides of the issue, i.e., effectiveness and non-effectiveness of the self-government system. Therefore:

Define: First, define local self-government system in India:

- Provide a brief mention of the 73rd and 74th Constitutional Amendments that led to local self-governance in India
- Mention the major local self-governance institutions such as gram Sabha and panchayat, zilla parishad, block-level institutions, and municipal corporations.

Describe: Describe the major points about how local self-government systems have been effective instruments (i.e., the successes of these institutions).Then describe the major points about how local self-government systems have not been effective instruments (i.e., problems)

Conclude: Finally, conclude with a simple two to three sentence 'analysis'. This should follow from the points provided above.

For example: From the above-mentioned, it is clear that there are many successes of local self-governance system in India. With better capacity building, laws, and implementation, their effectiveness can be increased for delivering effective governance to the people.

As you can see, you have to breakdown the question first. Then catch the keywords of the question and what it is asking you to answer. Then you can go ahead and start your answer and try to use a basic framework as follows (applies in most questions):

1. Define the main issue in the question (here it was local self-government institutions)
2. Argue the main points asked for (here it was effectiveness)
3. Conclude

Q2. Critically examine the Supreme Court's judgment on 'National Judicial Appointments Commission Act, 2014' with reference to appointment of judges of higher judiciary in India. (150 words)

Approach:
Same as above, follow the Framework (Define, Describe, and Conclude)

- **First**, define the NJAC judgment briefly in two to three lines.
- **Second**, provide the positive aspects of the judgment with respect to the appointment of judges. For example, judicial independence would have been compromised if the NJAC was not ruled unconstitutional by the Supreme Court.
- **Third**, provide the negative aspects of the judgment with respect to the appointment of judges. For example, overreaching of the Judiciary in legislative matters.
- **Finally**, conclude through an analysis of the above points. For example, from the above analysis, it is clear that judicial independence is a must to maintain separation of powers and exercise checks and balances. Hence, a better system of appointments must be proposed by the Legislative over the current one.

Q3. "Simultaneous election to the Lok Sabha and the State Assemblies will limit the amount of time and money spent in electioneering but it will reduce the government's accountability to the people." Discuss. (150 words)

Try to answer this question yourself through the framework I have provided before you go ahead and read my explanation!

Approach:
Same as above, follow the Framework (Define, Describe, and Conclude)

- **First**, define the concept of simultaneous elections. Try to use historical references such as the fact that it was widely debated in the Constituent Assembly Debates.
- **Second**, provide the positive benefits of having these elections. (Refer to the Law Commission Report on Elections.)For example, simultaneous elections will provide more time for policy making and execution for the government instead of going into election mode every one or two years.
- **Third**, provide the negative aspects of having simultaneous elections. For example, muscle power, money power, etc. will come to dominate unless more electoral reforms are ushered in.
- **Finally**, conclude through an analysis of the above points.

Q2. How do pressure groups influence Indian political process? Do you agree with this view that informal pressure groups have emerged as powerful as formal pressure groups in recent years? (150 words)

Approach:
Same as above, follow the Framework (Define, Describe, and Conclude). This is a simple question because it is one of the main topics in the syllabus itself and also given comprehensively in many resources.

- **First**, define pressure groups. Give some examples of both informal and formal pressure groups.
- **Second**, provide an explanation of how pressure groups influence the Indian political process under a heading, such as 'Pressure Groups Influencing Indian Politics'. For example, pressure groups such as the Confederation of Indian Industries (CII) publish various research papers and organize conferences with major political leaders to push their major agenda and views through political pressure.
- **Third**, provide two more points on the second part of the question—how informal groups have become powerful. For example, informal groups such as ASSOCHAM (The Associated Chambers of Commerce and Industry in India) have emerged as an influential industrial agency that provides many inputs on policy making to the government. Then also provide an alternative view of how they are not truly pressure groups but alternative political groups. Example: The AITUC (All India Trade Union Congress) plays an important politico-social role in the Indian democracy.

Finally, conclude through an analysis of the above points in favour of one or the other stance depending on the points you have provided.

Q5. Discuss the role of Public Accounts Committee in establishing accountability of the government to the people. (150 words)

At least, two to five such straightforward questions will be asked. Do not try to develop an opinion here, just provide the main points you remember.

Approach:
Define PAC, provide bullet points on its role, and conclude.

Q6. "To ensure effective implementation of policies addressing water, sanitation and hygiene needs, the identification of beneficiary segments is to be synchronized with the anticipated outcomes." Examine the statement in the context of the WASH scheme. (150 words)

This question is mainly looking for WASH scheme points. Here, the statement is specific and focuses on 'identification of beneficiary segments'. Therefore, include points about it as the main content to the answer.

WASH is a collective term for water, sanitation, and hygiene. Each of these three components is dependent on the presence of the other. For example, without toilets, water sources become contaminated; without clean water, basic hygiene practices are not possible. (UNICEF)

Then, provide various points of WASH and conclude.

Such questions can be a bit out of scope, as they are deal with international programmes that are still not popular in India. The key is to use generic points and discuss them around the context provided.

Q7. Does the Rights of Persons with Disabilities Act, 2016 ensure an effective mechanism for empowerment and inclusion of the intended beneficiaries in the society? Discuss. (150 words)

- This is also a straightforward question about this Act. Define the Act and provide some basic details in two to three lines.
- Provide the positives (effective mechanism) and negatives of the Act (not effective/ shortcomings).
- Conclude.

Q8. Hunger and Poverty are the biggest challenges for good governance in India still today. Evaluate how far successive governments have progressed in dealing with these humongous problems. Suggest measures for improvement. (150 words)

This is a simple question that can be divided into three segments by carefully reading the question. You will most probably know the content for the answer here but its presentation is the key here. To presents it you can use a table here. This can be as follows:

Provide an introduction with the definitions of hunger and poverty through statistics.

Successive governments	*Dealing with hunger and poverty*
1950–1965 (first-third plan era/post- . independence)	Imports of grains, ICDS (Integrated Child Development Scheme), and free ration programmes
1965–1990 (era of total command economy era)	Agricultural revolution, new health schemes
1990–2004 (post-liberalization era)	Market economy, PPP, etc.
2004–2017 (recent era)	DBT(Direct Benefit Transfer)and demand-driven era

After this, provide measures for improvement. This can itself be the conclusion.

This presentation is key here, as it will enable the examiner to understand your content and give better marks.

Q9. "China is using its economic relations and positive trade surplus as tools to develop potential military power status in Asia." In the light of this statement, discuss its impact on India as her neighbor. (150 words)

This is an important question. The statement is something but the question is something else. The statement is about China using its economic relations to develop military status in Asia, but the question is not about that. It is about the impact of China's development as an economic and trade power on India. So, it is a well-disguised question, where the UPSC is testing how well you read the main gist of the statement.

Approach:
Here, the Define approach will not work in a straightforward manner.Hence, define the rise of China as a trade power through examples. For example, China has emerged as the second largest economy and the largest trading/exporting country in the world. It has launched various economic initiatives such as CPEC (China Pakistan Economic Corridor) and Maritime Silk Road, which have much strategic and military value.

Then, give points on impact on India of these projects. These can be economic, military, soft power, social impact, etc. Conclude with two to three points on how India can counter the impact through its own projects such as Chabahar port project.

Q10. What are the main functions of the United Nations Economic and Social Council (ECOSOC)? Explain different functional commissions attached to it.

This is like the PAC question (Q. 5). It is mostly factual. If you do not know the answer to such questions or do not remember the facts, do not waste time. Move ahead with other questions first and come to this in the end. Just writing anything will not fetch marks. You have to maximize marks with the answers you know first and then come to the questions that you are not sure of.

Approach:

- Define ECOSOC.
- Provide bullet points on its functions.
- Mention different commissions and explain their role in a maximum of 1-3 lines maximum.
- Conclude.

Q11. Explain the salient features of the Constitution (One Hundred and First Amendment) Act, 2016. Do you think it is efficacious enough "to remove cascading effect of taxes and provide for common national market for goods and services"? (250 words)

This is a factual question just like Q. 10.

Approach:

- Define what the constitutional amendment is.
- Provide bullet points on its main features.

- Then, under a heading 'EFFECTIVENESS OF GST', explains how the amendment will remove the cascading effect of taxes and discuss these points in detail.
- Then, under a heading 'INEFFECTIVENESS', provide the shortcomings and how the amendment raises many problems as well.
- Then in conclusion, you can end by providing an analysis/summary on the basis of the above points, as in the examples I have shown in some other questions. For example, "On the basis of this analysis, it is clear that the 101st Constitutional Amendment will enhance tax buoyancy in India, remove the red-tapism for businesses, and remove multiple taxation. Hence, by addressing some of its shortcomings, it can prove to be a game changer for the Indian economy."

Q12. Examine the scope of Fundamental Rights in the light of the latest judgment of the Supreme Court on Right to Privacy. (250 words)

This is an expected question given the fact that the Right to Privacy and the Supreme Court's judgment on it was much in news this year. In this question, the examiner is looking for specific analysis by the aspirant. This is regarding the various fundamental rights impacted by the latest judgment of the Supreme Court.

Therefore, quoting those particular judgments as well as the articles and then analysing how the Right to Privacy judgment has impacted these is what this answer requires. You can structure it as follows:

- Provide a short introduction about Right to Privacy and the ongoing case.
- Provide a list of Fundamental Rights impacted by the judgment followed by the explanation.
- Form a conclusion.

Q13. The Indian Constitution has provisions for holding joint sessions of the two houses of the Parliament. Enumerate the occasions when this would normally happen and also the occasions when it cannot, with reasons thereof. (250 words)

Purely factual question.

Approach:

- **First**, define a 'joint session'.
- **Second**, provide points on 'when it is held', i.e., the occasions.
- **Third**, provide when it cannot be held and explain the reasons.
- **Finally**, conclude with a point about the utility of joint sessions and how, when it is summoned, it has helped in coming to some decisions on important constitutional matters.

Q14. To enhance the quality of democracy in India the Election Commission of India has proposed electoral reforms in 2016. What are the suggested reforms and how far are they significant to make the democracy successful? (250 words)

Very standard question, as you must have studied election reforms in the news regularly.

Approach:

- Define in brief the role of elections and electoral reforms (give past examples)
- Make a heading, 'Proposed Electoral Reforms in 2016' and then under it provide a bullet-point-wise list of as many as you can recall with a brief outline of each.
- Then make anther heading, 'Significance in Making Democracy Successful' and then provide points about how will they improve the electoral system.
- For example,

  Proposed Electoral Reforms in 2016:

  a. Making bribery in elections a cognizable offence

  b. Ban on exit polls and opinion polls

  c. Ban on government sponsored ads before elections

  d. Paid news

  e. Maintenance of accounts by political parties

  ...and so on.

Significance in Making Democracy Successful

i. Making bribery a cognizable offence will reduce the money power influence in elections, and so on.

You can also use a table to show the proposed reforms in one column and their significance in the next column:

Proposed Electoral Reforms in 2016	*Significance in Making Democracy Successful*
a. Ban on exit polls and opinion polls	Will ensure that public opinion is not influenced by select media houses and corporate supported parties.

There are many such reforms and they can be found in the "Electoral Reforms" report published by the Election Commission in 2016-17. The key is to know about the major recommendations of such reports and be able to discuss them as illustrated. Then, follow with the conclusion.

Q15. Is the National Commission for Women able to strategize and tackle the problems that women face at both public and private spheres? Give reasons in support of your answer. (250 words)

The question is asking about successes and failures of the National Commission for Women. Read the keywords 'Is the NCW able to strategize and tackle problems..."

Hence, use the same pattern/technique as I have mentioned: (1) Introduction of NCW with a few examples of major schemes/interventions, (2) Successes, (3) Failures, (4) Conclusion with a way forward.

Q16. 'The emergence of Self Help Groups (SHGs) in contemporary times points to the slow but steady withdrawal of the state from developmental activities'. Examine the role of the SHGs in developmental activities and the measures taken by the Government of India to promote the SHGs. (250 words)

Self-Help Groups (SHGs) are normally groups of women (15-20 in numbers) that work to provide alternative livelihoods to women or encourage small regular savings programmes. For example, Kudumbshree of Kerala and NABARD have funded the 'e-SHAKTI' programme that provides funding to thousands of SHGs in India for undertaking new women-run business opportunities.

Role of SHGs in Developmental Activities:

1. **Financing**: For example, the priority sector lending that GoI provides to SHGs and the low interest rates and relaxed repayment agreements.
2. **Corporate Linkups**: Various CSR programmes are spearheaded by SHGs now. For example, the Saheli programme of Amazon.com.
3. **Livelihood programmes**: The Deen Dayal Antodaya Yojana that encapsulates capacity building of SHGs for development activities. Also, the Priyadarshini scheme.
4. **Social mobilization** for health and sanitation awareness is a key part of various SHGs and many of these initiatives are led by women groups in villages and small talukas.

Conclude by giving either a way forward or just a simple conclusion (as provided in other questions).

Q17. "Poverty Alleviation Programmes in India remain mere show pieces until and unless they are backed by political will." Discuss with reference to the performance of the major poverty alleviation programmes in India. (250 words)

The Constitution of India provides for social and economic justice as key goals to be achieved by our government and society. For achieving this, many poverty alleviation programmes such as NREGA (Rural Employment Guarantee Scheme), National Old Age Pension Scheme, PMGAY (Gram Awaas Yojana), Maternity Benefit Scheme, and many others have been launched.

Need for political will:

1. Leads to quick and productive policy decision making.
2. Leads to swift executive and administrative decisions.
3. Directly enhances the grass-roots vision of the 73rd and 74th Constitutional amendments.
4. Reduces corruption.

Provide some examples about how political will leads to success in such poverty alleviation programmes. These can be found elsewhere in the book. For example, The Bangalore Action Task Force and Delhi Government's Bhagidaari programmes.

Q18. Initially Civil Services in India were designed to achieve the goals of neutrality and effec tiveness, which seems to be lacking in the present context. Do you agree with the view that drastic reforms are required in Civil Services? Comment (250 words)

The focus here should be to provide an introduction of the civil service reform recommendations so far, summarize major recommendations, and then conclude with a forward-looking statement. The key here is to note that not only do you have to provide a brief list of recommendations but also the reasoning behind why these reforms are needed. Hence, do not miss that part.

Introduction: Provide a short list of (two to three) reforms and the committees that recommended them. For example, Civil Services form the critical 'steel frame' of India's administration, which must be reformed from time to time to avoid it from 'rusting'. Various committees such as ARC (Administrative and Reforms Commission 1996), the Hota Committee (2004), and many others have proposed key reforms.

Reforms—The content should focus on the following points:

1. Training and capacity building
2. Civil Services Board
3. Fixed tenures
4. Domain expertise
5. Accountability and transparency

Why are these drastic reforms the need of the hour?

1. The socio-economic-politico milieu of the country has changed drastically. Greater economic opportunities, grass-roots politics, and emerging religious/caste dynamics need empowered as well as accountable bureaucracy.
2. The devolution of power with the 73rd and 74th Constitutional Amendments needs a new bureaucracy to handle the greater democratic dialogue.
3. Rapid urbanization presents new challenges.

You can add more points (but keep in mind the word limit of 250–275 words).

Q19. The question of India's Energy Security constitutes the most important part of India's economic progress. Analyse India's energy policy cooperation with West Asian Countries. (250 words)

India is a global giant of oil consumption and imports almost 90% of it. This makes India energy dependent on foreign sources, thereby making oil a key strategic resource like defence and telecommunications. It is also a key ingredient of India's interest in West Asia. India is dependent on imports for 80% of its oil needs, of which roughly 55% is sourced from the Persian Gulf region.

There are various key successes of India in energy cooperation in the region. India has also launched many programmes for energy policy cooperation in the West Asian Countries as follows: (the answer can be formed along these major points)

1. Look West
2. Strategic Petroleum Reserve System
3. SLOCs (sea-lines of communication)
4. TAPI (Turkmenistan-Afghanistan-Pakistan-India Pipeline)
5. Joint ventures between Indian and West Asian oil giants

Challenges and Failures

1. Bureaucratic hurdles and red-tapism
2. Massive fluctuations in world oil prices and the role of the OPEC (The Organization of Petroleum Exporting Countries) cartel
3. Regional geopolitical challenges such as the blockade of Qatar, a major gas producer.

Conclusion:

Form a conclusion that has one to two points on the way forward. For example:

Way Forward:

1. The Energy Security Policy document needs to be drafted
2. Constant dialogues with West Asian Countries on energy security and mutual cooperation in synergistic areas
3. A dedicated 'Energy Security Cell' in West Asian embassies

Q20. Indian Diaspora has an important role to play in South-East Asian countries' economy and society. Appraise the role of Indian Diaspora in Southeast Asia in this context (250 words)

This question is a bit unexpected as it is specifically asking about the Indian Diaspora in Southeast Asia. Normally, the Indian diaspora in USA, UK, and the Middle East is more talked about than that South Asia. East Asia Research Programme published an article about this in 2017, but it is almost unlikely that many aspirants would have read it.

Therefore, the strategy with such questions could be to answer them in a more generic way so that you can score some points. This 'generic' way could draw on your knowledge from the GS 1 history section, from which the section on the influence of India's historical ties in Southeast

Asia could be used. This could fetch good marks. Also, try to attempt this as one of the last questions if you do not know the specifics.

Approach:
First, define the term 'Diaspora'; specifically the strength of Indian diaspora in the world. Then, write two to three points about India's presence in Southeast Asia.

For example:
The diaspora of any country provides a human dimension to the links between two countries. They have a unique role in international relations because they find themselves in between two countries, sharing two cultures, having an emotional investment in two nations, and preserving social connections in two societies (refer to EARP.in).

From a historical perspective, Southeast Asia has been hugely influenced by India in art, culture, architecture, religion, and so on. For example, the Chola Empire sent many expeditions to this region and many Indians settled there permanently.

Now you can elaborate on further points such as:
The Indian diaspora plays various roles in this region:

1. Soft power
2. Trade ties and economic role (source of huge currency remissions to India)
3. Software development and outsourcing (ASEAN-India ties)
4. Role of Indians in politics and civil services of Southeast Asia (you can use the Singapore example, where a large number of Indians are bureaucrats)
5. Strategic role

Conclusion:
Form the conclusion along these lines:

The Indian government must promote a conducive environment to ensure that the diasporic community always remembers its relationship with the homeland. Government initiatives such as Pravasi Bharatiya Diwas, Pravasi Bharatiya Sammelan, and trade facilitation centres for overseas Indians are steps in the right direction (refer to EARP.in and ICRIER).

General Studies Paper 2, (CSE Mains 2018)

Q1. In the light of recent controversy regarding the use of Electronic Voting Machines (EVMs), what are the challenges before the Election Commission of India to ensure the trustworthiness of elections in India?* (10)

Answer:

The Election Commission of India (ECI) is the apex body that conducts the general and legislative assembly elections in India. The challenges before the ECI are as follows:*

*If you remember any relevant constitutional article, you can refer to it here as well to add depth to your answer, but it is not necessary·

1. **Paid news:**
   a. Paid news has been used to manipulate people's views about political parties. For example, in the state of Uttar Pradesh, almost 50–60 complaints of paid news were reported to the ECI.
   b. No concrete legislations or rules exist to address the menace of paid news at the present.
2. **Social media:**
   a. Media such as Face book, Whatsapp, and others have become a source of major news content and communication between people.
   b. A constant monitoring of these media during election periods and swiftly addressing any misuse has emerged as a must area for the ECI.
3. **Election expenditure**
   a. A Law Commission report on election reform has also highlighted the need to curb money power in elections.
4. **VVPAT(Voter verifiable paper audit trail)**
   a. Well-functioning VVPATs could provide paper trails that could address the concerns with EVMs and also provide audit capability.
5. **Voter awareness through SVEEP (Systematic Voters' Education and Electoral Participiction)**
   a. The SVEEP program of the ECI must be extended in order to educate the voters more broadly about their responsibilities.

How to study for such questions:

1. This is a current affairs question, based on recent news about EVMs and the Election Commission of India
2. Expanding on the basic points is enough here. In this question, the main matter is about the "challenges" faced by the Commission, so please focus on that, as the answer is required in only 150 words worth 10 marks.
3. Use capital or bold letters to highlight the main points such as VVPAT and social media, so that the examiner can check your answers quickly.
4. Give a brief introduction, a simple one. There is no need to write an introductory statement such as "Recently, the ECI has faced criticism for EVMs...." Just provide a background of ECI and go ahead with the challenges.
5. Conclusion is not needed in such short-format questions, as there is hardly any space for content.

Q2. Can the National Commission for Scheduled Castes (NCSC) enforce the implementation of constitutional reservation for the scheduled castes in religious minority institutions? Examine.

Answer:

The NCSC was set up as a Constitutional body to promote the social, educational, economic, and service interest of scheduled castes in India.

The NCSC has directed Aligarh Muslim University to implement the reservation policy after judgment of the Allahabad High Court, which declared AMU as a non-minority institution.

Why can NCSC enforce the implementation of constitutional reservation for SCs in such institutions?
Special office under the constitution

- It has been set up as a special body to address the socio-economic-politico problems of the scheduled castes and ensure their well-being to meet the ideals of the Constitution (specially the Right to Equality and Article 338) and therefore it can do so.

Why it cannot?

1. Even though the NCSC is a constitutional body, it does not have the necessary judicial or executive powers to do so.
2. The NCSC is not an implementation body but a policy maker. It can only provide recommendations to the government.
3. Religious Minority Institutions have special rights accorded by the Constitution as well. The National Commission for Minority Educational Institutions is the apex body for their oversight. Hence, the NCSC's enforcement could be questioned.

From this analysis, it's clear that the NCSC does not have a clear mandate to enforce, and hence the apex court's final judgment must be awaited in order to determine the status of minority institutions and reservations therein.

Q3. Under what circumstances can a Financial Emergency are proclaimed by the President of India? What consequences follow when such a declaration remains in force? (10)

Answer:

Article 360 of the Constitution empowers the President to proclaim a financial emergency. No financial emergency has been declared in India since independence in 1947.

Circumstances:

1. The President is satisfied that a situation has arisen due to which the financial stability or credit of India or any of its territories is threatened.
2. The President has the final and conclusive authority in this matter, but his/her authority can be challenged for a judicial review.
3. Both the Houses must approve this within two months. A financial emergency can be declared for an indefinite period once approved and the President can revoke it at any time.

Consequences:

1. The Centre can direct any state to observe any rules/regulations of financial propriety as it specifies.
2. The President may issue any direction to the Centre/states/Judiciary for reduction in salaries, allowances, etc. of public servants.
3. The President may direct the states to reserve money bills or financial bills for his/her consideration.
4. The Centre has full control over the states' finances.

This provision is a debatable one, as many constitutionalists have deemed it as "a serious threat on the financial autonomy of the states."

> If you remember any such statements or quotes that are relevant, you can use them in introductions or conclusions.

Q4. Why do you think committees are considered to be useful for Parliamentary work? Discuss, in this context, the role of the Estimates Committee. (10)

Answer:

A number of committees assist the Parliament to carry out its work. Two kinds: (1) Standing committees, which are permanent in nature. (2) Ad-hoc committees, which are temporary in nature.

Why these committees are are useful?

1. They reduce time and workload for an otherwise very busy Parliament.
2. They provide expertise in the specific areas they handle, such as Finance.
3. They ensure that the varied functions of the Parliament are efficiently handled.
4. They provide intensive scrutiny of the legislative matters of utmost importance.

Estimates Committee

The Estimates Committee examines estimates such as that of the budget and suggests 'economies' in public expenditure.

1. It reports on various parameters such as efficiency, administrative reform, and overall improvements needed.
2. It also suggests alternate policies to bring in administrative and economic efficiency.
3. It ensures that the estimates are within the prescribed limits.

Hence, it can be seen that the Estimates Committee provides expertise, reduces the burden of the Parliament, and undertakes the key work of scrutinizing the important public function of budget.

Q5. "The Comptroller and Auditor General (CAG) has a very vital role to play." Explain how this is reflected in the method and terms of his appointment as well as in the range of powers he can exercise. (10)

Answer:

The CAG [Article 148,149] is considered as the guardian of the public purse and controls the entire financial system of the country. Dr B.R. Ambedkar referred to the CAG as the most important officer under the Indian Constitution.

> If you remember any relevant constitutional article (here Articles 148,149), you can refer to it here as well to add depth to your answer, but it is not necessary.

Appointment:

1. Appointed by the President of India
2. Holds same precedence as that of a Supreme Court judge

Range of Powers:

1. Security of tenure:
    a. The CAG can only be removed by the President on the same grounds as that of a Supreme Court judge. This ensures that his/her work is not impacted by vested interests.
2. Eligibility for further office
    a. He/she is not eligible for further office in the Government, thereby ensuring his/her impartiality and highest level of ethics while in office.
3. Independence and working
    a. Salary is determined by the Parliament and it cannot be altered to her/his disadvantage.
    b. All expenses are borne by the Consolidated Fund of India, thereby ensuring independence.

c. CAG is an agent of the Parliament and prepares AUDIT reports of expenditure on behalf of the Parliament.

d. Reports are considered by the Public Accounts Committee (PAC) and the Committee on Public Undertakings.

Q6. "Policy contradictions among various competing sectors and stakeholders have resulted in inadequate protection and prevention of degradation to the environment." Comment with relevant illustrations.

Answer:

How to approach such abstract questions:

It is very unlikely that you will actually remember such a statement from the news or reports you might have read. Such abstract and seemingly out-of-place questions require you to cite some concrete examples (the question also mentions "relevant illustrations"); stick to the word limit as much as possible and give two to three really strong points to fetch maximum marks. It also needs a good conceptual understanding.

I am giving a broad overview of the answer here, not a complete answer. You can build your own answer using such points.

Answer:

Various sectors and stakeholders compete for the same resources, which has led to the degradation of the environment. This is due to (add more points):

1. Limited availability of environmental (forest, land, water) resources that could be used for developmental purposes.
2. Competing claims for development by the state (government) and forest dwellers/tribals, who have traditional rights to the resources.

Examples/Illustrations:

1. Bullet train development
2. Dam development
3. Mining rights

Solutions:

The government has started the District Mining Funds in order to provide some funds to the tribals/inhabitants. Use such current examples to improve your answer.

Q7. Appropriate local community level healthcare intervention is a prerequisite to achieve 'Health for All' in India. Explain.

Approach:

1. Provide basic definition of 'Health for All'.
2. Provide points for the need of local community level healthcare intervention with existing provisions.
3. Conclude.

I am giving a broad overview of the answer here, not a complete answer. You can build your own answer using such points.

Answer:

Health for All is a World Health Organization (WHO) programme to ensure full primary healthcare to promote human dignity and well being.

As often said, "It takes a village to raise a child;" local community interventions are key to achieving "Health for All" in India:

1. Malnutrition starts at pregnancy, not after birth
    a. If a pregnant mother has proper nutrition, the chances of a low-weight birth and other deficiencies reduce significantly. Hence, community focus on the mother's nutrition is the need of the hour.
2. Sanitation
3. Immunization
    a. While some top-down led immunization programmes have been successful, communities still remain unaware of the many necessary supplemental immunizations.
4. Awareness at the local community level
    a. The local community is largely unaware of basic health interventions.

Steps in India:

1. **A village-level health committee** has been set up as a part of the gram Sabha to enable local community discussions about health outcomes in the village.
2. **Anaganwadi and ASHA workers** are focused solely on the local community solutions and interventions to ailing health outcomes in India. Greater institutionalization and strengthening of these institutions will further expand Health for All.

Q8. E-governance in not only about utilization of the power of new technology, but also much about the critical importance of the 'use-value' of information. Explain. (10)

Answer:

Information is a highly valuable commodity. It has a tremendous value in terms of the insights it can provide to improve governance, thereby improving the quality of life and service delivery to millions of citizens. This 'use-value' of information through e-governance can be utilized as follows:

1. **Big data** E-governance naturally collects many gigabytes of user information. For example, crop insurance disbursals made online can be used to study crop failure patterns and the impact of climate, inputs, and marketing through big data. This is tremendous use-value.
2. **Trends analysis** For example, the government can run a trends analysis on agriculture export and import data to educate farmers about market trends.

3. **Cross-use in various applications** Beneficiary (citizen) data gathered from education can be used in health services and vice versa. Such cross-applications can truly enhance the value of e-governance and its impact on the beneficiaries.
4. **Understanding gaps in implementation** Various shortcomings of the schemes can be understood by carefully studying the data generated through e-governance, thereby enhancing its use-value.

Note: Aspirants should note that such questions are hard to prepare for well in advance. Therefore, it might happen that your answer is not satisfactory or you end up leaving it altogether. It is not something to worry about, as we cannot really do much about one or two questions!

Q9. "India's relations with Israel have, of late, acquired a depth and diversity, which cannot be rolled back." Discuss. (10)

Answer:
India-Israel relations have reached new defining heights. The two countries have many similar world views and areas of congruence. India and Israel are both deeply religious countries, stricken with domestic and international challenges and with many overlapping strategic interests in the following areas:

1. **Fighting terrorism (security)**: Israel's hi-tech capabilities in countering terrorism along the border can provide India with the many capabilities it needs for itself.
2. **Agriculture and water**: Israel has developed water-efficient technologies. In line with India's "MORE CROP PER DROP" policy in agriculture, a partnership in this area is natural.
3. **Defence production and trade**: Various Israeli companies have entered into agreements with Indian companies and startups to develop defence technologies after the recent investment deregulation in India.
4. **People-to-people exchanges**: Israel has also decided to start an annual exchange of bilateral visits by 100 young people from science-related educational streams.

Apart from these areas, India and Israel are entering into areas of cooperation such as oil and gas, cyber security, films, and startups. These areas are indicative of diverse and broad-based engagement between the two countries, which will only gain further momentum in future.

Q10. A number of outside powers have entrenched themselves in Central Asia, which is a zone of interest to India. Discuss the implications, in this context, of India's joining the Ashga bat Agreement, 2018. (10)

Answer:
Central Asia has become a hotbed of 'the new great game' that is unraveling in the region. Its natural resources, trade potential, and geo-political importance has led to entrenching of powers such as Russia, China, USA, and many others in the region.

Implications of India joining the Ashgabat Agreement, 2018

1. International North-South transport corridor (INSTC): It would enable India to utilize the existing transport and transit corridor to facilitate trade and commercial interactions with the Eurasian region.
2. Trade with Central Asia: It would make it easier for India to reach out to Central Asia, which houses strategic and high-value minerals including uranium, copper, titanium, etc.
3. Competitive Trade with Euro-Asian Transit System: Container transport plays a significant role, and for India to join the competitive situation in the Euro-Asian transit system, active participation in transportation projects becomes essential.
4. Connecting to Afghanistan via Chabahar: Setting up the port and opening up the INSTC (shown in Fig. B.1) has been essential for India and it has already sent shipments of wheat to Afghanistan through the Chabahar port. This corridor opens a new door of relations to the region.

It is clear from the above analysis, that India's position and interest in Central Asia will be further boosted by participation in the Ashgabat Agreement.

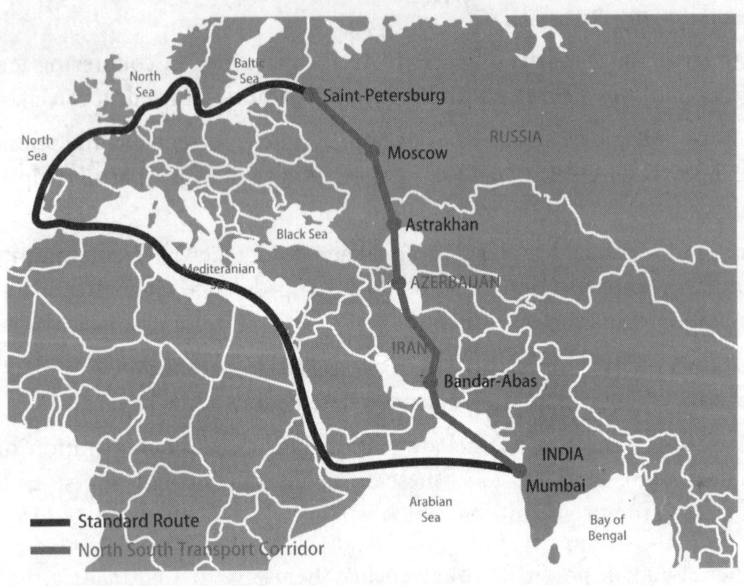

Figure B.1: International North–South Transport Corridor (INSTC)

Q11. Can the Supreme Court Judgment (July 2018) settle the political tussle between the Lt Governor and the elected government of Delhi? Examine. (15)

Answer:

The Supreme Court recently passed a judgment interpreting Article 239AA, which is the key originating point of tussle between the two parties.

Why should it settle the political tussle?

1. The SC has ruled that the LG of Delhi had to act as per the aid and advice of the Council of Ministers of the Delhi Government except in matters of land, police, and public order.
2. It has also ruled that the LG cannot interfere in each and every decision of the Delhi Government and Delhi Government need not concur with the governor in all matters.
3. The power given to the LG is not for routine matters but only for valid reasons when it becomes necessary to safeguard the interest of the Union Territory. Hence, it cannot be used freely.
4. LG has been termed as "Administrator".

Why will it not?

1. The Court has said that Delhi government *must communicate all decisions to the LG office,* even though it does not need concurrence of LG office. This creates a room for reinterpretation of the judgment.
2. The Court has held that Delhi is not a *'state'* and *occupied a special status under the Constitution*, thereby further complicating the role of an elected body of legislators in the non-state entity of Delhi.

What is more important here is the spirit and words of the larger judgment, which point towards the efforts of collaboration between the LG office and the representatives.

It has clearly said that the Union and state governments must embrace a collaborative federal structure by displaying harmonious coexistence and interdependence so as to avoid any possible constitutional discord. Unless this is understood by both the sides, the political tussle is likely to stay.

Q12. How far do you agree with the view that tribunals curtail the jurisdiction of ordinary courts? In view of the above, discuss the constitutional validity and competence of the tribunals in India. (15)

Answer:

The Law Commission Report on Tribunals has defined a 'tribunal 'as an administrative body established for the purpose of discharging quasi-judicial duties.

The 42nd Amendment Act of 1976 provided for Articles 323A and 323B in the Constitution of India, which led to the establishment of Administrative Tribunals.

Hence, they are constitutionally valid quasi-judicial bodies.

How they curtail jurisdiction of ordinary courts:

1. **Conflicting judgements**: Many times, tribunals pass conflicting judgments from high court or Supreme Court rulings, thereby curtailing their jurisdictions.
2. **Appointment of judges in tribunals**: The Supreme Court has ruled that tribunal judge appointments are equivalent to those of high court judges, thereby creating a conflict between the jurisdictions of the courts.

3. The tribunals have been set up to reduce the workload of courts, but in doing so, they often pass overzealous decisions outside their jurisdiction, which often leads to the denial of timely justice to the aggrieved parties.

How they don't:

1. **Judicial review**: The power of judicial review of high courts and the Supreme Court is a basic feature of the Constitution and no tribunal order lies outside its scope.
2. **Appeals to high court and Supreme Court**: High courts and the Supreme Court accept appeals of tribunal judgment on the merits of the individual case.
3. An administrative tribunal is neither a court nor an executive body. It stands somewhere midway between a court and an administrative body. Hence, it is not a purely judicial body.

Competency of Tribunals

1. Pendency of cases not resolved: Over 3.5 lakhs are pending in five major tribunals, thereby not achieving the core idea behind establishing them, i.e., resolving the delay in delivering justice.
2. Benches not established: Access to justice through tribunals not yet achieved, as they are not uniformly present in all parts of India as envisaged.
3. Lack of uniformity in appointments: The system of appointments in tribunals has not been completely streamlined yet.

Hence, it is clear from the above analysis that tribunals serve an important purpose, and a streamlined, well-supervised tribunal system can lead to quicker justice delivery in India.

Q13. India and USA are two large democracies. Examine the basic tenets on which the two political systems are based.

Answer:

	India & USA
Constitutionalism	Both democracies are based on a set of fundamental values enshrined in their constitutions. In both democracies, the Constitution limits the power of the government to deprive citizens of their natural rights.
Liberty	Both democracies prescribe liberty of thought, expression, belief, faith, and worship as one of the core values. This has to be assured to every member of all the communities.
Equality	Both democracies ensure equality of status and opportunity to every citizen for the development of the best in him/her.

Separation of powers	Both democracies have strict separation of powers of the Legislature, Executive, and the Judiciary. However, there are a few exceptions in the Indian democracy where there are overlaps in the Executive and Legislature.
Independent Judiciary	Both have independently functioning judiciaries headed by the Supreme Court.

Differences:

Rights

Even though fundamental rights are guaranteed in both democracies, in USA they are considered as natural rights but in India they have been granted by the Constitution. Therefore, the difference between the 'due process of law' vs. 'procedure established by law' arises.

Socialism

While India has declared itself to be a socialist country with a focus on equitable distribution of public goods, thisis not the case with USA. The Indian Constitution directs to prevent concentration of wealth and power in a few hands.

Secularism

Secularism implies that India is not guided by any one religion or any religious considerations. At the same time, the Indian state is not against religion. It allows all its citizens to profess, preach, and practise any religion they follow.

On the other hand, USA is a secular state but not in similar terms as India. USA has separated the state and the church entirely. American Presidents take the oath of office on the Bible, unlike India where it is done on the Constitution.

Q14. How is the Finance Commission of India constituted? What do you know about the terms of reference of the recently constituted Finance Commission? Discuss. (15)

Answer:

Article 280 of the Indian Constitution provides for setting up of the Finance Commission. It is constituted by the President of India every 5 years. The main tasks of the Finance Commission are:

1. It decides the distribution of revenue between the Centre and the states.
2. It also specifies the underlying principles on which grants-in-aid are given to the states.

The 15th Finance Commission has been constituted recently, and the following are the major terms of reference:

1. It will review the current status of deficit, debt levels, and fiscal discipline followed by the Centre and the states.
2. It will recommend a fiscal consolidation roadmap.

3. It will foster higher inclusive growth in the country, guided by the principles of equity, efficiency, and transparency.
4. It will review the present arrangements on financing disaster management initiatives under the Disaster Management Act.
5. It will also study:
   a. The impact of GST on revenues
   b. The impact of the recommendations of the 14th Finance Commission (devolution of funds to the state government)
   c. Progress made in moving towards the replacement rate of population growth
   d. Progress in sanitation, solid waste management, etc.

Major Issues with terms of Reference:

- Census data: The 14th Finance Commission used the 1971 census data for determining the devolution of taxes, duties, and grants-in-aid. The Central Government asked the 15th Finance Commission's terms of reference to use the 2011 data.
  i. This puts the southern states at a considerable disadvantage in devolution of funds as they have been successful at controlling population growth, while the northern states have grown at a faster rate comparatively.
  ii. This could lead to lower resource allocation to the southern states.

The Centre has noted that:

- Finance Commissions will use both qualitative and quantitative criteria
- The Terms of References of the 15th Finance Commission rightly balance both the "needs" represented by the latest population and the "progress towards population control."
- Also, it recognizes the efforts of all the states that have done well in population control.

The need of the hour is to address the concerns of stakeholders and evolve principles that lead to an equitable distribution of resources among the states and between the Centre and the states.

Q15. Assess the importance of the Panchayat system in India as a part of local government. Apart from government grants, what sources can the panchayatsidentify for financing d e - velopmental projects? (15)

Answer:

The 73rd Amendment to the Indian Constitution gave constitutional teeth to and formalized the Panchayati Raj (PR) system in India. It now consists of a three-tier system of governance: gram panchayat, panchayat samiti, and zilla parishad (with some exceptions in a few states).

Importance of Panchayat System

1. **Decentralization of governance:**
   a. The gram Sabha is the soul of the PR system. It can hold meetings to discuss issues, create a village level development plan, and appoint implementation agencies in concurrence with the executive.

   b. This decentralization could solve the problem of top-down approach of governance.
   c. It enables local people and leaders to address local problems directly.
2. **Participative governance**: The system envisages the participation of each and every resident of the village to ensure true participative democracy.
3. **Representation of women**: A 33% reservation in panchayats ensures that the concept of women in leadership roles is emerging from the very grassroots and enabling a greater say of this gender in governance matters.
4. **Grass-roots accountability**: It also brings greater accountability, as development projects are conceptualized and executed at the local level itself.

Sourcing for financing projects by panchayats

1. **Local taxes**: The gram panchayats can collect taxes locally on water, places of pilgrimage, local temples, and markets. These funds can be used for financing developmental projects within the village. However, many gram panchayats have not evolved these functions due to lack of awareness, manpower, and capacity.
2. **Proportion of land revenue**: Gram panchayats can also get a certain proportion of land revenue from the district as a grant from the state. This provides additional sources for development. This has been implemented in some states such as Maharashtra.

The PR system is not merely a Gandhian idea, but a true democratic tool that can transform India's rural governance. Better financing, training, and awareness can lead to efficient and timely delivery of developmental projects through this institution.

Approach to the question:
This is a standard question and study from traditional sources such as Yojana, this book, and the Internet should be able to address it.

Q16. Multiplicity of various commissions for the vulnerable sections of the society leads to problems of overlapping jurisdiction and duplication of functions. Is it better to merge all commissions under an umbrella Human Rights Commission? Argue your case. (15)

Approach:
In such questions, more often than not, you will need to provide an answer created by common sense laced with your knowledge. Here is a basic overview (not a complete model answer):

Answer:
India has set up various commissions to address the cause of equitable development as mandated by the Constitution. For example, the National Commission for backward castes, safai karamcharis, women, unorganized sector, human rights, and many others.

Advantages of an Umbrella Human Rights Commission:

1. Single point of reference for all cases
2. Single-point evaluation of progress and justice delivery
3. One body to advice the government about issues faced by these sections

4. Quick decisions to reach justice
5. Cuts red-tapism
6. Accountability

Disadvantages:

1. Dedicated commissions are able to understand and address section-specific issues
2. Lack of overlapping of issues across sections
3. Specialization of functions is needed

Provide a conclusion that analyses the above points and reaches a logical conclusion.

Q17. How far do you agree with the view that the focus on lack of availability of food as the main cause of hunger takes the attention away from ineffective human development policies in India? (15)

Answer:

Hunger continues to be a major human development problem. According to the Food and Agriculture Organization (FAO) report, almost 200 million people (15% of the population) are still malnourished in India due to hunger.

India has produced a record amount of food grains, 280 million tons, in 2017, which is considered enough to meet the total demand.

However, lack of availability (which leads to hunger) occurs due to the following reasons:

1. Food waste
2. Unstable markets
3. Climate change and agriculture instability (lack of proper supply chains and distribution systems)
4. Lack of technological development in agriculture
5. Poverty trap

On the other hand, ineffective development policies are also a cause of major hunger problems. These are:

1. **Poor implementation by design**: Various schemes have failed to meet their intended purpose. For example, the MUDRA Loan scheme has not solved the problem of creating livelihoods, as many entrepreneurs lack the essential skills and knowledge to utilize such loans.
2. **Poor governance and rule of law**: A key condition for schemes and policies to succeed is the presence of rule of law and good governance. However, lack of these leads to the failure of well-thought policies.
3. **Lack of awareness**: A key problem has been the lack of awareness about policies amongst the public. For example, despite the introduction of the Panchayati Raj System in India, many states have not devolved powers to the grass-roots. Therefore, awareness is key for success of policies.

Hence, it can be seen that both shortage of grains caused by artificial/extraneous reasons as well as poor policy lead to hunger. Both must be addressed simultaneously to solve this problem.

Q18. The Citizen's Charter is an ideal instrument of organizational transparency and account ability, but it has its own limitations. Identify the limitations and suggest measures for greater effectiveness of the Citizen's Charter. (250 words)

Answer:

The Citizen's Charter is a public statement that defines the entitlements of citizens to a specific service. It covers the following as per the Administrative Reforms Commission (ARC):

1. Standards of service delivery
2. Condition to be met by users
3. Remedies available to users if they don't get the service

Hence, Citizen's Charters are effective tools to ensure citizen-centric governance to promote transparency and accountability. For example, the Income Tax Department has implemented Citizen's Charters across its offices in India.

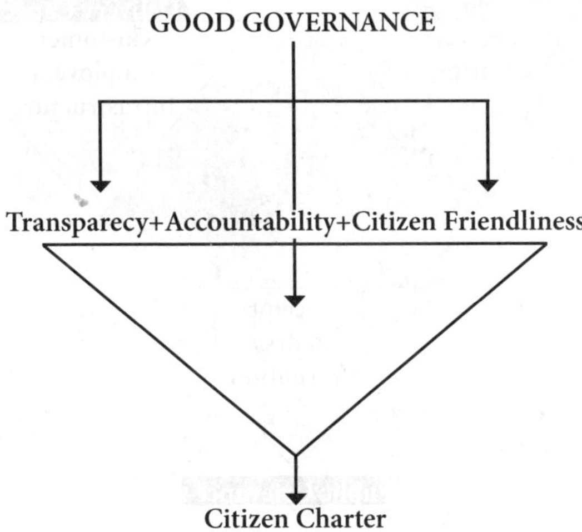

Figure B.2: Features of the Citizen's Charter

Limitations:

1. **Capacity development and training**: Lack of proper understanding among government officials leads to poor citizen interface. Bureaucratic red-tapism also leads to poor implementation.
2. **Legal enforcement**: The Citizen's Charter is not legally enforceable and, therefore, is non-justifiable. This reduces its efficacy.
3. **Awareness of citizens:** Citizens remain largely unaware of the charter and its grievance redressal mechanism, thereby making its demand-driven feature useless.

4. **Variance in standards**: There is no single standard to guide the charter formation; hence they vary across organizations, making monitoring difficult.

The Citizens' Charters initiative was introduced in India in 1997. However, implementation has faced various problems as outlined above. Measures that can be taken to solve these problems are as follows:

1. An effective awareness campaign for all the stakeholders including government officials and citizens must be undertaken at this stage.
2. Right to Service (RTS) Acts: Many states are coming up with RTS Acts to enforce the right to service for citizens. This provides the much needed legal force to Citizen's Charters.
3. Monitoring and Implementation (SEVOTTAM): Immediate adoption of the Sevottam model to address implementation, grievance redressal, and others problems.

[Such figures (in reality, they will be rough drawings) can be drawn to improve your presentation of the answer. Please do provide a title or explanation for the figure, without which it will seem out of place.]

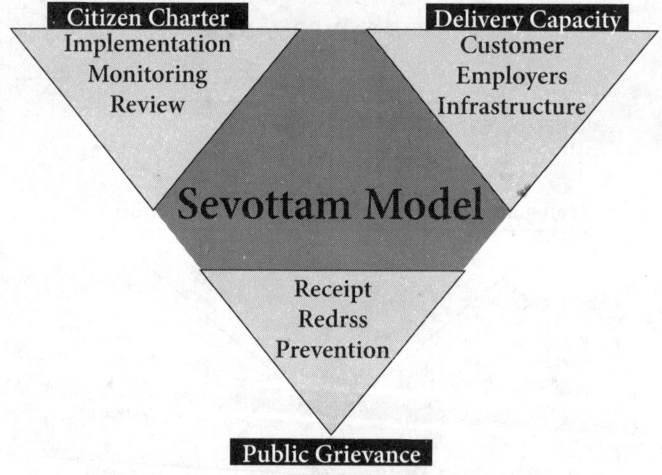

Figure B.3: The Sevottam model

Q19. What are the key areas of reform if the WTO has to survive in the present context of 'Trade War', especially keeping in mind the interest of India? (15)

Answer:

A joint report by the WTO, IMF, and the World Bank has issued an emergency call to reform the multilateral trading systems due to US's retreat from the prior arrangement. Due to the increasing threats of 'Trade War' by the US, various key reforms are needed:

1. **Focus on e-commerce**
   a. New rules are needed to govern the investments in e-commerce and e-services.

   b. India has emerged as one of the most dynamic markets for e-commerce, with large global players such as Amazon already functioning here.
      i. This poses a direct threat to the traditional Indian supply chain of millions of small traders and shops that are present in the country.
      ii. Hence, reforms are needed in this area, as these are key for Indian markets.

2. **Better dispute settlement mechanism**
   a. WTO dispute settlement systems have been problematic for developing countries like India.
   b. For example, the recent contested decisions in exports of dairy and agriculture products from USA to India and that of mangoes to Europe have shown that developing countries are at a natural disadvantage (lack of level playing field).
   c. The US also opposes and fails to implement rulings that go against it.
   d. Hence, the WTO needs to revive this mechanism.

3. **Like-minded countries**
   a. More agreements are needed with countries that have similar mindsets when it comes to trading.
   b. India is already pushing for such 'plurilateral accords', such as those with ASEAN, Japan, and Australia.

A new era of trade is emerging and the WTO must rethink its policies to remain an institution of relevance in times to come.

Q20. In what ways would the ongoing US-Iran Nuclear Pact Controversy affect the national interest of India? How should India respond to its situation?

Answer:

Approach: First, provide a short introduction of the US-Iran Nuclear Pact and the controversy, within 30-40 words. Basically, define the main issue in the question first, as done in Q. 18 on Citizen's Charters.
Second, handle the main part of the question, i.e., the impact on the national interests of India. Here, the following quick points should come to your mind:

1. **Energy security**—do not just write "oil needs," etc.; use keywords such as energy security; draft your answer as if a bureaucrat has written it.
2. **Regional security**
3. **Strategic ties with US could be impacted**—increasing defence, communications, energy, technology exchange, and trade ties.
4. **India's image might get impacted on an international level**
5. **Trade relations**—India's exports of rice, processed food products, raw materials, diamonds, and machineries.

6. **Impact on proposed strategic projects such as Chahbahar Port to counter China's influence will be impacted**—Also draw rough sketch of the port connecting India with Iran to Central Asia; Fig. B.4 is just an illustration.

7. **Historical Cultural Ties**

Third, move on to the next part, i.e., "What should be India's response...." Here you can start with something like "With deepening strategic ties with the US, India finds itself in a catch 22 situation...."

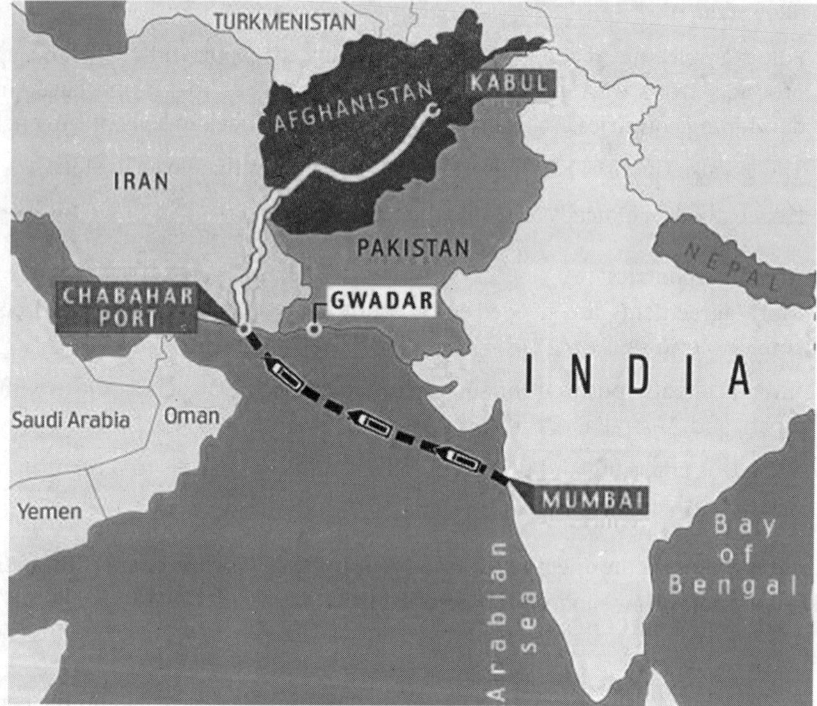

Figure B.4: India's outreach to the Middle East

India's response (think of a maximum of three to four points):

1. A comprehensive bilateral dialogue with the US to resolve the issue. Possible multiple-partite talks with Iran and other stakeholders such as Russia and USA.
2. A continuation of all possible historical ties and exchanges with Iran in order to maintain continuity in relations.
3. Urgent delegations to both US and Iran and associated countries to resolve these matters and reaffirm India's efforts to achieve a neutral and win-win situation for all parties.

You may notice that I have not focused on the Conclusion much. It is something that is not strictly needed, but can be used where the need is felt. Here, both the answers already require a solution to the given problem; hence, a conclusion is not needed.

Appendix C

Solved Practice Sets: Main Examination

Practice Set 1

Instruction: Answer the following questions in not more than 200 words each. Contents of the answers are more important than their length. All questions carry equal marks. (15 marks each)

Q1. The rights-based approach is giving rise to a new trend in Indian constitutional governance, that is, the DPSPs are getting preference over Fundamental Rights. Identify such trends and analyse their pros and cons .

Answer:

The rights-based approach refers to fulfilling various economic, social, and political ends of a society by viewing them as inalienable and inseparable 'rights' and not just as obligations.

For instance, as provided by DPSP earlier, educational rights for 6 to 14 year old children were not fundamental in nature. The passage of the RTE Act has made this a fundamental right, which is justiciable.

Similarly, DPSPs such as legal aid for the poor, nutrition for all sections of the society, child rights, and so on are also viewed more and more to be fundamental rather than just as directive objectives to be fulfilled by the state.

This could even lead to a compromise of rights by the government. For instance, Aadhaar identification to deliver various services could compromise on citizens' basic right to privacy, as established in the R. Rajagopalan Case by the Supreme Court.

The need of the hour is for the state to be able to view fundamental rights as complementary to the directive principles that have to be fulfilled and protected side by side.

Q2. After establishment of the NITI Aayog, the role and significance of the Inter-State Council seem to have eroded further. In the light of this statement, discuss the relevance of the Inter-State Council and inter-state coordination.

Answer:

The Inter-State Council has been envisaged in the Constitution of India itself. The founding fathers believe that such a body will enable the achievement of cooperative federalism and enhance centre-state relations.

Relevance of Inter-State Council

First, this is a high-powered body constituted by the prime minister, cabinet minister, and chief minister. Any important issue affecting national integration and state welfare can be discussed by it.

Second, it can be a platform for the states to amicably discuss problems such as river water disputes, interstate trade, and common economic and social principles.

Third, as envisaged by Pandit Nehru, the Inter-State Council is a forum for discussion, communication, and deliberation among the states' heads and the Central Government.

The NITI Aayog has overtaken this role, as it also comprises the chief ministers and prime minister in the governing council. In this situation, the role of the Inter-State Council should be made clear and its mandate be reinforced as envisioned by the Constitution as recommended by the Sarkaria Commission as well.

Q3. There is the contention that the NHRC is more than an extension of the government, rather than an independent overseeing agency, and hence the label of being a' toothless tiger' is not justifiable. Critically examine.

Answer:

The National Human Rights Commission (NHRC) has been established to address human rights violations in India and fulfilits mandate for the UN Commission on Human Rights (UNCHR) as well.

Problems due to Lack of Independence of NHRC

First, it has not been accorded constitutional status and hence it can be used to fulfil only practical ends.

Second, the NHRC lacks the ability to investigate cases of human rights violations independently due to lack of staff and expertise in the field. This results in influence over its investigations by externalagencies such as the CBI.

Third, the NHRC's recommendations are not binding on the government. This undermines its ability to address human rights.

Independence can be ensured by:

1. Its members should be nominated by a larger panel.
2. Only a retired Chief Justice of India should be able to head the NHRC, thereby increasing its stature and independence.

3. Working with NGOs would help the NHRC by keeping executives from influencing its working.

Way Forward

Therefore, reforms are needed to further enhance the effectiveness of the NHRC by giving it more investigative powers and making it totally free from executive control.

Q4. There are two contrary views regarding 'sedition' law in Section 124-A of the Indian Penal Code. One section wants its scope to be expanded and another section wants its scope to be restricted or even for it to be abolished, so that the freedom of speech does not get obstructed. Critically analyse their views.

Answer:

Section 124 of the Indian Penal Code has a long and muddled history. It was used by the British during the freedom struggle to charge Gandhiji and Bal Gangadhar Tilak of seditious activities. Even today, it opens up a gamut of issues:

1. Section 124 can be used by the government to hassle the critics of government policy. This is against the Freedom of Speech under Article 19.
2. It can also be an instrument of self-censorship, thereby muffling citizens' voices.
3. It can be used to serve political vested interests and as a tool in inter-party politics.
4. Fundamentally, it has no place in a modern liberal democracy of India, as it is regressive in itself and morally deviant.

The need of Section 124A

1. As opined by the Supreme Court in the Kedarnath Case, Section 124 is constitutional only if any speech, writing, or form of expression attempts to incite violence or bring down the government by force. This is reasonable, as India is still an evolving democracy with regional, communal, and ethnic problems.
2. Also, at the same time, the apex court has said that government criticism cannot be termed as sedition regardless of how harsh it is.
3. Problems such as cross-border terrorism, national security, and communalism are so prevalent and growing that this section may be able to serve its purpose.

Way Forward

The onus lies on the government of the day to not use Section 124 to meet political ends, but address only grave constitutional issues with this powerful section.

Q5. Traditionally, sports have been seen as a public-spirited non-profit sector, but due to fierce competition and commercialization, the sector is facing governance and regulatory challenges in recent times at both the national and international levels. In the light of this statement, suggest a suitable model for the governance of sports.

Answer:

Sports have been an integral part of human history, which is evident from the long tradition of the Olympics. In India, the guru-shishya tradition also originated in the background of sports.

However, this noble field is facing many national- and international-level problems, as shown in the following table:

Table: Problems being faced by the field of sports at the national and international levels.

National level	International level
1. Corruption in major bodies such as the Sports Authority of India and the Athletics Federation of India is not unknown.	1. Corruption and commercialization of bodies such as the FIFA and the Olympic Federation.
2. Lack of a standard national sports policy.	2. Lack of a global framework guiding the national programme.
3. Lack of institutional coordination in India between the Centre and the states.	3. Lack of consensus among nations.

Suitable government models:

1. Creation of a national sports policy that defines the vision, mission, and the institutional structure of Indian sports.
2. Sports charter that incorporates transparency and accountability.
3. Three-tier bodies at the Centre and the states in the district should promote sports at the grass-roots level.
4. Appointment of leading sportspersons as advisors and members. For example, Haryana has done this and benefitted immensely in the governance of sports.

Similarly, the recognition of a body at the international level needs to be freed from commercial interference by corporates. National appointees should be considered for the governance of FIFA, Olympic Association, and so on.

Q6. Is India emergency free? Enumerate the major factors responsible for the internal emergency in 1975 and critically analyse how today's factors differ from those back then, which can make India emergency free?

Answer:

Articles 352 and 360 underline the conditions for the declaration of a national emergency. The 44th Constitutional Amendment has made various changes, which make it very difficult to declare emergency today. These are:

1. A written cabinet note is required instead of just verbal communication by the prime minister to the President.
2. Approval by both houses in session within a specified time limit.
3. Declaration to revoke the emergency can be passed even by the Lok Sabha itself.

Factors that make emergency possible

1. It must be noted that national emergency is also a means to address an immediate threat on the nation through war or armed rebellion.
2. Due to our hostile and unpredictable neighbours, rising regional problems, and cross-border terrorism, an emergency cannot be outrightly ruled out. Hence, an emergency is harder to declare, but the chance still exists.

Factors that led to the Declaration of National Emergency in 1975

1. India had already seen two major wars in 1962 and 1971, which had hampered national integration and security.
2. India had a fast-growing government influence with nationalization, and further reduction of the private sphere in the economy.
3. The Indian government was still dominated by one party at the centre, but multiple regional parties had emerged, which contributed to political tussle not seen before.
4. The emergency provisions themselves were not put to test and had a few loopholes.

Today many of these issues have been resolved after the 44th Amendment, liberalization, and a vibrant democratic dialogue in the country. Hence emergency is harder to impose.

Q7. While the alternative dispute resolution (ADR) mechanism helps in relieving the pressure of the Judiciary, it can also be seen as an abdication of the state's responsibility to provide a modern and efficient judicial system. Critically examine.

Answer:

Alternative dispute resolution (ADR) refers to institutions that are established to carry out mediation, arbitration, and conciliation among people to resolve disputes outside the court.

Examples: Gram Nyayalaya, Traditional Lok Adalat, and soon.

Benefits

1. Eases the burden on the Judiciary by taking care of the mundane cases. As per NALSA, over 25 lakh cases are pending in Indian courts and ADR can play a critical role in clearing these.
2. Resolves disputes using the principal of natural justice and common sense at village and district levels.
3. Offers a cheap and quick means of justice dispensation.
4. Provides advice based on historical and traditional knowledge at the village level and in panchayats, thereby making justice more accessible to people.

Drawbacks→possibly an abdication of state responsibility?

1. The directive principle of state policy (DPSP) envisages the objective of providing swift and quality justice. ADR is such a system outside the judicial system.
2. ADR promotes informalization of the justice system, which is against the principle of judicial responsibility.

3. ADR runs parallel to the integrated judicial system envisioned by our founding fathers. Hence it is against ethical and constitutional principles.
4. In many cases, ADR does not bring justice but gets roadblocked by the societal idea of patriarchy, women's relegated position in society, and caste differentiation.

Hence, ADR presents an effective solution but also has some fundamental flaws.

Way Forward

A more comprehensive institutional structure for ADR under the integrated judicial system can be a solution to the above-mentioned problems.

Q8. The object of anti-defection law was to bring down political defection and not freedom of speech. However, its effects are seen more on curtailing freedom of speech rather than defection. Discuss the causative factors for such unintended consequences. In your view, what steps should be taken for its effectiveness?

Answer:

Anti-defection law was incorporated under the 10th Schedule of the Constitution to counter the problem of legislators switching parties for wrong or politically vested interests. This problem had become extremely grave and a blot on the Indian democratic Parliamentary system. However, the anti-defection law has also encountered some problems:

1. Legislators are not able to express their dissent on party policies that are not principally sound.
2. Legislators often find it difficult to raise their concerns when they feel that party policy is adversely affecting their constituency.
3. Freedom of speech and expression is effectively shunted in favour of the will of party supremos.
4. The very spirit of debate and discussion is thwarted.

Step to remedy these problems and the way forward:

1. Anti-defection law could be amended to allow debates and discussion without consequences for a legislator.
2. Its provisions could be limited to measure voting in no-confidence motions for critical aspects only and not for every legislation.
3. The merger of parties may be allowed only in a defined situation.
4. The role of the Speaker as neutral observer and authority can be strengthened by creating a non-partisan committee headed by the Speaker in case of adjudicating the anti-defection case.

Q9. In order to be truly independent and effective, the CAG must be free from both governmental control and should have adequate power. In the light of this statement, analyse the need for bringing changes in the appointment of CAG and amendment of the Audit Act that governs the working of the CAG.

Answer:

CAG is appointed directly by the President of India. No specific qualifications have been prescribed for this appointment.

Changes needed to ensure the relevance of CAG

1. An appointment committee that evaluates the merits of candidates could make the process more holistic.
2. A set of required qualifications as part of the procedure of selection will greatly increase the credibility and independence of the CAG.
3. With the advent of ever-expanding audit duties in the states as well as at the Centre, the CAG must also adhere to a strict ethical guidelines framework to enable greater effectiveness.
4. The Audit Act could be amended to make audit reports open to judicial and public review to ensure greater accountability.
5. Dr Ambedkar envisaged CAG as the most important constitutional office. Constant changes to meet dynamic economic, social, and constitutional needs are required to keep the CAG relevant.

Q10. The deadly nexus between unaccounted money and politics has led 'money power' to not only distort free and fair elections but also diminish India's democratic credibility. Discuss the repercussion of this system of government on the people.

Answer:

Money power has emerged as a serious challenge that is undermining the democratic election process.

1. The ability of a rich person to just 'buy' votes seriously violates the principle of free and fair elections envisaged by the Constitution.
2. Political parties are funded under a much opaque process, which harms their public mandate.→Political leaders are prone to becoming champions of the interests of corporates and rich people rather than those of the common people.
3. The rule of law, a critical pillar of democratic credibility, is affected negatively by money power.
4. Merit and not money should determine political leadership in a democracy. Election of individuals wielding money power leads to the promotion of the policy of nepotism and kinship, disregarding the real needs of the masses. Our Constitution envisages a welfare society but neo-capitalism has crept into aggravate the problem of inequality through money power.

Way forward

1. The Election Commission has a recommended a new section under the Representation of People Act, 1951 to effectively counter money power.
2. Political parties can voluntarily come under the ambit of RTI to help address the transparency and accountability issue.

There are over 50% Members of Parliament today with assets over INR 1 crore. Their interest must be aligned with the people's interests to ensure healthy democracy in India. Hence, appropriate action by themselves on this issue could raise the confidence of the common people in politics and help us navigate through this issue.

Q11. In recent times, the relevance of the upper chamber of the Parliament has been debated as a deliberative house, on the one hand, and a federal house that protects the interest of the states, on the other. Give your view on the role of the upper chamber.

Answer:

The upper chamber of the Parliament of India, or the Rajya Sabha (RS), has a central role to play in our democracy and the Indian federal structure.

Role in democracy

1. The RS acts as a second chamber for the review of major decisions to ensure that thoughtful, well-discussed, and effective laws are made.
2. The RS ensures that the Lok Sabah's hasty and populist decisions are avoided.

Federal role

1. The RS enables the states to raise concerns about national legislations that could affect their interests. For example, the Land Acquisition Act, 2013and GST Act, 2016 failed to ensure that the interest of states is not affected adversely.
2. The RS represents the concerns of the states at the centre to address their grievances.

Drawbacks

1. Small states are under-represented; for instance, the northeastern states face problems in voicing their concerns due to low representation.
2. Political interests lead to the RS acting as a roadblock instead of as a reviewing chamber for major legislation.
3. The RS has become a house of 'disruption' instead of house of 'dissent'.

Way forward

The Rajya Sabha has immense potential to be used effectively to achieve national interest. Smaller states should be allowed greater voice and the members should be held accountable for the outcomes of their actions as well. This will lead to more effective functioning of the RS.

Q12. To deter the use of PILs to defame or acquire fame, a petitioner's locus standi, their direct stake in the case, should be clear. They should also be liable to punishment if the charge levelled is proved incorrect. Comment.

Answer:

The public interest litigation (PIL) has emerged as a powerful tool for the public to bring their grievances to court and seek respite. However, it has also been used as 'publicity' interest litigation to further personal interests. For example, the PIL to seek planes and SUV cars for a judge in the UP district court was an attempt to gain publicity.

Fine on frivolous PILs

PILs that have no public character should be rejected outright. Fines that discourage such PIL sin the future could also be considered. This will save the court's time and maintain the integrity of purpose of PILs.

Petitioner's own interest and stake to be made clear

- The Supreme Court is free to reject PILs not filed by at least one of the affected parties in the case.
    i. Such rejection can be done at the committee level even before the PIL is brought to the bench.
    ii. This would save time and resources for the courts.
- Finally, the public must itself be wary of PILs on their behalf. Bogus PILs without the participation of the actual affected party should be condemned; their cultural disapproval could lead to a decline in such cases.

Q13. Opinion polls tend to prejudice the minds of the voters, thus, affecting free and fair elections. Their validity has also been questioned. Since free and fair elections are at the core of a healthy democracy, such polls should be banned. Critically comment.

Answer:

Opinion polls are carried out before and after polls to predict the voting behaviour of the public.

Benefits

1. They help political parties and candidates to gain a feel of the people's moods and make changes in their strategy accordingly.
2. People can raise major public concerns through polls to pressurize the political party to act on the public grievances.

Drawbacks

1. They could have undue influence on people's perception of voting trends, and the parties could misuse this to drive votes in their favour through unfair means.
2. They commercialize and commodify the process of elections, instead of making it a public event. Media channels use them to drive viewership instead of opinion.
3. They shift focus from the manifesto to unnecessary things.

Way forward

1. The Election Commission has already banned opinion polls for a certain period of time during the elections to decrease their adverse impact.
2. A comprehensive media policy and guidelines are the need of the hour in this respect.
3. Self-regulation should be seriously practised by media, not to misuse opinion polls.

Q15. Simultaneous holding of elections for the Lok Sabha and the state assemblies is desirable but not feasible. Critically examine.

Answer:

Simultaneous elections for the Lok Sabha and state assemblies took place from the first election in 1952 until 1967. The rise of regional coalitions led to the falling of various governments during their midterms, leading to changes in the calendar of Indian elections.

Challenge posed by the trend

1. Elections are going on year after year, leading to discontinuance in policy-making and implementation.
2. Heavy spending on elections year after year adversely affects this process. Money power in elections is becoming more pronounced due to this.
3. State resources such as teachers, vehicles, officials, etc are devoted time and again to elections, which affects daily public functions such as schools, government and private offices, and the economy.
4. There is a greater chance of communal violence and crime; their frequency may increase as well.
5. The political leadership focuses on elections rather than on welfare policies and matters of national and regional importance.
6. The staggered election cycle also breeds nepotism, favouritism, and the practice of extending favours.

Feasibility and Way Forward

A Parliamentary committee, a Law Commission report, and the Election Commission have all recommended that the election cycles be matched. However, this is not practical unless regional governments agree.

→A possible solution suggested by the Election Commission is midterm election.

A solution is needed to solve the several problems created by the staggered election cycle. The above-mentioned recommendation can be studied further to bring a consensual change to the Indian election calendar.

Q16. Discuss the pros and cons of the need for a national court of appeal. Is it a suitable strategy to reduce the burden on the apex court and enhance the speed and quality of judgment? Justify your view.

Answer:

A national court of appeal has been envisaged as a court where all appeals from high courts can be heard, except matters of constitutional importance.

Such a court of appeal could be established across different regions, and thereby mundane cases of civil nature that do not have constitutional and national repercussions can be heard here instead of taking up the Supreme Court's time.

Pros:

1. Reduces burden on the apex court.
2. Faster disposal of regular cases at the appeal court itself.
3. Helps in achieving the goal of natural and social justice envisioned by the Directive Principles of State Policy.
4. This is a line with international practices such as in USA and UK, where apex courts only hear constitutional matters.

Cons:

1. It is against the spirit of integrated judiciary envisaged by the Constitution.
2. Will lead to possible conflicts between the apex court and the court of appeal if the procedures and jurisdiction are not clearly defined.
3. Difficult to implement, as it will need wide consensus in the Parliament, and among states and judicial levels.

Strategy and way forward:

The Union Government has already discussed such a court even though the apex court itself did not view such an appeals court favourably. Hence, an agreement is needed among all stakeholders to study this alternative.

To achieve swift justice and solve the problem of 'justice delayed is justice denied', the solution to this problem should be worked out carefully.

Q17. The onus on the regulatory bodies for the pharmaceutical sector is to ensure a healthy supply of quality drugs at affordable prices to the Indian masses. In the light of this statement, discuss the deficiencies and limitations of the current regulatory regime and suggest suitable remedies.

Answer:

The Ministry of Chemicals and Fertilizers houses the Department of Pharmaceuticals, which overlooks the regulation of the pharmaceutical sector in India.

Deficiencies

1. Arbitrary regulation has resulted in mispricing and non-availability of critical drugs.
2. The absence of a national medicine policy and procedure framework has led to haphazard policymaking in the sector.
3. Lack of resources and trained professionals, as well as the nexus of officials with industry interest are also concerns.

Strengths

1. A consistent policy to make affordability the most critical aspect of the decisions has helped the public in general.
2. The National Drug Pricing Authority has published strict guidelines for fixing prices and formulation of drugs.

Way forward:

1. Creating a separate ministry for the pharmaceutical sector.
2. A national policy recommended by the Parliamentary Committee on Drugs is needed.

Q18. The talk of a Uniform Civil Code has nothing to do with gender justice. It is for the 'integrity of the nation' that uniformity in law is required. Critically examine.

Answer:

The Uniform Civil Code has been long debated but still remains a missing piece in India's democratic system. It is envisaged under Article 44 of the DPSP but faces stiff legal and societal challenges. Moreover, it encapsulates a 'national character' because it:

1. Fulfils the 'Right to Equality' guaranteed to every citizen by Articles 14 and 15, regardless of ethnicity, race, sex, caste, and so on, and ensures the dignity of individuals.
2. Fulfils the dream of having a consistent rule of law in the society. This is a foundation of the nation.
3. Ends discrimination and achieves the principle of brotherhood and fraternity as envisaged by the Preamble.

On the other hand, the Uniform Civil Code (UCC) also poses challenges for the society, as follows:

1. In a diverse and varied country like India, it will be difficult to enforce.
2. It may even lead to popular dissent and violence thereby threatening integrity.

Therefore, UCC is the need of the hour, as it ensures the dignity and integrity of individuals, which leads to national integration. A societal consensus must be achieved on it before legal provisions are passed for its implementation.

Q19. What is the underlying rationale behind a governor's discretionary powers? How is the governor's office meant to act as a bulwark against abuse of power by an elected state government? Explain with suitable examples.

Answer:

The governor has been envisioned as a critical link between the Centre and the state in the Indian federal system. This position has been accorded numerous powers such as nominating the leader of the majority party, chief minister, government tribal advisory council under the 5th Schedule; holding state legislative for President's assent; or even recommending Presidential rule in a state.

Need of such widespread powers

1. To ensure that the constitutional machinery in the states remains intact and state governments do not misuse their wide powers.
2. To ensure that the state legislation does not impinge over the Centre's powers, and therefore the governor can send state legislation for the President's assent.
3. The governor is a means of communication and interchange of ideas between the states and the Centre, and not necessarily a roadblock in the state executive. For example,

- Various state legislations on tax that violate the principle of free interstate trade stated by the Constitution have been reserved by governors for President's assent.
    i. Without these provisions, such legislation could have violated the principle of cooperative federalism.

4. To ensure that the state executive works in the interest of tribal and indigenous people, as envisaged in the Forest Rights Act and other central legislations.

Hence, the role of governor is critical in upholding Article 1of the Indian Constitution, i.e., India is a 'union' of States.

Q20. GST: Is it truly a threat to fiscal federalism in India or ushers in a new era in the fiscal relations of the Union and states? Critically analyse.

Answer:
GST has been ushered in by the 101st Constitutional Amendment, which opens a new chapter in the economic and federal structure of India.

Threat to federalism

1. Takes away the power of the states to tax their residents, thereby violating a critical federal feature of the Constitution.
    i. Even Dr Ambedkar himself vehemently defended the states' right to tax, as it enables them to fulfil regional development requirements.
2. Reduces the states' ability to raise more funds for regional development schemes and in events such as disasters.
3. The GST Council provided veto power to the centre on GST issues, thereby threatening federal balance.

Benefits of GST outweigh federal concerns

1. GST actually enhances federalism by increasing the amount of taxes that will accrue to states.
    - This will enable the state to address local and regional problems with greater funds.
2. Fulfils the vision of free interstate commerce envisaged in the Constitution of India.
3. Creates one single national market, reduces the tax burden on citizens, and makes India more competitive.
    - Will enhance ease of doing business and schemes such as Make in India and others

Hence, the benefits of GST are so wide and massive that its problems are outweighed. Going forward, the states and Centre should coordinate in the efforts of the GST Council to truly make GST a successful economic reform.

Practice Set 2

Instruction: Answer the following questions in not more than 200 words each. Contents of the answers are more important than their length. All questions carry equal marks. (15 marks each)

Q1. Would the creation of an institution by itself eliminate corruption in government institutions? Is external institutional mechanism a substitute for integral vigilance? How can internal vigilance be strengthened?

Answer:

Institutions are organizations that comprise a set of clearly defined mechanisms, processes, procedures, and policies for regulatory functions. These include institutions such as RBI, SEBI, FSSAI, TERI, etc. Judicial institutions include courts of law and other institutions include the police and so on.

Institutions by themselves cannot eliminate corruption.

- They require autonomous and credible leadership and clear agenda to eliminate corruption.
- For instance, despite a strong set of powers, CBI has been termed as a 'caged parrot' by the Supreme Court because it is unable to operate independently.

Similarly, the Central Vigilance Commission (CVC) lacks investigative infrastructure due to which the institution of CVC is unable to control corruption.

External institutional mechanism to substitute for internal vigilance:

Institutions such as the Lokpal have been envisaged as an external mechanism to check corruption by:

1. Addressing grievances of citizens against corrupt political leaders and officials.
2. Ushering accountability and transparency.
3. Giving strength to other mechanisms such as RTI.

However, they must be supported by internal vigilance. This is because

1. Internal vigilance is like self-regulation—the best form of regulation.
2. Internal vigilance is more effective in addressing lacunae in the internal processes.

As recommended by the Paris plan on effective institutions, internal vigilance can be strengthened by:

1. Setting up an enforcing agency to work internally.
2. Providing judicial backing and power to internal vigilance.
3. Providing investigative powers to internal vigilance institutions.

Practice Set 2

Instruction: Answer the following questions in not more than 200 words each. Contents of the answers are more important than their length. All questions carry equal marks. (15 marks each)

Q1. Would the creation of an institution by itself eliminate corruption in government institutions? Is external institutional mechanism a substitute for integral vigilance? How can internal vigilance be strengthened?

Answer:

Institutions are organizations that comprise a set of clearly defined mechanisms, processes, procedures, and policies for regulatory functions. These include institutions such as RBI, SEBI, FSSAI, TERI, etc. Judicial institutions include courts of law and other institutions include the police and so on.

Institutions by themselves cannot eliminate corruption.

- They require autonomous and credible leadership and clear agenda to eliminate corruption.
- For instance, despite a strong set of powers, CBI has been termed as a 'caged parrot' by the Supreme Court because it is unable to operate independently.

Similarly, the Central Vigilance Commission (CVC) lacks investigative infrastructure due to which the institution of CVC is unable to control corruption.

External institutional mechanism to substitute for internal vigilance:

Institutions such as the Lokpal have been envisaged as an external mechanism to check corruption by:

1. Addressing grievances of citizens against corrupt political leaders and officials.
2. Ushering accountability and transparency.
3. Giving strength to other mechanisms such as RTI.

However, they must be supported by internal vigilance. This is because

1. Internal vigilance is like self-regulation—the best form of regulation.
2. Internal vigilance is more effective in addressing lacunae in the internal processes.

As recommended by the Paris plan on effective institutions, internal vigilance can be strengthened by:

1. Setting up an enforcing agency to work internally.
2. Providing judicial backing and power to internal vigilance.
3. Providing investigative powers to internal vigilance institutions.

Way forward:

1. Creating a separate ministry for the pharmaceutical sector.
2. A national policy recommended by the Parliamentary Committee on Drugs is needed.

Q18. The talk of a Uniform Civil Code has nothing to do with gender justice. It is for the 'integrity of the nation' that uniformity in law is required. Critically examine.

Answer:

The Uniform Civil Code has been long debated but still remains a missing piece in India's democratic system. It is envisaged under Article 44 of the DPSP but faces stiff legal and societal challenges. Moreover, it encapsulates a 'national character' because it:

1. Fulfils the 'Right to Equality' guaranteed to every citizen by Articles 14 and 15, regardless of ethnicity, race, sex, caste, and so on, and ensures the dignity of individuals.
2. Fulfils the dream of having a consistent rule of law in the society. This is a foundation of the nation.
3. Ends discrimination and achieves the principle of brotherhood and fraternity as envisaged by the Preamble.

On the other hand, the Uniform Civil Code (UCC) also poses challenges for the society, as follows:

1. In a diverse and varied country like India, it will be difficult to enforce.
2. It may even lead to popular dissent and violence thereby threatening integrity.

Therefore, UCC is the need of the hour, as it ensures the dignity and integrity of individuals, which leads to national integration. A societal consensus must be achieved on it before legal provisions are passed for its implementation.

Q19. What is the underlying rationale behind a governor's discretionary powers? How is the governor's office meant to act as a bulwark against abuse of power by an elected state government? Explain with suitable examples.

Answer:

The governor has been envisioned as a critical link between the Centre and the state in the Indian federal system. This position has been accorded numerous powers such as nominating the leader of the majority party, chief minister, government tribal advisory council under the 5th Schedule; holding state legislative for President's assent; or even recommending Presidential rule in a state.

Need of such widespread powers

1. To ensure that the constitutional machinery in the states remains intact and state governments do not misuse their wide powers.
2. To ensure that the state legislation does not impinge over the Centre's powers, and therefore the governor can send state legislation for the President's assent.
3. The governor is a means of communication and interchange of ideas between the states and the Centre, and not necessarily a roadblock in the state executive. For example,

- Various state legislations on tax that violate the principle of free interstate trade stated by the Constitution have been reserved by governors for President's assent.
    i. Without these provisions, such legislation could have violated the principle of cooperative federalism.

4. To ensure that the state executive works in the interest of tribal and indigenous people, as envisaged in the Forest Rights Act and other central legislations.

Hence, the role of governor is critical in upholding Article 1of the Indian Constitution, i.e., India is a 'union' of States.

Q20. GST: Is it truly a threat to fiscal federalism in India or ushers in a new era in the fiscal relations of the Union and states? Critically analyse.

Answer:

GST has been ushered in by the 101st Constitutional Amendment, which opens a new chapter in the economic and federal structure of India.

Threat to federalism

1. Takes away the power of the states to tax their residents, thereby violating a critical federal feature of the Constitution.
    i. Even Dr Ambedkar himself vehemently defended the states' right to tax, as it enables them to fulfil regional development requirements.
2. Reduces the states' ability to raise more funds for regional development schemes and in events such as disasters.
3. The GST Council provided veto power to the centre on GST issues, thereby threatening federal balance.

Benefits of GST outweigh federal concerns

1. GST actually enhances federalism by increasing the amount of taxes that will accrue to states.
    - This will enable the state to address local and regional problems with greater funds.
2. Fulfils the vision of free interstate commerce envisaged in the Constitution of India.
3. Creates one single national market, reduces the tax burden on citizens, and makes India more competitive.
    - Will enhance ease of doing business and schemes such as Make in India and others

Hence, the benefits of GST are so wide and massive that its problems are outweighed. Going forward, the states and Centre should coordinate in the efforts of the GST Council to truly make GST a successful economic reform.

Q2. Over-regulation will stifle the voluntary sector, but no regulation poses a threat to democracy itself. In the light of this statement, analyse the provisions of the Lokpal and Lokayuktas Act, 2013, which necessitate it for senior management personnel working with NGOs to disclose their assets and liabilities if the NGOs receive foreign donations and funds from the Union Government.

Answer:

NGOs play a central role in the Indian democracy. Some key public legislations such as RTI and Lokpal are a result of NGO work.

The Lokpal and Lokayuktas Act, 2013 addresses NGO senior management as public officials and puts them in the same category as government officials.

Additionally, the Act also requires NGO personnel to disclose all assets and liabilities.

This poses following problems:

1. Invasion of right to privacy with right to life (Article 21) of a private citizen.
2. Possible harassment by vested interest for ownership of even hereditary assets or high salary.
3. Exit from profession by capable management from NGOs to the private sector in lieu of such intervening legal provisions.
   - Over-regulation leading to problems akin to those that were caused by the License Raj in the pre-liberalization era.

Positive aspects of Lokpal provisions:

1. Monitoring of foreign funding and influence on public policy and NGO action by the government.
   - Ford Foundation has been accused of disturbing development efforts in many countries such NGOs could be monitor rise in national interest.
2. Checking corruption and money laundering and instances of black money used through NGOs.
   - A large section of laundered funds are sent/received through NGOs.

Therefore, it seems necessary from serious crisis of foreign funding and corruption that the provisions of the Lokpal Act are necessary for the overall benefit of the society.

Q3. Universities are meant for education and not for politics, and hence student politics should either be strictly regulated or banned. Critically examine.

Answer:

University is a sacred space, where the principles of objectivity, knowledge, curiosity, and civic duty are inculcated.

Indian universities have active political bodies such as All India Student Association (AISU) and ABVP.

Positives:

1. Historical tradition of having politically active student bodies from the days of national freedom struggle.
   - Many universities such as Calcutta University and others were the hotbed of economic, social, and political critics of the British Empire.
2. Political activity includes a sense of citizen participation and consensus in decision-making.
3. It is a training ground for future leaders.
4. It is a forum for students to voice their grievances.
5. It ensures that students are well-informed and active about national, regional, and international issues.

Negative impacts:

1. Interference of national political parties may hamper the functioning and autonomy of university administration.
2. Focus shifts from academics to politics, thereby not fulfilling the role of college education.
3. Emotionally charged politics leads to violence and loss of property and polarization on the campus.
4. The student body gets divided on the basis of caste, religion, language, regional affiliations, etc.

It appears from analysis that political activities should be limited in university due to these adverse effects.

The experiences of JNU and Jadavpur University have shown that political interest can deviate student bodies.

Q4. Traditionally, efforts to address the issue of accountability have focused on improving and/ or strengthening the 'supply side' of the democratic government social audit and bringing attention to improving the 'demand side' of democratic governance. Elucidate.

Answer:

Supply-side mechanism

Supply side of governance refers to provisions such a citizen charters, RTI, and grievance redressal mechanisms to address citizens' problems and enhance public service delivery.

This has a limited impact on governance as:

1. Lack of awareness about the supply-side mechanism leads to their underutilization by citizens.
   - For example, citizen charters are barely available to citizens.
2. Lack of clarity leads to major loopholes and delays, and the one-sided approach does not fulfil the government's goals.

Demand-side mechanism

Demand-side mechanism refers to provisions such as social audit and citizen report card (CRC).

- These are more effective (in reference to citizen charters) as they:

1. Lead to greater awareness among citizens.
2. Enable consensus-driven and citizen-centric government.
3. Allow for more responsibility and accountability of local government officials.
4. These are two-way mechanisms, thereby ensuring conversations between those who govern and those who are governed.

Examples

→Social audit in Andhra Pradesh has greatly enhanced the quality of food grains available under the Food Security Act.

→Citizen report card by Bangalore action task force (BATF) has improved municipal work there.

Therefore demand-side mechanism must be implemented to increase democratic governance.

Q5. While there are many successful stories about the benefits of SHGs, many are concerned about the future of the SHG movement in India. Are SHGs heading towards the right direction of women empowerment? Explain with a suitable illustration.

Answer:

SHGs (self-help groups) have greatly transformed the lives of millions of households by empowering women. As on date, there over 8 crore individuals availing its benefits, and over 17,000 crore rupees have been mobilized through the SHG bank-linking programme as well (E-Shakti programme).

Are they heading in right direction?

Benefits:

1. Financial inclusion has been enabled by SHGs by bringing crores of households within its net.
2. Women empowerment by providing them livelihood options.

→Additionally, women are empowered as they can share information, discuss problems, and create consensus-driven solutions for the community.

Example:

1. Kudumbshree in Kerala has enabled land ownership for millions of women in SHGs.
2. Myrada in Karnataka has provided financial literacy for women in SHGs.

Problems:

1. Hidden default rates in SHG loans can lead to financial distress for women.

2. Forced appropriation of funds or fund misuse by the male head of the family can lead to domestic violence problems.
3. Excessive growth in SHGs can lead to financial improprieties by some ill-intentioned individuals.
4. SHGs' high interest rate can create inordinate financial burden.

These challenges in the growth and future of SHGs can be addressed by greater community participation and consensus-driven solutions for SHGs.

Q6. What safeguards are required to protect honest officers from harassment? Are the provisions of taking prior sanction of the government before registration of cases necessary? How can it be ensured that this does not become a shield for corrupt officers?

Answer:

Honest officials have often faced the wrath of vested interests in public office. For instance, Mrs Durga Shakti Nagpal, an honest IAS officer from UP, faced political vendetta in public office while discharging her duties.

Safeguards required:

1. Fixed 2–3 year term in office for all public officials as recommended by the ARC report.
2. Written and video-recorded evidence for all meetings with political leaders.
3. Clear protocol policy and rules for execution of tenders, projects, and programmes, so as to minimize political interference.

Existing provision—Prior government permission

1. The Constitution has provided various safeguards. However, they have both positive and negative outcomes, as follows.

Negative

1. Cases are not filed against corrupt officers due to political support.
   - Current officials misuse power in the shadow and protection of such shielding laws.

Positives

1. Honest officials can really discharge their duties without political threats.
2. The actions of the officials are guided by public interest and non-populism.

Ensuring that it does not become a shield:

1. It is recommended by the 2nd ARC report that an independent ombudsman such as Lokpal can be given powers to freely and fairly investigate officials.
2. Granting greater investigative power to the Vigilance Commission will also result in internal vigilance.

Q7. How is media as a pressure group different from an interest group? Discuss the role of media including social media as a pressure group in influencing public policy.

Answer:

Media is regarded as the 'fourth pillar' of our democracy. This is due to the media's ability to report without bias, start public debates, keep a check on the Executive's as well as the Legislative's over-reaching powers and work as an agent of change.

Media is different from interest groups

1. It does not have to represent the vested interest of a particular group or class of people.
2. It functions as an information sourcefor the public.
3. Pressure groups such as FICCI, CII, and other trade unions focus on a few individuals' particular interests, but media represents a larger community and has greater national interest in mind.

Similarities

1. Both can duly influence public opinion.
2. Both can lead to a considerable change in public policy.
3. Both are also driven by a narrow interest if they are owned by a small group.

E.g., some media channels are owned by business groups and functions for their own interest.

Role of social media and media in influencing public policy:

1. Social media can reach out electronically to people.
    - For example, Change.org can be used directly by citizens for launching petitions to elected leaders.
2. Social media can also greatly impact public opinion and perception as it is run by the public itself.
3. Media debates and prime time shows can evoke emotions and inform people about their rights.
4. It can demand greater transparency, accountability and consensus-driven decision-making by the government.

Q8. Should thecivil society work as a watchdog—holding institutions to account and promoting transparency and accountability, or should it work shoulder to shoulder with the government in the process of governance and development. Analyse.

Answer:

Civil society refers to various civic organizations such as NGOs and media that represent matters of public Interest.

Role as a watchdog

1. The civil society as a watchdog has led to the passing of transformational acts such as the RTI and Lokpal.
    - Without such Acts, the governance standards would have been low and citizens would be underserved with information and justice.
2. As a watchdog, it can also ensure that the executive branch does not misuse power and arbitrariness in governance is removed.
3. It also enables a critical analysis of our various institutional functioning.

For instance, the Association of Democratic Reforms (ADR) has exposed money power and crime by reporting on these metrics in the Parliament.

Role: Shoulder-to-Shoulder

1. Measures such a social audit and citizen report card cannot be fulfilled without the cooperation of civil society.
2. Many government schemes are also effectively implemented by the civil society (NGOs). For example, Akshay Patra provides mid-day meals in many schools.
3. The civil society also enables the government to get critical feedback from all stakeholders.

Hence, if both the approaches are used together, they can enhance governance and enable NGOs etc. (civil society) to work as the third arm of the government.

Q9. RTI has enabled people to participate in the process of development, which has resulted in the reduction of corruption and the establishment of an open and participatory government system. Critically examine.

Answer:

RTI was ushered in 2005, and in the last decade or so, it has enabled millions to access government files, challenge government undertakings, and win critical cases with the help of information.

The RTI has promoted greater transparency by allowing citizens to access information pertinent to public service in a timely manner.

It has promoted awareness among the citizens.

It has helped policy makers to take the 'Rights Based Approach' to policy making. This has led to key changes in the government such as ushering in the Lokpal, release of millions of rupees delayed by the bureaucracy in compensation to farmers, exposure of corruption scams such as 2G, 3G, coal scam, and Vyapam scam.

Deficiencies:

1. Murders of activists and whistleblowers such as Satyendra Nath in the NHAI Case has led to the citizens fearing to using the RTI.

- Over 200 murders reported since 2005.80 plus in Uttar Pradesh alone as per the NCRB.

2. Public official soften delay RTI due to low fine.
3. Ignoring of RTI by political parties despite Chief Information Commissioner's order.
    - This has led to the undermining of RTI's power and efficacy.

Way forward

1. Provide witness-protection-type of security to RTI activists.
2. Close loopholes of the RTI by bringing in legislative changes.
3. Bringing political parties under CIC's RTI and enhancing CIC's power to punish in case of disregard of its order.

Q10. Is social media destructive for the democracy or is it essential for the democratic government? In the light of this statement, analyse the recent trends.

Answer:

Social media has brought millions of people to the forefront by giving them a voice in our democratic governance.

It has worked both as an enabler and disabler (disruption).

Essential →Enabler

1. Twitter has become a mouthpiece of citizens for good governance.

    For example, the various problems faced by train passengers can be reported through the Railways' Twitter account, which leads to results within hours.
2. Facebook, Twitter, etc. are also channels of self-reporting by citizen reporters.
    - They post photos and videos coercing the authorities to take instant action.
3. They are also instruments of mass and digital movements, where opinion, demand, and action are immediately mobilized. They also enhance transparency and accountability through 'social documentation'.

Disrupting →Disabler

1. Violence and mass exodus can be triggered by false reports and social media.

    For example, the Northeastern citizens left Bangalore in March on the false report of attack on them.
2. Social media can be used by terrorism to hire/influence youth and radicalize them, thereby weakening democracy. A case in point is ISIS recruiting online on Facebook.
3. Can lead to poorly thought conclusions and hysteria and false reports, thereby threatening the right to privacy under Article 21.

Hence, social media is a two-edged sword and its use must be judicious.

Q11. The citizens' charter, which promises a morally time-bound delivery of services, will be ineffective as long as it is not made legally bound. Examine.

Answer:

The citizens' charter promises a certain level of standards, quality, timelines, and delivery of public services. They also outline the grievance redressal mechanism.

For example, the income tax department has an elaborate and enforceable citizens' charter.

Pros of legally binding charters:

1. Citizen will be able to seek full delivery of services they are entitled to.
2. Public officers will be required to deliver service or face legal consequences.
3. Legal accountability will ensure relief for older citizens, women, SC/ ST and other marginalized sections.

For example: legally enforceable character in Sweden and Finland has greatly enhanced efficiency and effectiveness in public office.

Cons:

1. Undue legal burden on the Judiciary even in small grievance cases.
   - Already courts are burdened with over 25 lakh pending cases.
2. Public officials will face greater challenges in carrying out their duties due to legal repercussions.
   - Creativity may be hampered in public policy.
3. Legal cost, thereby taking such services out of the reach for the poorest citizens.

Solution and way forward

1. Create an internal ombudsman in each government office to address grievance and corruption cases.
   - Self-regulation is the best form of regulation as recommended by the 2nd ARC report.
2. Create public hearing and social audits as essential features.
   - E.g., NREGA has still not been fully equipped with a social audit in many states despite this provision.

Q12. Is a career-based bureaucracy, with public servants ascending up the ladder with time, the best solution for achieving outcomes in governance? Or is a position-based bureaucracy with each key office open to choice and competition with guaranteed tenure a better option? How can such a competition and choice be fostered/institutionalized?

Answer:

Competition and choice are integral features of a dynamic, effective, and efficient civil service.

Career-based promotions on age basis create following problems:

1. Civil servants become incentivized to protect their own interests rather than think creatively about the public's problems and solutions.
2. The influence of political leadership could become imminent in such a system.
3. Demotivation of capable officers due to age, and not merit, as a factor.
4. Most competent officers are not able to apply for choice postings due to lack of meritocracy, thereby reducing competition.
   - Competition for best post on the basis of merit, performance, and expertise must be considered.

Advantages of position-based competitive bureaucracy:

1. Experts will be placed in desired positions

   E.g.: A financial expert in a finance office could be more efficient and effective.
2. Will promote career planning and continuing education among civil servants.
3. Will reduce political interference and vested interest.

Institutionalization of such systems:

1. Allow merit-based lateral entry.
2. Enable cross-cadre appointments on the basis of merit and appointments.
3. Provide security of tenure.
4. Eliminate age-based promotions.
5. Put age limit on certain posts so that age-appropriate officers are selected for certain posts.

Q13. In a democracy, which role will be considered the most appropriate for civil services: regulating public affairs or playing a direct role in the development and transformation of society? Substantiate your view.

Answer:

Civil services have been referred to as the 'steel frame of Indian government' since British time. Today it plays role not only of steel frame but also of a dynamic institution that can facilitate development.

Regulating public affairs:

1. Regulation can be left to autonomous institutions such as RBI, SEBI, FSSAI, TERI, and judicial institutions.
2. Regulation of public affairs by civil servants can be limited to extreme situations, such as public order by police; the rest can be enforced by institutions meant for such functions.
3. Regulation by civil servants opens possibility of corruption, inspection raj, and hindrance in public affairs.

Role in development:

1. Civil servants can act as facilitators of social and economic change.
   - This can be achieved by their constructive participation in executing government programmes. Educating society about its rights and building transparency and accountability in systems.

For example:

Civil services can enhance 'functionaries' of panchayat raj institutions by devolving funds and functions to them, instead of blocking such efforts.

Q14. Discuss the current challenges for managing the e-governance projects in India that are not doing well or falling short of expectations. What steps have been taken by the government in recent times to overcome them?

Answer:

E-governance has the potential to transform India into a knowledge economy and improve the delivery of services to public.

Challenges:

1. Digital divide:
   - As revealed by World Networking Report released by World Economic Forum, India is highly prone to being left out from digital economy and society due to e-illiteracy.
2. Lack of e-government software in vernacular languages leaves out both officials and citizens.
   - For instance, the Centre's e-NAM platform has been criticized for lacking the local language translation feature.
3. Interoperability:

   Due to excessive number of software and e-platforms, convergence of programmes not achieved.

   E.g.: NREGA and Skill India are finding difficult to converge due to interpretation issues.
4. Lack of connectivity:

   Broadband highways have not been rolled out even in 40% of villages yet, rendering e-governance impossible.

Steps to overcome issues

1. Translation of software in local languages has been envisaged as a 'mission mode' scheme under Digital India.
2. Digital India is creating single-window websites for various cross-connected platforms with help of National Informatics Centre.
3. Mission mode laying of broadband under 'Bharat Net' programme.

4. Launch of 'unified payment interface' should facilitate payment, and Aadhaar's legislative backing should enhance JAM Yojana as well, which will provide a boost to e-governance.

Q15. There is a need to strike a balance between the rights of women, the unborn foetus, and the legitimate interest of the state to prevent selective sex determination. In the light of this statement analyse the Supreme Court of India's recent landmark decision to allow a 24-year-old rape survivor to terminate a 24-week pregnancy.

Answer:

The right of foetus conceived due to rape raises myriad of ethical, legal, and rights-based questions.

For foetus

Ethical questions:

1. Abortion leads to loss of life of an unborn foetus, which is morally wrong
    - If sex of foetus is known, it is even more perverse on part of a person to abort it.

Legal questions:

- Sex-based determination and abortion are simply illegal under the PCPNDT Act.

Rights-based questions:

- The foetus has right to life under Article 21, as it is a living creature.

For mother:

Ethical questions:

- The Mother's mental state maybe very fragile in case of a rape and conception thereafter.
- She may not feel fit to raise the child.

Legal questions:

- The mother cannot abort due to laws in place against such abortion.
- However, she also has a legal right due to crime committed against her.

Rights-based questions:

- Mother may not be able to lead a dignified life as envisaged under Article 21.This presents a deep challenge. In the landmark decision, the Court sided with mother in light of extreme mental trauma, physical pain, and threat to her life posed due to medical reasons.

In such cases, various opinions—medical, ethical, constitutional, and even based on international experience—have been recounted to favour mother's right due to imminent threat to her mental and physical being.

Q16. It is very difficult to define public purpose in the case of land acquisition. What do you understand by 'public purpose' and how can it be misused to promote the State's interest instead of public interest? Explain.

Answer:

'Public purpose' refers to any cause that leads to direct benefits to all sections of the society.

For Instance: Hospitals, education, institutions, housing for the poor, women's centres, etc. are causes of public benefits.

Steps by State

1. States have routinely acquired land in the name of public purpose and passed it on to builders for housing and commercial use.
    - Such cases have been filed against DLF Corporation in Haryana and many others.
    - Right to property not respected in spirit of law.
2. Commoditization of land has taken place due to such acts.
3. Tribal resources have been procured and allotted to mining companies.
    - Rehabilitation and resettlement not done as per provisions
    - Forest Rights Act routinely flouted in the name of public purpose.

Consequences

1. Alienation of farmers, tribals, and marginalized sections.
2. Greater inequality in society.
3. Poor outcome for the public:
    - 'Public plunder' instead of 'public purpose'.
4. Violation of environmental laws in cases such as POSCO and Art of Living exhibition/ festival on Yamuna banks.

Way forward

1. Public purpose be strictly defined by a community of all stakeholders.
2. Limit such purpose to very few cases only.
    - Case-by-case approach by communities consisting of all sections of society.
3. Use of PPP mechanism to provide public service instead of outright acquisition of land for public purpose, etc.

Q17. The Maintenance and Welfare of Parents and Senior Citizens Act, 2007 seeks to make it a legal obligation for children and heirs to provide maintenance to senior citizens. It also permits state governments to establish old age homes in every district. Give your reactions to the statement.

Answer:

India comprises over 85 million old age persons (over 60 years of age) and the number will reach 300 million by 2030.

This will make India home to largest population of old age persons.

Clearly their interest and welfare are highly relevant.

Problems that led to this Act:

1. Dignity: Old people were often dislodged from their homes by their children, leading to homelessness and loss of dignity.
2. Livelihood: Due to high informalization of our employment sector, many old people lack society security, pension, etc.
3. Food security: Old age has specific dietary needs and the ill treatment by children threatens their food security.
4. Medical care: Intensive care is a necessity in this phase of life and the Act must ensure such provision as well.
5. Homes: State have been provided funds to establish old-age homes to ensure the elderly are taken care of in case of homelessness.

International obligation

India has also signed the Madrid Agreement for a barrier-free society. This requires provision for old population as well.

This Act only legalizes what is otherwise a moral and ethical duty of the society. Old-age persons are a repository of knowledge, experience, joy, and support. They must be treated with utmost respect, as envisaged by the Act.

Q18. Discuss the need for statutory status to IIMs. In your view how should a balance be ensured by the law between autonomy and accountability?

Answer:

IIMs have played a critical role in management and financial education in the country. A new IIM Act is envisaged to given them statutory status.

Needs and benefits:

1. Enable IIMS to grant internationally equivalent degrees in management instead of a diploma as per present practice.
2. Enable IIMs to increase fees and enhance financial resources for better infrastructure.
3. Provide full autonomy on course structure, hiring, and tenure of professors.
4. Enable IIMs to partner with foreign institutions on equal footing.

Autonomy and accountability:

1. An independent board of directors can ensure accountability of the IIM administration.
2. Annual reports to the government can be presented in the Parliament.
3. Fees can be made market-driven, but special provision for scholarship to marginalized sections, SC/STs, and women can be created to maintain autonomy as well as accountability.

4. Accreditation, inspections, and other such measures can be carried out by an independent body and international organization to ensure accountability.

Steps

In committee discussions, the government has already consulted with all IIMs and the Ministry of Human Resource Development on the changes.

Q19. The MCI has not served its purpose with regard to the regulation of the medical practice in the country, highlighting the problems. Discuss the scope for a new regulatory regime.

Answer:

Medical Council of India (MCI) is an autonomous organization that oversees accreditation of medical schools (colleges), pattern of various medical exams, and licensing of medical professionals.

Problems:

1. Rampant corruption has been reported in MCI with respect to accreditation of colleges.
2. MCI has been unable to increase number of doctors in India, leading to acute shortage in the profession.
    - WHO has reported that India has about 35–40% shortage of doctors in private and public hospitals.
3. MCI has been unable to enhance the quality of doctors and many licenses have been awarded to undertrained professionals as well.
4. MCI has not addressed the problems of shortage of medical colleges and rather awarded licenses to politically connected families/individuals instead of professionals.
    - This has led to widespread commodification of degrees and the ethics of the profession have been compromised.

NEW REGULATORY REGIME:

A new Parliamentary committee has recommended scrapping of MCI and rethinking governance in the medical field.

1. Establish a national health authority to oversee and regulate medical (doctor) licenses.
2. Establish a separate body to regulate university/medical college licenses.
    - This will bifurcate the two functions and enhance credibility.
3. Create a national policy governing medical standard and ethics.

Q20. The very practice of setting-up of the Pay Commission every 10 years is flawed. It will never satisfy all the sectors in its jurisdiction. Therefore, the practice should be discontinued and every government sector should be allowed to have its own Pay Commission. Critically examine.

Answer:

The Pay Commission is set up to undertake salary review of government employees. It accounts for inflation, quality of life, private sector salary, etc. to review such emoluments of employees.

Problems with 10-year system:

1. The time phase is too long, as inflation and other development factors change rapidly, year after year
   - Shortened time frame of 2–3 years needed, as done in UK and US.
2. Tends to favour Group A employees over Group B, C, D, etc. and hence the gains of Pay Commission are uneven.
3. Too centralized and does not meet varying needs of different government departments and sectors.

Recommendation and way forward

1. Provide internal pay commissions to each department
   - Base pay hikes on performance review done by departmental seniors.
2. Frequency of pay hikes to be left to departments and hikes to come from own departmental budgets.
   - This will lead to move productive and efficient performance by departments themselves.
3. Focus on Group C, D employees, as they are least paid.
   - Greatest hikes should start from bottom and then move upward.
4. Gender budgeting in such pay hikes as well.
   - Such policy will enhance the effectiveness of Pay Commission and rationalize its output/outlay as well.

Practice Set 3

Instruction: Answer the following questions in not more than 200 words each. Contents of the answers are more important than their length. All questions carry equal marks. (15 marks each)

Q1. What do you understand by the term growth potential? What in your view is the growth potential of the Indian Railways?

Answer:

Growth potential can be defined as the prospective ability of an organization or company to increase its footprints, presence, and impact on all stakeholders.

Indian Railways growth potential:

The 12th Five-Year Plan and Shri Bibek Debroy Committee have laid out a bright plan for growth in the Railways due to its immense potential in various respects.

Economic potential

1. Freight: Railways served over 50% of freight in 1980 but it has declared below 27%in 2017 as per the economic survey.
    - It can regain freight market share from the roadways and airlines.
2. Upgradation of infrastructure:
    - Due to lack of investment, the Railways cannot grow in infrastructure coaches, track axles load, etc.
    - It needs over INR 2 lakh crore in the next 5 years to do so.
3. Spillover effect on other industries due to wide-reaching impact of Railways.
    - The potential for employment growth.

Methodological problems

1. Railway budget used for populist announcements.
2. Outdated accounting system.
3. Poor organization structure.
    - Tariff Authority and Development Authority need to be separated for more autonomous decision-making.
4. Lack of human resources development: All these deficiencies are reflected in year after year losses in Railways.

Remedies

As proposed by Bibek Debroy Committee:

1. New accounting system as per international standards.
2. Create a Railway Regulatory Authority.
3. Separate non-strategy functions such as Railways schools, hospitals, etc.
4. Create a separate manufacturing arm of Railways.

Q2. Should India develop and pursue a permanent solution to the public stockholding of food despite having received enough guarantee in its favour? In light of this statement discuss the strategy India should adopt at the WTO.

Answer:

India has been able to attain an indefinite hold on the reduction of agriculture subsidies in WTO meeting, at Bali and then in the Doha round.

However, this will be up for discussion again as:

1. Developed countries are eager to get access to large Indian and other developing markets for their agriculture products.
2. Developed countries want to protect farmer interest in light of decreasing commodity prices.
3. Tying agriculture prices to 1985 prices, as discussed in the WTO, will give undue advantage to developed countries.
4. Millions in India are without food and income security.

How India should maintain the status-quo and hold negotiations:

1. India should put its farmers' interests first and form a strong coalition with like-minded developing countries.
2. National Food Security Mission and National Food Security Act to ensure India's food security and livelihood security.
3. Impending climate changes are also a consideration in this overall negotiation.
    - Will lead to reduced food production, thus making stocking important.
4. Malnutrition, hunger, and poverty are still major problems and Food Policy in India must be independent to fulfil Sustainable Development Goals (SDGs).

Hence, India should strategize in its own interest with other LDCs (least developed countries) regardless of pressure by WTO.

Q3. "Everybody should be given a basic minimum income as an entitlement and not as compensation for work"—explain this statement in the light of the newly proposed universal basic income. Also bring out the different viewpoints and highlight the benefits and hurdles in its implementation.

Answer:

Universal basic income (UBI) refers to the payment of specific minimum allowance to the citizens of a country to ensure their income security.

- It is given unconditionally to all citizens.
- For example, a recent referendum was held in Switzerland to provide minimum basic salary to all citizens but was voted down.

Viewpoints and benefits:

1. Enables 'rights-based' approach to security; minimum and assured livelihood/income source.
2. Guaranteed minimum standard life as a citizen can spend entitled on education, health, food, and income-generating activities.
3. Ensures redistribution of wealth in a welfare country like ours, thereby leading to greater equality.
4. 'Socialist' principle of our Constitution (as stated in the Preamble and Directive Principle of State Policy).
5. Provides women, senior citizens, and disadvantaged groups with much-needed support.

Counter-views

1. Huge expenditure on an already burdened fiscal bill.
   - Indian government pays $10 billion (INR3.5 lakh crore) in 10% of the budget on subsidies already (too expensive).
2. It is a 'dole' to citizens; might disincentivize some to depend on state support.

Hurdles:

1. Implementation is difficult due to massive size and scope.
2. Potential leakage and corruption could defeat the purpose.
3. Could face physical hurdles like Universal Healthcare.

The government can utilize the Aadhaar coding to plug the leakages. The JAM trinity could be used to implement this. Finally, such UBI would also help fulfil the sustainable development goals (SDGs) for India.

Q4. UPI can revolutionize the financial sector. Explain the present working architecture of the UPI. Highlight the various stakeholders involved in it. What is the issue regarding its successful implementation? Suggest measure to overcome such impediments.

Answer:

The universal payment interface (UPI) is an agent mobile application through which individuals can transfer payments to each other simply by using their UPI ID or mobile number in any bank account.

Impact:

It will enable financial inclusion, affordable micropayments by millions of working Indians, eliminate black money, and create a cashless economy over the long term.

Working architecture:

User → UPI → Receiver

Mobile 1 →access on mobile phone → send money to receiver→mobile 2

The RBI clearing system also figures in between these steps.

Stakeholders:

1. Government
2. Citizens:
    - Migrant workers
    - Bank users
    - Women (working class and homemakers)
    - Students
    - Senior citizens
3. Business communities
4. Banks
5. Regulatory institutions

Issues on implementation

1. Lack of awareness would lead to failure.
2. E-illiteracy and problem of digital divide would create less adoption.
3. Muted response by banks.
4. Competition from private services such as Paytm and e-wallets.

Measures:

1. The government could use community service centres (CSCS) in villages to facilitate awareness.
2. Rope in private players to offer a cross-hybrid platform for greater coverage.
3. Launch UPI in vernacular languages to minimize the digital divide.
4. Offer UPI with bank accounts to increase acceptance.
5. Rope-in the post office network of 1.5 lakh post offices to roll out UPI in villages.

Q5. Recently the Lok Sabha has passed a bill to amend the existing Securitization and Reconstruction of Financial Assets and Enforcement of Security Interest (SARFAESI) Act and the Debt Recovery Tribunal (DRT) Act. Examine the significance of these amendments.

Answer:

Amendments to SARFAESI Act and DRT Act have paved the way for adoption of the Insolvency and Bankruptcy Code of India.

Significance:

1. India faces exit problems for its businesses as pointed out by Economic Survey 2016. This leads to:
   - Capital trapped for investors who are unable to move it from failed firms to more efficient ones.
   - Workers lose out as they are not provided timely retirement bonus when companies close.
   - Long (5–10year) process of exit discourages FDI.
   - Entrepreneurs are unable to move to new ventures; human capital is also wasted.
   - Litigation is expensive and long, and all stakeholders—employees, management, and investors—lose out.
   - NPAs (non-performing assets) increase drastically, as seen recently.

This problem has been dubbed the Chakravyuha Challenge by Economic Survey 2016.

Amendments in SARFAESI and DRT Acts will address this problem by:

1. Paying way for evolving a code those provisions for:
   - Time-bound resolution of such in insolvency proceedings.
   - Protection for workers for up to 2 years of lost wages.
   - Protection for creditors to dissolve firms in case of non-resolution.
   - Creation of institutional mechanism: Insolvency professionals and insolvency agencies certified to undertake these matters.

Hence, this will enhance the ease of doing business for Indian firms.

Q6. The apparel industry is labour intensive and India possesses a large labour pool while also enjoying a historical advantage in this sector. Yet, India is ceding market share to export from Bangladesh and Vietnam. How can India's productivity in the textile sector be improved?

Answer:

The textile sector has provided the highest number of employment in the manufacturing sector in India (12th Five-Year Plan).

- Includes labour-intensive cloth and yarn milk processing cotton.
- Also includes design, distribution, and printing services for textiles.

Market share loss:

1. Indian textile exports have lost out to Bangladesh and South Asian countries due to various factors (productivity loss).
   a. Input process has risen in India for cotton, dyes labours, etc.
   b. Regional trade agreements have impacted India's ability to cope.
      - TTIP and TPP agreements will mean a death nail for such exports.

   c. Restrictive labour laws have made it harder for companies to compete.
      - Laws such as Industrial Disputes Act are problematic.
   d. Poor technology investment and the lack of forward integration in design and fashion have impacted the ability to compete.
      - Other countries have invested massively in technology Upgradation.

Productivity improvement steps:

1. National Textile Policy has been revamped to enhance competitiveness by
   a. Investment in new technology through government grants.
   b. Changes to labour policy to enable some space for the manufacturer but also provide safety for workers:
      - Greater skill training.
      - Managerial training to increase productivity.
   c. Focus on improving access to cheap inputs by strengthening the value chain.

Q7. Pulses, India's most consumed protein-rich food group, have continued to push food inflation upward even as the prices of most other item have cooled off. Examine the reason for their high prices, impact on the poor, and the measures needed to cool off their prices.

Answer:

The prices of pulses have increased manifold across India despite food inflation touching down to 4% recently.

- The prices of arhar, moong, gram, etc. have doubled in urban and rural centres alike.

Reasons for high prices:

1. Government policy
   a. MSPs (minimum support price) favour cereals such as rice and wheat, which has led to skewed production of cereals and lower production of pulses.
   b. Lack of focus on investment in irrigation, and 80% pulses are grown in rain-fed areas (Economic Survey).
   c. Pulses are grown in poor soil quality land due to the lack of soil health education.

This lack of supportive government policy has lead to low productivity in pulse production.

2. Demand-supply mismatch
   - The rise in population has created a sudden rise in high-protein pulses, but the demand is not matched by the supply.
3. Monoculture and focus on water-incentive crops such as sugarcane has driven out pulse production.
4. Black marketing and hoarding is rampant.

Source of Food Security:

1. Lack of nutritious and affordable diet.
    - Already malnutrition rates are as high as 47%. Lack of pulses will only intensify this problem.
2. Effect on ability to work and livelihood insecurity.
    - Women will be adversely affected, as they already lack nutrition compared to men.

Steps to cool off prices:

Short-term steps:

1. Blanket ban on hoarding and crack down on such operations.
2. MSPs to farmers and import subsidies to decrease prices.

Long-term steps:

1. Investment in irrigation and land improvement programmes such as Krishi Sinchai Yojana should be done on mission mode.

Q8. Reform that relies only on technological solutions may not give the desired effect. In the light of the recent launch of the national agriculture market scheme (eNAM), Karnataka Rashtriya Electronic Market Services (ReMS) is said to be a lesson for the eNAM scheme to succeed. Examine.

Answer:

eNAM will enable the farmer and consumer to come together to facilitate the sale and purchase agricultural commodities more efficiently. It will lead to:

1. Less wastage
2. Lower prices for consumers
3. Higher prices for producers/farmers
4. Quick payment for farmers
5. Reduction of the tax burden

eNAM is not simply a technical solution. It uses e-governance to deliver good governance and creates a market mechanism for farmers by:

1. Ridding farmers of social and economic dependence on money lenders and middlemen.
2. Empowering farmers by making them a direct stakeholder in their business.
    - The Rashtriya Electronic Market Services of Karnataka achieved empowerment goals by

a. Capacity development and training of farmers.

b. Ensuring that the digital divide does not hamper farmers' ability to sell online.

c. Creating awareness among buyers and handholding them to participate.

d. Using the platform to extend credit facilities information regarding demand from buyers to help the farmers plan better.

Hence, technology solutions assisted by human intervention can lead to eNAM success.

Q9. The Union Government is pushing for the imposition of Aadhaar-based biometric authentication in the public distribution system. Discuss the progress made in the PDS so far and the likely impact of compulsory Aadhaar-based biometric authentication of PDS reform.

Answer:

India's PDS system is the largest network of public service delivery through fair price shops in the world. Its importance is highlighted by the fact that it serves over 800 million urban and rural Indians every year.

Problems plaguing PDS:

1. Urban bias in coverage.
2. Leakages are rampant.
3. Poor quality of grain delivered.
4. Lack of timely delivery.
5. Identification of beneficiaries/ BPL population

Progress made:

1. The opening of over 65,000 centres in the rural area to address urban bias.
2. Use of the geographical information system to plug leakage caused by divergence of food trucks.
3. Use of SMS notification to users/buyers directory to play delivery leakage (used successfully in Jharkhand).
4. Grain inspections are more regular and stricter.
5. Use of targeted PDS programme and SECC (socio-economic caste census, 2011) for targeting has been envisaged.

Aadhaar Compulsory on PDS Receipt

Merits:

1. Leakages will be plugged due to biometric authentication.
2. The government can quickly respond to the various problems in PDS through the consumption data gathered.
3. Better targeting of the recipients of the National Food Security Act.

Demerits:

1. Privacy concerns due to the breach of biometric data.
    - The use of Aadhaar has been challenged in the Supreme for breaching right to privacy (which is implied under Article 21). The Supreme court has ruled against mandatory use of Aadhaar with exceptions (providing of public services and schemes)
2. Misuse of public data by authorities or lack of data available to track cyber attacks.

Q10. The Government of India recently decided to build a high-speed rail corridor between Mumbai and Ahmedabad at a very high cost with Japanese financial and technical assistance. Does India need a project such as this at such a high cost? Comment.

Answer:

A high-speed rail corridor between Mumbai and Ahmedabad will put India on the map of advanced rail connectivity.

Despite its high cost, it has both its advantages and disadvantages.

Advantages:

1. Economic:
   a. Connectivity will enhance trade, business, and commerce between the two industrial centres.
      - Will boost state GDP.

   b. Infrastructure investment will create millions of jobs and employment.
   c. Spillover effect on manufacturing industry, as machines, coaches, engines, track, etc. will be manufactured domestically.
      - It will boost employment as well.
2. Decongest and free up the capacity of Railways to serve people.
3. Technological transfer from Japan will help India develop the Railways.
   - The world experience of high-speed railways in Europe, Japan, and China has been extremely positive for their economies.
4. Inexpensive financing at 0–1% interest rate from Japan is attractive.

Disadvantages:

1. Funds and resources of this scale could be invested in other areas, such as to alleviate health, hunger, and poverty problems.
2. Airfares on this route are already cheap; hence this is not a financially viable option.
3. Will lead to the displacement of millions of farmers and tribals along the development route.

This concern can be addressed by rehabilitation program for the displaced population and also a better financial structure for the project. Overall the merits outweigh the demerits.

Q11. Relatively low-cost maternal and early life health and nutrition programmes offer a very high return on investment. Despite this social and economic wisdom, why does India continue to have one of the worst indicators for child and maternal health?

Answer:

India has a high IMR (infant mortality rate)—42 per 1000 births—and an MMR (maternal mortality rate) of 78 per 1 lakh births.

These have been rated as one of the worst in the world, on par with sub-Saharan Africa as per WHO.

India missed its IMR and MMR goals in Millennium Development Goals (MDGs) and even the Lancet Report indicates this is the prime reason for poor health outcome in India.

Why bad outcomes?

1. Sanitation—open defecation is prevalent among 500 million people.
   - WHO has indicated that early exposure to defecation and faecal material leads to stunting, diarrhoea, etc.
2. Mothers are routinely ignored for proper nutrition post the birth of babies.
   - This affects the mother and baby's health.
3. Institutional deliveries are low at 78% (non-institutional deliveries indicate high mortality of both child and the mother).
4. Lack of immunization.
5. The girl child suffers due to the lack of post-birth breastfeeding, which has been rated as one of the top factors of early death by the Lancet Report.

Government efforts:

Steps to improve IMR and MMR through nutrition have been taken through programmes such as

a. Janani Suraksha Karyakram
b. National Rural Health Mission
c. Institutions such as ASHA workers, Anaganwadi workers, and ANMs (Auxiliary Nurse Midwives).
d. Integrated child development programme (ICDS)

Further integration with the Swachh Bharat Abhiyan (defecation-free India) should bolster efforts to decrease such cases.

Q12. The small saving schemes are neither so small nor limited exclusively to the low-income earners. In fact, most of the tax incentives that are provided to them go to the relatively well off. Highlight the major policy flaw associated with such a scheme.

Answer:

Small savings schemes consist of investment programmes offered by the government to enable financial security and financial inclusion of small savers.

Example: Kisan Vikas Patras, Post Office Saving Schemes offered by post offices, etc.

Economic Survey 2016-17 has indicated the following policy flaws in these:

1. Large, affluent farmer corner benefit of the scheme.
   - 90% of benefits from the scheme reused by just 10% of wealthiest farmers.
2. Small farmers are unable to access this benefit due to lack of awareness.
   - Only 23% of farmers are aware of small saving schemes.

3. Interest burden of these schemes becomes too high when the market interest rate declines.
    - Government fails to adjust the rates due to populist reactions to the schemes.
4. Such schemes are not demanded driven and have a low impact on addressing financial inclusion problems.

Solutions:

1. Put a cap on use of schemes on basis of farm income.
    - Limit to bottom 50% farmers only.
2. Make interest rate and adjust the table to market changes.
    - Market float as practised by private bodies.

Q13. According to a report by Global Financial Integrity (GFI), fraudulent misinvoicing of trade transactions was revealed to be the largest component of illicit financial flows (IFF) from developing countries. What do you understand by raid misinvoicing and how does it affect developing countries?

Answer:

Trade misinvoicing refers to under-invoicing of the amount in the bill of trade as compared to its actual amount.

For example, an Indian trader bills an export shipment for $1500, when it should be $2500 as per agreed terms between the trader and foreign client.

This has been an increasing trend, and accounts for 20–30% of our trade amount in the world as per GFI.

Problems created by this practice

1. Underreporting of trade done by the country—affects the balance of trade figures.
2. Black money transaction and money laundering done via this.
3. Loss of tax revenue for the government.
4. Could lead to illicit trade.
5. Used to export primary articles such as gems and agricultural products, thereby affecting credit terms for farmers and primary producers.

Way forward

1. Automatic invoicing should be promoted.
2. Strict regulatory framework by WTO and national government needed.
3. Administrative mechanism at ports must be strengthened to put a check on such practice.

Q14. The Indian ports sector plays a vital role in sustaining growth in the country's trade and commerce. What are the problems faced by the ports sector in India? What measures have been taken to address them?

Answer:

India has 12 major ports and over 200 minor ones across 7500 km of coastal line.

Ports account for over 90% by trade volume of all international trade, clearly underlining their vital role in the economy.

Problems:

1. Cluster-based approach for developing port-industrial townships not followed.
   - Leading to ports that are not well-connected by roads and the Railways network.
2. Land acquisition problems for the development of port townships.
   - Township is essential to boost activity at ports.
3. The livelihood of fishermen is directly affected by port development.
4. Lack of financing leading to slow development of ports.
5. Poor container capacity and lack of latest equipment causes the delay in ship loading and unloading.
6. Indian ports have over 95% capacity utilization and the longest waiting period for vessels. Inefficient administration.

Measures:

1. Ministry of Shipping has allowed PPP (public private partnership) development of ports.

   Example: Ennore Port was developed and has been a successful venture.
2. Shipping conclave by the government to enhance investment in the sector for developing multimodal infrastructure to support ports.
3. Addition of shipping industry to 'infrastructure status' by the Ministry of Finance.

Q15. The government has decided to create a new banking giant by merging the State Bank of India with its associated banks. Discuss the merits and demerits of this move. Also, bring out the challenges in its successful implementation?

Answer:

State Bank of India is the largest bank in India, and figures among the top 10 banks in the world.

Due to the large number of associate banks such as State Bank of Bikaner, Hyderabad, etc., banking is affected in following ways:

1. Lack of lending ability to large infrastructure projects.
2. The management is not standardized.
3. Local politics influences the associate banks negatively and impacts profitability.

A new large SBI has the following merits:

1. Ability to lend to a large infrastructure project of national importance.
    - India requires one trillion dollars in next 5 years period to develop the infrastructure it needs.
    - SBI merger could facilitate this.
2. It will ward off political interference, as the management will come under one umbrella and become autonomous.
3. Ability to raise funds internationally.

Demerits:

1. To big to fail problem like Lehman brothers in the USA. Financial crisis could impact economy adversely.
2. Ignoring local banking needs of small customers.
3. Losing regional focus and creating the problem of handling transparency in dealing.

Challenges in implementation:

1. Latest risk management to comply with the Basel norms.
2. Dealing with employee union during the merger of banks.
3. Serving customers with same diligence as before.
4. Protocol, policy, and regulation must be very comprehensive.

Q16. What are the relative merits and demerits of GDP as a tool to measure the economic performance of nations? Has it outgrown its utility? What ultimate measure can be used to measure the well-being of a nation? Examine.

Answer:

GDP measures the total output of an economy in government expenditure, private consumption, and investment in export/import.

This provides a holistic number of purely financial terms to measure economic performance.

Merits:

1. Simple to calculate and easy to compare with other countries; accepted worldwide.
2. It is a widely adopted measure to understand the outcome of economic activity.
3. Used to develop the budget programme, plans, and scheme by the government.
4. Used by IMF and World Bank as well—international banking.

Demerits:

1. Not comprehensive—misses the human development aspect, as pointed out by Dr Amartya Sen.

2. World Bank Report 2015 has highlighted the need for a human behaviour approach to measure growth, not just an economic approach.
3. Does not capture some production factors in the economy:

   -for example: lack of gender equality in GDP as work done by women at home is not captured in this measure.
4. Not inclusive in nature; inapplicable when comparing large and small countries.

Hence, it appears that GDP has outgrown its utility because today growth is not a sufficient measure of economic success. Even SDGs focus on poverty as a multi-dimensional issue.

Other alternative:

1. A mix of various indexes such as:
   a. Human development index (HDI)—education, health, and gender equality to income
   b. Happiness index developed by the World Bank.
   c. Inequality index and gender index could be used in addition to the above-mentioned measures.
   d. All the above could be used to develop an adjusted GDP for the above factors.

Q17. The US economy is driven by consumption and the Chinese economy is driven by production while the Indian economy is driven by trade and services. Which category do Indian start-ups belong to? Discuss their strengths and weakness.

Answer:

India has become home to over 12,000 start-ups, the third largest start-up ecosystem in the world. Indian start-ups serve all three sections—consumption, production, and trade and services.

Consumption:

1. There are new Indian start-ups in the area of food services, such as Zomato and Foodpanda, boosting urban consumption.
2. Retail start-ups such as Flipkart and Snapdeal also focus on this.

However, these start-ups have an urban bias, not rural focus.

Production:

1. Many start-ups are delivering new defence technology, as the new defence policy emphasizes on indigenous design, development, and production.
2. Indian start-ups are leading in the production of 3D printers as well as software production.

Services:

1. Start-ups such as Paytm in financial services, Mitra in peer-to-peer lending, and other various education start-ups are serving such needs.

2. Various start-ups are focusing on providing weather and field-related (soil testing etc.) information to farmers.

Strengths of start-ups in India

1. Led by the extremely brilliant talent of engineering and management professionals.
2. Serving the huge market demand both in India and abroad.
3. Leading to employment creation.

Weaknesses

1. Ecosystem is weak as compared to USA and Israel due to early phase.
2. Financially bubble created, leading to a poor decision by management.
3. Informalization of workforce.

Government has launched Start-up India programme to boost the start-up environment and also a national aspiration fund to invest in new start-ups. This should enhance the nurturing of startupsin India, leading to their success.

Q18. It is said that in India there is an emphasis on increasing farm productivity, but this might not always align to greater profitability for farmers. In this regard, do you think the government should also focus more on farmer welfare? Give your argument.

Answer:

Farmer welfare is directly related to farm productivity because:

1. Greater farm productivity will increase farmer wages.
2. Greater farm productivity will make food security and livelihood security achievable dreams.
3. It will also ease the burden of farm subsidies, which can be allocated to farm investment.

The World Bank Report 2016 has shown a direct relationship between health, education, and gender equality as farm productivity increases.

- A $1 increase in productivity has given multiple effects of $3 on various welfare measures such as sanitation, health, education, and nutritional security.

The government should, therefore, focus on:

1. Farm and land improvement by enhancing soil quality and irrigation.
2. Seeds and fertilizers policy that promotes healthy use of inputs.
3. Greater insurance coverage for farmers.
4. Easy credit facilities.
5. Rationalizing MSP structure.

Q19. What do you understand by climate-smart agriculture? Illustrate with examples the various technologies used in climate-smart agriculture to combat climate change effects. Give innovative suggestions in this regard and critically evaluate such innovations.

Answer:

Climate-smart agriculture can be defined as sustainable agriculture practices that adapt to changing climate patterns.

Features of climate-smart agriculture:

1. Crops not affected by erratic monsoons/climate changes.
2. Higher yields despite harsher climate—more productive yield.
3. Use of satellite technology for efficient sowing, growing, and harvest.
4. Less labour intensive, more environmentally friendly.

Example of techniques:

1. GIS (geographical information system) sends timely updates to farmers about the weather.
   - Satellite imagery of field and soil health to get higher yield.
2. Use of drip irrigation and sprinkler methods for higher crop per drop.
3. Use of fortified seeds for better nutrition per unit and use of, more effective fertilizers.

   E.g.: Neem-coated urea for greater impact of fertilizers on crops.
4. Use of soil health cards to understand the nutritional needs of the soil.
   - Government has launched Paramparagat Krishi Vikas Yojana for more sustainable and climate-smart agriculture practices.

Innovative measures:

1. Use the Internet of things and 3D printing technology for R&D in agriculture.
2. Promote the use of programmes to link with national extension services and farmer development centres.
3. Student satellites have been launched by IIT Bombay receiving for climate prediction services.
4. Develop third-generation mobile app for farmers.

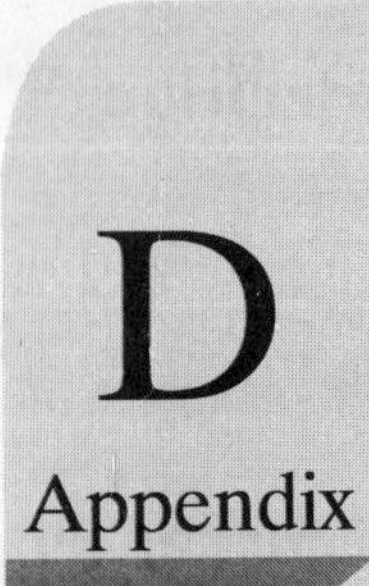

Appendix D

Additional Reads for Main Examination

This chapter provides analytical insights on key issues related to the topics mentioned in the syllabus of General Studies Paper II. You can read these to enhance further conceptual understanding of various topics in GS 2 syllabus.

Separation of Powers

The three organs of the government—the Executive, Judiciary, and Legislature represent the people and their will in our country, and are responsible for the smooth running of a democratic government in our society. The Legislature is the law-making body, the Executive is responsible for the enforcement of all such laws, and the Judiciary deals with the cases that arise from breaches of law. Thus, they are all interlinked organs of the government and their roles and functions tend to overlap with each other, as it is not possible to separate the three from each other completely.

This has not only been the cause for serious political debate in our country but has raised many philosophical and jurisprudential debates among legal scholars and the law fraternity. Whether there should be a complete separation of powers or a well-coordinated system of distribution of powers thus becomes the focal point of contemplation.

Key points:

1. According to the Directive Principle of State Policies, Article 50 requires the State to keep the Judiciary and Executive separate.
2. The Judiciary is independent, and its judgments, conduct of judges, and matters cannot be discussed in the Parliament by the Legislature.
3. Power of judicial review
4. Power of impeachment of the judges is a check on judicial powers.

5. Powers, privileges, and immunities are provided to Members of Parliament.
6. The functioning of the houses is provided immunity from judicial scrutiny.
7. The Legislature has the power to impeach the President and the executive head.

The powers of the Executive, Judiciary, and Legislature are not strictly separated:

1. The Executive is a part of the Legislature itself.
2. It is responsible to the Legislature.
3. The Westminster type of Parliamentary government requires close coordination of the Indian Executive and the Legislature.
4. According to Article 74, the President has to act as per the directives of the council of ministers.

The Supreme Court's Kesavananda Bharati case is an important case in this regard, as it says that while the Parliament has the power to amend the Constitution under Article 368, it cannot change the 'basic features' of the Constitution. These basic features entail a limit on the amending power of the Legislature in terms of separation of powers as well. In Indira Gandhi v. Raj Narain (1975), the SC upheld that adjudication is a judicial function and cannot be exercised by the Parliament even under amending power.

Relevance of Rajya Sabha

Equality of Seats in Rajya Sabha with Lok Sabha

The need for equality of seats in the RS with the LS arises owing to the following reasons:

1. First, states that need urgent developmental effort and institutional reforms from the centre have the least voice due to their small proportion in the Rajya Sabha. For example, the Northeastern states are regularly at low priority during much of the work in the Rajya Sabha.
    - Nine states in India have just one member each in the Rajya Sabha.
    - Just 10 populous states occupy nearly 70% of the total elected membership of the upper house.
2. Some smaller states have expressed resentment at their inability to make their voice felt at the Centre.
3. The number of seats in the Lok Sabha anyway is directly linked to the population and there is no need to duplicate the principle.
4. Large states with many Rajya Sabha seats can use them to politically influence the outcome of many important bills for their own vested interests.
5. Debates in the RS have become one-sided in favour of large states.
6. Equality of seats will truly allow us to meet the goals of cooperative federalism.

Drawbacks:

1. This could also lead to a situation where smaller states could block reform even if it is for the benefit of the larger populations in big states.

Abolition of Legislative Councils

Need for legislative councils

a. To check on hasty actions of the assembly

b. To allows more debate on various topics

c. Individuals who are experts in their respective fields and are not able to get elected in popular elections are able to contribute to the law-making process

The need to abolish legislative councils

a. They do not have effective power, as the assembly can reject all the amendments proposed by it.

b. Leaders with connections, or people related to political leaders, but who lose elections are nominated to these councils.

c. They strain state finances—approximately INR 100 crores are required to establish these, and then INR 20 crores per year to run them as per the standing committee.

Procedure

a. A state must pass a resolution with special majority in the assembly to create or abolish it.

b. The resolution must then be passed by the Parliament as well.

The Standing Committee of the Parliamenthas recommended a National Policy with regards to creating the second chamber in various states.

Educational Qualifications in Elections

The Supreme Court has upheld the constitutionality of the Haryana Law that disqualifies candidates without the requisite educational requirements for panchayati seats.

Positive effects of the Decision

- Able leadership: Education imparts some level of technical education and better understanding of various social, economic, and political concepts.
- Role model: Educated person scan prove to be better role models for the rural masses with respect to concepts such as maintaining sanitation, reducing open defecation(having a functional toilet), and promoting the spirit of education.
- Educated leaders can ensure that education is promoted in rural areas, independent of gender.

Negative effects of the Decision

- Omission of women: The decision will limit the participation of women in panchayati raj institutions, as their literacy rates are almost 10–15% below those of men.
- It is against the principle of 'one man one vote', which is against the right to equality as per article 21, as it puts people with education on a different plane and questions can be raised on its impact on the right to universal suffrage.
- The black-marketing of fake degrees and certificates could increase.
- STs and SCs could be isolated from the democratic process.
- Not being able to provide education to the masses and the high level of illiteracy in India are failures of the government functioning itself, for which citizens should not be made to suffer unduly.
- It is against the principle of direct democracy.

Simultaneous Elections

From the first elections in 1952 until those in 1967, the election cycles in the states and the Centre have matched, and all elections have been held together. However, from 1967, due to the emergence of regional parties and the coalition era, the state governments were often dissolved before they completed their full tenure of five years. This led to staggering of the election cycle in India. The challenges of staggered elections are as follows:

- Expense: In its2017 report titled 'Proposed Electoral Reforms 'to the Law Commission, the Election Commission has estimated that the cost of holding multiple elections would be almost 50% lower than holding staggered elections.
- Hold on developmental activities: Since the enforcement of the Model Code of Conduct (MCC), various developmental activities come to a halt during elections.
- Government officials and security forces have to be deployed every time elections are held.
- Due to the money and muscle power involved, communal forces come into action and immoral activities start taking place.
- The advantages and disadvantages of simultaneous elections are as follows:

Advantages

- Decrease expense
- Continuation of developmental policies and programmes
- Judicious use of government apparatus for deployments on election duty
- Reduced use of money power and muscle power

Disadvantages

- It is a challenge to the federal structure of India
- Voters tend to vote for the same party during elections held simultaneously
- National issues dominate the agenda, and regional issues take a backseat

Panchayati Raj

Gandhiji's vision of making every village a Republic was translated into reality with the passage of the Constitution (73rd Amendment) Act in 1992.Under this Act, panchayati raj institutions (PRIs) were given constitutional status, and a three-tier panchayati raj system was formed to ensure people's participation in rural development. With 496 panchayats at district level, 5905 at block level, and 2, 30,762 at village level, India is today the world's largest functioning democracy.

However, PRIs face a host of challenges:

1. Unscientific distribution of functions
2. Incompatible relations between the three tiers
3. Inadequate finances
4. Lack of cordial relations between officials and people
5. Lack of conceptual clarity
6. Undemocratic composition of PRIs
7. Political and caste factionalism
8. Problems faced by the Panchayats(Extension to Scheduled Areas) Act (PESA), 1996in scheduled areas

PESA and its challenges

The Panchayats (Extension to Scheduled Areas) Act (PESA), 1996was envisioned to enable local self-governance in various tribal scheduled areas. However, this act faces many challenges both at the institutional and ground level, as follows:

- State's reluctance to implement and adopt the PESA: While all nine states have notified the Act, there are ambiguities in their own rules framed about it. This is hindering its quick adoption in their scheduled areas.
- Administrative and bureaucratic reluctance
- Power struggle between tribal communities and bureaucracy
- Transfer of funds, functions, and functionaries to the lower level government has not taken place after devolving statutory powers to the gram Sabha and panchayats.
- Clear rules have not been laid out with respect to the management of minor forest products and land, thereby making it more ambiguous to implement the PESA. This is impacting the traditional and environmental rights of tribals.

- Tribals in these areas already have established customs to address their governance problems. In some cases, they are not very open to adopting a new panchayati system.
- Financial autonomy is merely on paper and the Governor's mandatory report is not prepared.

The PESA is a most powerful legislation that can play an instrumental role in recognizing the rights of the tribal population in scheduled areas over natural resources, thus transforming their quality of life. It is almost true that due to lack of political will, their rights have been disregarded strategically.

Though the Central Government has taken several measures to implement the Act in letter and spirit, the lack of initiative from the concerned state government is quite evident. The Central Government should take appropriate action to eliminate the loopholes in the central legislation immediately followed by a strong direction from the political government to abide by the constitutional mandate. The state government should follow the guidelines issued by the central government to incorporate changes in the state Acts proposed by state-level study reports, take appropriate measures to amend state laws that are in conflict with the provisions of the PESA, and take initiatives to enhance the capacity of the government machinery and stakeholders who play a vital role in the actual implementation of the Act at the ground level.

Civil society organizations that have been fighting proactively for the issue have to play a strategic role in building awareness among the stakeholders at each level and in organizing the politically divided tribal communities. So, a multi-pronged strategy to address the issue from different aspects is the need of the hour.

The Forest Rights Act, 2006 and the PESA have established a framework for local self-governance in demarcated (or 'scheduled') areas; yet their full implementation is fraught with many challenges. Indigenous tribes constitute about 8% of India's population and both the Forest Rights Act and PESA go a long way in ensuring constitutional protection and empowerment of these people.

The Virginius Xaxa committee has painted a bleak picture of the status of tribals.

The Forest Rights Act recognizes the rights of tribal communities over trading in forest produce. The problems in implementation of the provisions of the Act are as follows:

- The Ministry of Environment and Forests had changed the law to throw open 40% of the country's forests to private sector management. Allowing the private sector to use these lands for monoculture could have a ruinous impact on the ecosystem. In these areas, the tribal communities have control over only 10–15% of the forest land.
- In Maharashtra, the control over forest resources has been appropriated by the forest department, granting them control over the lucrative trade in tendu leaves and bamboo running intercourse of rupees.
- Absence of land record, low literacy, corruption, and collusion between the elite section of the society and the forest officers derail the process.
- Slow implementation (in Madhya Pradesh, only 23% of the land has been distributed yet, after 10 years) and cumbersome process add to the woes.

- States override the FRA clause under the pretext of development without adequate compensation and rehabilitation.

These problems can be remedied through the following actions:

- Amending the state laws in accordance with the FRA and the PESA.
- Empowering the gram Sabha (financially, through training, and by providing information).
- Recruiting more officers from the community.
- Preparing the Governor's report on time.
- Solving the land-grabbing issue by setting up a fast track court.

The participation of the civil society and activist judiciary further add teeth to the twin laws that epitomize real swaraj as envisioned by Gandhiji.

Anti Discrimination Legislation: A Constitutional Perspective

India remains among the few countries with a constitutional commitment to a liberal democracy that nevertheless lacks comprehensive anti-discrimination legislation.

The Indian constitution was framed keeping in mind rights, disabilities, beliefs, marginalization, and the problems encountered by all sections of the society. However, some problems exist, holding India back, as described in the following.

Discrimination against lower castes

The social integration of lower castes is still lacking, as casteism and untouchability are widespread. Further, discrimination against women and disabled people is still prevalent. Despite several empowerment measures, some guaranteed by the Constitution itself, atrocities against Dalit and other lower castes continue unabated. The societal prejudice against these people manifests in violence against them, or they being deprived of equal rights.

Discrimination against women

The fact that we are still debating whether women have the right to enter temples or mosques presents the sorry status of women. The patriarchal nature of the society has led to the perpetration of kangaroo courts in the form of Khap panchayatsthat still treat women as second-grade citizens. The concept of marital rape is not yet recognized. Despite several well-intentioned measures taken by the government, women still face discrimination in several walks of life.

Discrimination against Lesbians, Gays, Bisexuals, and Transgender

While transgender suffer primarily due to societal biases, lesbians, gays, and bisexuals face discrimination by law in the form of Section 377 of IPC. The recent surrogacy bill approved by cabinet discriminates against the adoption of children by same-sex couples. The SC while hearing the curative petition in the Naz Foundation case directed the legislature to take anti-discriminatory measures.

Discrimination against citizens on issues of Freedom of speech

The constant uproars over freedom of expression manifested in cases such as banning the book of Perumal Murugan, Madhorubagan (One Part Woman), and unabashed usage of sedition laws violate the fundamental tenet of liberalism.

Communalism

Progressive rational and scientific ideas are not accepted well by fringe groups that backfire against such ideas, as is evident by the murder of social activist Narendra Dabholkar and activist Govind Pansare.

The various provisions of the Indian Constitution with respect to fundamental rights, fundamental duties, directive principles, and various legislations provide significant commitment to prevent discrimination. It provides for Fundamental Rights against any form of exploitation and untouchability, and ensures that these are absolutely intolerable in our modern, liberal society. The Fundamental Duties call citizens to perform their civic duty by condemning any form of discrimination against women. The Directive Principles make it a state objective to aspire for a country with all social and economic rights. This has been achieved by enabling legislation such as free legal aid to the poor and marginalized sections under the NALSA (National Legal Services Authority).

The SC/ST Prevention of Atrocities Act is a strict law that imposes many punishments on discriminatory attitude and action. However, the Judiciary should play a key role to ensure strict enforcement.

Women in Local Governance

Overcoming the stereotype bias that has always prevailed, women from all walks of life have been successful leaders. Examples of stupendous success have been stories such as those of Meena Behen, first woman sarpanch from a village in Gujarat to build roads to enable accessibility for women during pregnancy. Despite success in leadership roles, women continue to be confined to the four walls of their homes in the patriarchal social environment in rural as well as urban areas. The problems faced by women in these situations are as follows:

1. The practice of electing only male sarpanch heads sidelines women in their political leadership roles.
2. Women have to perform domestic tasks despite their active life in panchayats and local leadership, which puts additional burden on them.
3. Women face the patriarchal attitude of their suggestions and ideas being considered inferior to those of men.
4. Devolution is so uneven and inadequate that often even the ablest of women are crippled for want of the rightful allocation of functions, finances, and functionaries, without which effective PR is rendered impossible.

Domestic Violence

The National Family and Health Survey has estimated that there is a 33% chance of women in the age group 15–49 facing domestic violence of some sort. This is a worrying figure, and steps need to be taken urgently to ensure the welfare and security of women in their own homes.

Steps taken by the government

The Parliament has enacted several laws to protect women from domestic violence at the hands of the husband or his relatives:

- The Dowry Prohibition Act, 1961
- Introduction of Section 498A in the IPC(1983)
- Domestic Violence (DV) Act, 2005

These have been hailed as landmark legislations giving voice to silent sufferers.

Misuse

In various cases, the relatives of the husband are wrongly implicated, who then have to undergo the rigours of the criminal justice system. Thus, there is a demand for these laws to be amended. In 2017, the issue was raised in the Rajya Sabha.The amendment is needed due to low conviction rates—as per the NCRB (National Crime Records Bureau), out of the 426 cases registered under the DV Act in 2014, only 13 were convicted.

The low rate of conviction doesn't reveal the extent of misuse or abuse of the law as other factors like compromise, lack of evidence etc. also play a role in non-conviction. The real causes of misuse, as identified by the Law Commission in its 243rd report, are as follows:

- The mechanical and casual manner in which the police exercises their right to arrest. It has to be remembered that the right to arrest is a tool to prevent any further harm to the victim. This tool must be used sparingly, as it results in irreversible harm to the reputation of the accused, which reduces the chances of any reconciliation later on.
- Second, matrimonial disputes are inherently different from other criminal cases due to the scope as well as need for conciliation between the parties.

Recommendations of the Law Commission report

1. The police must follow the guidelines of arrest as given by the SC in D.K. Basu vs. State of West Bengal.
2. The necessity of arrest has to be properly established.
3. A mechanism of dispute settlement such as conciliation and mediation must be mandatorily initiated before making any arrest, unless the facts disclose an aggravated form of cruelty.
4. The option of compounding of the offence should be available to parties.

National Consumer Disputes Redressal Commission

Organization

Post liberalization, since 1991, the Indian society has witnessed a dramatic rise in consumer-oriented products. This has led to increasing disputes between consumers and sellers as well. For example, increasing purchases of residences in urban centres have led to a rise in the instances of disputes between builders and residents.

In this context, the National Consumer Disputes Redressal Commission (NCDRC) has become an increasingly important institution. It is the Commission's responsibility to resolve these consumer cases, empower the consutmers, and help the economy function in a smooth manner. The NCDRC empowers the customers in the following ways:

- Its three-tier structure helps in quick and fair resolution of disputes at the district, state, and national level.
- The quasi-judicial nature of the Commission helps in both investigation and judgment as well as in creating rules to empower consumers.
- The Commission ensures that the rights of consumers are protected and better trade practices are promoted.

The government has incorporated the Consumer Protection Act, 1986 to oversee the NCDRC. It has also taken various initiatives such as the Jago Grahak Jago campaign to spread awareness among consumers. The recommendations of the Commission are as follows:

1. Partnership with industry associations to promote better seller behaviour with buyers.
2. Single-window online portal to register complaints and offer resolution.
3. Coordination with regulatory bodies such as FSSAI to bring all matters of consumer interest less than one forum.

Scrapping of Rail Budget

Indian Railways is not just a means of transportation but also a thread that connects the entire nation through exchange of ideas, people, culture, art, and goods. It plays a critical role in the Indian economy, polity, and society. Unfortunately, the Railways have faced many financial and infrastructural challenges in the last two decades.

One major reform recommended by the Bibek Roy Committee (and accepted by the government in September 2016) was to scrap the rail budget altogether. The various merits of this step are as follows:

- The Rail Budget has been a means of promoting populist measures such as announcing new trains in the constituencies of the respective railway ministers and so on.
- The Budget has never focused on addressing the structural requirements of the Railways. Scrapping it will democratize the Railways and promote a more agile and efficient railway system.

- This scrapping upholds the vision of maximum governance.
- The Budget has lost its efficacy since 1924, when it was a large portion of the government expenses. The latest edition was smaller than even the defence budget.

The demerits of this recommendation are as follows:

- Mere economic fixes are not enough for the Railways. The focus needs to shift to leadership, management, cultural changes in organization, etc.
- Following the merger of the Rail budget with the Union Budget, it could further take attention away from reforms in the Railways.

Way forward

The future of the Railways lies in manpower development through capacity development, introduction of more freight lines to decongest the railway traffic, and provision of better amenities and attractive fares to people. This can be achieved through incremental reforms (as suggested by Economic Survey 2014).

Goods and Services Tax

The goods and services tax (GST) has ushered in a new tax regime in India which will introduce one single tax for all indirect tax transactions across the country. The various benefits of the GST are as follows:

1. It will help the country to achieve the objectives of free trade and commerce throughout the territory, as laid in Article 301 of the Constitution.
2. It will lower the burden of indirect taxation on Indian people. Indirect taxes have grown rapidly and are regressive in nature as they tax the rich and the poor at the same rate. The introduction of GST will lower the effective tax rate and thereby the help poor manage their expenses better.
3. It will simplify taxation filing and payment by MSMEs, thereby enhancing the tax base of the government. This should increase the tax collections for the government.
4. It will unify the tax rates across the country on manufacturing, thereby promoting manufacturing in states where it is not mainstream at present due to tax differences with other states. This will promote Make in India.
5. It is expected to boost economic growth by 0.5–1%.
6. It will help Indian products compete internationally, as the taxation rate on value-added products will reduce.
7. It will reduce the collection costs for the government as well as the filing costs for corporates, thereby increasing the efficiency of tax collection.

The drawbacks of the GST are as follows:

1. It will impinge on the financial independence of the states, thereby hurting the spirit of cooperative federalism in the country. This has been addressed by providing equal voting rights to the states in the GST Council.
   a. However, questions remain over how it will affect the ability of the states to address regional developmental problems.
   b. Also, the centre has veto power in the GST council, thereby raising concerns over the states' ability to further their interests effectively.
2. It will lead to large loss of revenue for state governments. This has been resolved by compensating the states for any loss in revenue by the Centre.
3. Its implementation, if done poorly, could lead to an economic downturn in the economy.
4. **Federalism:** Does GST enhance federalism? If we look at large peer countries, the US does not have a centralized GST. In fact, many states in the US have the power to impose income tax in addition to state-level sales tax. In the European Union (EU), each member-state (country) has retained fiscal autonomy. The Maastricht Treaty only forced members to remain within the limit of fiscal deficit of 3% of gross domestic product (GDP). Even this ceiling was breached early on by EU's two biggest members, France and Germany. After the sovereign debt crisis starting with Greece, and after Brexit, all bets are off. The fiscal rebellion may spread. China does have a national GST, but the spending and resource raising autonomy given to its provinces (states) is immense. Indeed, the governors' performance is purely linked to capex and GDP growth, and they enjoy de facto fiscal autonomy. Thus, in comparison to the US, EU, or China, the GST in India will greatly curtail the fiscal autonomy of states. It is unlikely that we will have income tax powers bestowed on state governments.
5. **Progressivity:** The GST is an indirect tax. The poor bear a disproportionate burden of indirect taxes. India has a very low direct tax-to-GDP ratio. The ratio of direct to indirect taxes in India is 35:65. This is exactly the obverse of the situation in most of the developed world. Income tax rates have steadily reduced, whereas service tax rates have gone up from 5% in the mid-1990s to 15% at present. Swachh Bharat and Krishi Kalyan cesses are recent examples of new indirect taxes. Less than 5% Indians file income tax returns, but almost all Indians pay indirect tax in one form or another. A starting GST rate of 18% (as per current discussion) will hurt the poor more than the rich. Early discussion was around a GST rate of 12% or 13%, which has now drifted to 18%. At 20% or higher, we might as well not have a GST.
6. **Legislative cap on GST:** Excise duties on petrol and diesel were raised almost a dozen times from 2015-2017. These are indirect taxes. The excise duty hikes did not require any Parliamentary approval because the frequent tax hikes were executive action (can be done directly by government of India without any deliberation in the Parliament). If GST can be tweaked upward just by the Executive, it will become more and more regressive, worsening income inequality. Hence a legislative cap (via the bill, not necessarily in the Constitution) is needed to prevent future misuse. One must bear in mind that the tax

buoyancy (and elasticity) of a tweak from 18% to 19% is much higher and hence easier than widening the direct tax net. We need to curb this temptation to increase taxes through a legislative restraint, i.e., a cap on the GST rate

7. **Council governance:** GST disputes will be thrashed out in the GST council. Small and large states will have equal voting powers. Is this fair? Large producing states such as Maharashtra already fear losses in excess of INR 14,000 crore in the first year itself. It is asking for a larger reimbursement. Other voting states may 'gang up' against Maharashtra and veto such a proposal. What if a larger state wants to impose a higher sin tax or give a bigger subsidy at the lower end of the GST slab, since they can afford it? Will the current governance framework provide such a leeway?
8. **Tax disputes:** The power of the sales tax commissioner at the state level enables speedy resolution of disputes. However, the excise framework uses the process of appeals and tribunals, involving interminable delays. This distinction is called the revision versus review approach. Will the GST lean the excise way or the sales tax way? Will we soon have a mountain of disputes and long judicial delays?

Federalism and GST

In the Constituent Assembly debates, Dr B.R. Ambedkar vigorously defended the right of the States to tax their residents. He said this would enable the states to exercise the mandate for development and growth given to its representatives by the people.

Impact on States

1. The states will not be able to levy special taxes to help in the relief and rehabilitation of people during natural disasters, thereby exposing them to adverse outcomes after such disasters.
2. They will not be able to finance local schemes related to any social or economic issues such as Swachh Bharat and these will be purely planned and financed by the Centre only.
3. Small scale/tribal industries might be destroyed: The states will not be able to protect their own local industries run by tribals, minorities, and other groups with traditional products from manufactured products in other states. This could destroy their small-scale industries.
4. The veto power of the Centre in the GST Council can be used to sideline issues important for the states.

Political Parties under RTI

Background

- A petition by the NGO Association for Democratic Reforms (ADR) had said that political parties should be declared 'public authorities' to bring them under the RTI Act.

- The petition had also urged the court to ask political parties to declare all donations, including those below INR 20,000.
- Thus, the Supreme Court had issued a notice to six national parties, including the BJP and the Congress, asking them why they could not come clean and explain their hesitation to disclose the complete details of their income, expenditure, donations, and funding, including donor details, to the public under the RTI Act.

In June 2013, the Central Information Commission (CIC) deemed national political parties to be 'public authorities' under the RTI Act, to whom the provisions of the Act would now apply.

Need for Political Parties to be Public Authorities

1. Political parties are institutions of public importance as they comprise leaders who are elected by the people. This requires complete transparency and accountability.
2. Public finance is becoming a significant roadblock in achieving the true potential of our democracy. Hence, the funding of political parties must be made public under the RTI.
3. This move will raise the confidence of people in the political leadership, and help in the image makeover of the parties as well.

Unwillingness of Political Parties to Entertain RTI Applications

1. The Union Government (in 2017) conveyed to the Supreme Court that political parties must not be brought under the RTI as they are not public authorities.
2. The nature of funding provided to political parties is mostly opaque.
3. It could lead to the exposure of strategic and tactical information held by political parties for elections and other political work.

Centre's arguments

1. Political parties are not public authorities, as they are not set up under the Constitution or any law enacted by Parliament. Hence, they cannot be treated as an institution or establishment.

2. If political parties come under the RTI, it will affect their smooth internal functioning.
3. Political rivals will start using the RTI instrument with malicious intent.
4. There are already provisions in the Income Tax Act, 1961 and Representation of the People Act, 1951that demand the necessary transparency on the financial aspects of political parties. These mechanisms ensure transparency in the financial dealings of the parties.
5. Information about political bodies is already in the public domain on the website of the Election Commission.
6. It will curb the complete independence and autonomy of political parties, as they will come under the public scanner through the RTI instrument.

The 255th Law Commission Report (Titled 'Electoral Reforms' by Law Commission of India) has attempted to highlight the problems that a democracy has to face because of unregulated funding in elections.

Universal Basic Income

The basic idea of a universal basic income (UBI) is that everybody should be given a basic minimum income as an entitlement and not as compensation for work. In a referendum held in 2016, Switzerland rejected the idea of UBI.

Benefits of UBI

- UBI would help to partly offset the rapid rise in economic inequality observed in recent years.
- As a means of economic safety net, especially during times of recessions the UBI would be the simplest means to support the economically vulnerable sections.
- Robots:
    - o Another point stems from the potential obsolescence of work in a robotized world. As robots take over more and more of the tasks hitherto performed by human beings, robotized production systems will be capable of producing goods of mass consumption on an almost unlimited scale.
    - o On the other hand, human workers no longer required or paid to do most jobs would lack the purchasing power to buy these goods of mass consumption.
    - o If mass consumers lack the purchasing power to buy the goods produced for mass consumption, whether for reasons of income inequality or work obsolescence, then the markets for mass consumer goods will collapse.
    - o The only way out of this impasse of chronic under-consumption is to revisit the link between income and work, hence the UBI.
- Better targeting
    - o According to the Shanta Kumar Committee Report, nearly half the subsidized food grains distributed through the targeted public distribution system (TPDS) for BPL families do not reach the intended beneficiaries.

- o The UBI would completely do away with targeting and all the challenges that come with it.
- o Leakages would also be minimized if UBI is administered using the JAM (Jan Dhan Yojana, Aadhaar, and mobile connectivity) trinity, the IT-enabled technological innovation.
- o The only challenge with UBI is that it would be expensive, as it would entail a large budget. Some studies peg it at as much as 8–10% of GDP. However, the cost can be simultaneously made up for with savings from the leakages in ongoing subsidies.

Lodha Committee Recommendations and the Role of Supreme Court

- o Economic and emotional importance of cricket: Given the level of economic and emotional importance of this game, constant reform is necessary to ensure that it does not become an avenue for corruption.
- o Internal reform not in sight: If internal reform within the BCCI is not in sight, than the government does have a role in ensuring that reforms are put into place.
- o Check oncorruption: The IPL-governing council should appoint a three-member probe panel to look into alleged corruption and match-fixing with two former high court judges on the panel.

Recommendations

1. The radical 'one member, one vote' formula suggests that if a state (such as Maharashtra or Gujarat) has three associations, one of them will have full voting rights, while the other two will be relegated to associate members. The BCCI does not agree with this recommendation.
2. Ministers and bureaucrats will not be allowed to hold positions on the Board, nor will those holding positions in their state associations or those above 70 years of age.
3. The BCCI and IPL should have different and separate governing bodies.
4. There are limits on the term of the BCCI President and their re-appointment as well.
5. The RTI Act should be applicable to the BCCI.

Sports Governance in India

- The sports activities in the country need governance due to the following challenges:
  - o Sexual harassment
  - o Infringement of media ethics

- o Organizational issues
- o Employment issues
- o Sports injuries, with regard to the issues of liability
- o Sports policy with reference to the competition law, etc.
- o Betting

- The National Sports Development Bill, 2013 has been introduced by the government. The impact of the bill needs to be assessed.
- No law school in India consists of sports law as a subject in its curriculum, and there is no specialization course available in the country to train or groom a potential sports lawyer.

Women in Sports

Women's professional sports should be encouraged, promoted, and popularized for the following reasons:

- The probability of India winning at women's world sports events such as the Olympics will improve.
- Sports as an alternative career avenue for women should be encouraged, which will lead to greater participation by women and will raise the quality of women's sports in India.
- Women sports stars can further the cause of the fight against social evils such as female foeticide and dowry system.
- Research papers show that participating in sports lowers stress levels and improves confidence, which can be effective in countering the increasing suicide rates and obesity among urban Indian women.
- Can have a positive spill-over effect for women into other sectors such as the armed forces.

Steps that can be taken to popularize women's games are:

1. Equal remuneration to women and men in sports, as was done in Wimbledon in 2007.
2. Extending the Lodha Panel's recommendation of including women in Player Associations to participate in decision-making for all sports.
3. Obliging sponsors to sign sponsorship deals with both men and women teams as a single unit, especially in cricket, where the asymmetry is high.
4. Comprehensive coverage of women's sports in national channels and disseminating information about women sports stars through interviews, documentaries, etc.
5. Setting up of a Commission to look into cases of asymmetric funding, infrastructural deficiencies, lack of women coaches, etc.

Euthanasia

Euthanasia refers to the painless killing of a patient suffering from an incurable and painful disease or in an irreversible coma. In her book 'A very easy death', Simone de Beauvoir describes the plight of her dying mother in the hospital as 'death by intensive care'. The plight of a dying patient and that of having to decide on whether or not to opt for euthanasia can only be understood by the closest family members, relatives, and friends. Additionally, the debate on euthanasia cuts across various ethical, legal, political, social, and individual human rights. The long vegetative state (42 years) of beloved nurse Aruna Shanbaug and the plight of the Supreme court in allowing euthanasia for her led to the opening of a debate on euthanasia in India. The arguments against this decision were as follows:

a. Neglect of healthcare by state: The Court noted that the provision of euthanasia may encourage or incentivize the state to not take care of critical patients. In fact, in Holland, the legalization of euthanasia has led to a severe decline in the quality of care provided to terminally ill patients.

b. Commercialization of healthcare: The court wisely noted that the life of a person cannot be entrusted in hands of the commercial health sector (doctors), who will not refrain from putting to death many older and disabled patients in hospitals.

c. Malafideintent: Unscrupulous elements in the patient's family or relatives circle may not ethically consider the best alternative for the patient.

d. It is a violation of the constitutional right to life (Article 21).

Thus, active euthanasia has been completely banned in India. The arguments in favour of euthanasia are:

a. The implicit constitutional right to die with dignity.

b. Organ transplantation encouraged: Terminally ill patients may be encouraged to donate their organs, thereby allowing another patient the right to live.

c. The burden of the caregiver: The caregiver must provide every possible treatment regardless of financial, legal, and personal reasons, as it is the only ethical thing to do.

d. Right to refuse care: The right to refuse care is recognized by the law and effectively gives way to passive euthanasia.

Judicial Pronouncements

In the Gian Kaur case (1996), the Supreme Court interpreted the constitutional Article 21'sright to life as a clause that does not include the right to die. In this light, the Supreme Court ruled in 2011 that only passive euthanasia can be administered in India. Passive euthanasia means that only withdrawal of life support or nutrition is allowed, and doctors cannot administer any medicine or drug to actually snuff life out of the patient. Additionally, the family members need to get permission from the relevant High Court. The HC chief justice would form a bench of two judges as well as appoint three reputed doctors to administer such a decision. The doctors must provide a report to the next of kin and the state government in this regard.

Legislative Action

The government has framed a new Passive Euthanasia or Medical Treatment for Terminally-Ill Patients(Protection of Patients and Medical Practitioners) Bill, which allows for a 'living will' or 'advance medical directive' by the patients beforehand in terms of medical treatment when they become ill. A patient (above 16 years of age) will have full authority to refuse medical care to him or herself, and allow nature to take its own course. Information regarding such a decision has to pass on to parents, relatives, friend, etc. by the medical practitioner.

Censorship

India is home to a multitude of views, literature, and a thriving news media and movie industry. Issues regarding the role of the Central Board of Film Certification (CBFC) have emerged recently. The Boardhand lesissues regarding both the constitutional rights as well as the creativity rights of individuals in the nation. One of the issues is that of 'excessive censorship' by the CBFC, which owes its origin to changing societal values. The new generation has an entirely different set of values with respect to marriage, relationships, and openness in public, and so on. For example, the cutting of drug scenes from the movie Udta Punjab has been considered against the Freedom of Speech and Expression as per Article 19 by many. On the other hand, many consider it the government's duty to block any expression that is against the overall welfare of the society.

Merits of Censorship

- The various destabilizing forces at play can be controlled and prevented from creating chaos in the society.
- It ensures that sensitive material about religion is not used to create violence.

Demerits of censorship

- Stifles free speech and expression.
- Takes away the right from individuals to judge opinions on the basis of their own understanding and inclinations.
- Impacts creativity and innovation in society.

Clearly, the demerits of censorship outweigh its merits and suggest that censorship should be minimized altogether. For example, the banning of Talisman Nasreen's book Ko in Bangladesh has effectively suppressed the voice of women's rights in the country. Similarly, many Indian artists have complained of facing harassment during film certification procedures, thereby feeling discouraged.

Way Forward

- As recommended by the Shyam Benegal Committee on film certification, the mandate of the CBFC should be to 'certify' films and not censor or filter them.
- The CBFC should simply recommend certifications such as 'adult', 'suitable for all', etc., and only recommend extreme cases to higher level committees.

Road Safety in India

The road transport sector plays a major role in the economy of the country and bears 75% of the total load of passenger and freight transportation. Its share in the India's GDP is close to 4.5%. Yet, India is a road safety disaster of inhuman proportions. An official report on Road Safety released by the Union Road Transport and Highway Ministry said that 1.46 lakh people lost their lives in road accidents in India in 2015, which is the second highest number in the world. Hence, there is an immediate need for road safety rules.

Group of Ministers (GoM) Recommendations

1. Formation of a National Road Safety and Traffic Management Board that will advice the government on road safety standards and guidelines.
2. Engineering defects in roads should be addressed.
3. There is a need to strengthen the rural transport system, for which the Centre will roll out a scheme.
4. The Central Government would provide 50% funding (rest from the states) to introduce new transport vehicles in the luxury and semi-luxury categories.
5. Transport utilities to be improved, exempting STU (state transport undertaking) buses from taxes and deregulating the luxury segment to shift people from using personal conveyance to using public transport.
6. The issues of hill states to be addressed separately.
7. It seeks to raise the accident insurance cover along with covering property loss as well in the insurance.
8. The mechanism for helping accident victims needs improvement, along with trauma care facilities, by launching a comprehensive scheme.
9. To liberalize intra-city taxi permits and other automobile aggregation policies, such as improving parking facilities for taxis and other public transport vehicles.
10. Steps to promote low-cost last mile connectivity solutions and barrier-free movement of freight transport across the states.

As a signatory to the Brasilia Declaration on Road Safety, India is committed to reducing the number of road accidents and fatalities by 50% by 2020.

Good Samaritan Guidelines in Save LIFE Foundation PIL

1. The Good Samaritan will be treated respectfully and without any discrimination on the grounds of gender, religion, nationality, and caste.
2. Any individual, except an eyewitness, who calls the police to inform them of an accidental injury or death, need not reveal their personal details such as full name, address, or phone number.
3. The police will not compel the Good Samaritan to disclose his or her name, identity, address, and other such details in the police record form or log register.

4. The police will not force any Good Samaritan while procuring information or anything else.
5. The police will allow the Good Samaritan to leave after having provided the information available to them and no further questions will be asked of them if they do not desire to be a witness.

Even when Good Samaritans agree to become witnesses, the guidelines accord them protection and comfort. They ensure that:

1. If a Good Samaritan chooses to be a witness, they will be examined with utmost care and respect.
2. The examination will be conducted at the time and place of the Good Samaritan's convenience and the investigation officer will be dressed in plain clothes.
3. If the Good Samaritan is required by the investigation officer to visit the police station, the reasons for the requirement shall be recorded by the officer in writing.
4. In a police station, the Good Samaritan will be examined in a single examination in a reasonable and time-bound manner, without causing any undue delay.
5. If a Good Samaritan declares himself/herself to be an eyewitness, they will be allowed to give their evidence in the form of an affidavit.

Defamation as Criminal offence

"I may not agree with what you have to say, but I will defend to death your right to say it"
— Evelyn Beatrice

Free speech and expression forms the very foundation of any liberal, progressive democracy. The provision of Article 19(1) in the Constitution highlights the wisdom and foresight of our constitution-makers in regards to the concern of free speech. However, the presence of a draconian provision of the IPC (Section 499: Defamation as a Criminal Offence) has led to much uneasiness in the society regarding the ability to speak, dissent, and disagree without the fear of criminal charges. The recent Supreme Court judgment that upheld the criminal nature of defamation opens up a Pandora's Box in this debate. The Court has upheld Sections 499/500 and 199(2) of the IPC.

Significance of Freedom of Speech and Expression

1. Freedom of Speech and Expression: The status of defamation as a criminal offence as per Sections499 and 500 of the IPC leads to the suppression of the freedom of speech and expression guaranteed by Article 19 of the Constitution.
2. Speech and expression are the very fundamentals of a liberal democracy, and without these rights democracy cannot be achieved as a whole.
3. Self-censorship is also a regressive outcome of these sections, as it renders individuals afraid of pursuing free speech without fear of criminal prosecution.

4. Misused by large corporates and powerful individuals: Due to the high legal costs and complex legal mechanisms involved, it is frequently used by powerful individuals and organizations to stifle dissent, disagreement, and sometimes even open reporting against them.
5. Historical burden: India continues to carry the burden of Sections 499 and 500 of Lord Macaulay's Indian Penal Code of 1860, which prescribes two years' punishment in case of defamation.
6. Outlawed elsewhere: No other modern democracy prescribes defamation as a criminal offence anymore. This statute has already been outlawed in most of the progressive democracies in the West as well as in countries such as Sri Lanka.

Judicial Pronouncement

The Supreme Court has upheld defamation as a criminal offence. It has observed the following:

1. "Mutual respect is the fulcrum of fraternity that assures dignity. It does not mean that there cannot be dissent."
2. Article 21: The right to reputation is also a constituent of Article 21.
3. Free speech not absolute: Free speech cannot be used by media to injure an individual's reputation; free speech is a "highly valued and cherished right."
4. While free press is the heart and soul of political intercourse and is a public educator, an individual's reputation is precious and cannot be maligned by the media.
5. Role of media as a "public educator": Media to act like a "public educator" and make formal and non-formal education possible at a large scale, particularly in a developing country like India.
6. Hence, the press must observe "reasonable restrictions" and play its role of "advancing public interest by publishing facts and opinions without which a democratic electorate cannot make responsible judgments."

The court provided two different strokes on the issue of free speech. In the first, it regards the "freedom of speech and expression as the first condition of liberty."In the other, it reins in this liberty by cautioning that free speech is "not an absolute value under our constitution." It also says that voice of dissent or disagreement has to be regarded and respected and not to be stifled as "unpalatable criticism."The Court also referred to defamation as a "crime against the society, and not just an individual."

The advocates of making the right to free speech absolute by removing the criminal aspect from defamation argue that this ruling makes free speech difficult and suppresses it effectively due to the threat of prosecution. They say that labeling defamation as criminal has a chilling effect on the press.

Sedition (IPC Section 124A)

Gandhiji described sedition law as the prince of the Indian Penal Code. It was used freely against our freedom fighters in an attempt to muzzle their anti-colonial writings, speeches, and voices.

No fundamental right in our Constitution is absolute. Freedom of speech and expression guaranteed by Article 19(1) (a) can be reasonably restricted on the grounds specified in Article 19(2).

It is notable that during constituent assembly debates, our founding fathers deleted "sedition" as a permissible ground of restriction under Article 19(2) on freedom of speech. However, it remains a criminal offence under IPC section 124A and provides for inter alia sentence of life imprisonment and fine upon conviction.

In Kedarnath vs. State of Bihar, the Supreme Court opined that vigorous words in writing and very strong criticism of the measures of the government or of the acts of public officials would be outside the scope of Section 124A.

Recent invocations of sedition law:

- Amnesty International.
- Actor-politician Divya Spandana faced sedition charges for her comments about Pakistan in2016.

Stringent fines are applicable on those, including lawyers, who invoke Section 124A casually for trivial cases.

Need for sedition law

Ours is still an evolving democracy with multitudes of ethnic, linguistic, and communal problems faced regularly by us. In this sense, sedition law is necessary to curtail speeches that can lead to public violence and disorder.

Disadvantages of sedition law

1. It effectively silences many authors and thinkers to present honest critiques about the government.
2. It insulates the government from healthy discussion, criticism, and feedback from the citizens.
3. It creates fear among people to present their view.
4. It renders the constitutional right of speech and expression powerless (Article 19).
5. It raises questions on the moral duties of the State to protect citizens instead of silencing them.
6. It is against India's commitment to enhancing human rights (which includes freedom of speech and expression) in international forums such as the UN Human Rights Commission.

Bonded Labour

Bonded labour, also informally known as bandhua mazdoori, has been a long-standing problem in India. Bonded labour are persons who have 'pledged' their labour and services as security for repayment of debt or other obligations. Many times, the children of bonded labour are forced into the bonded labourship if they are not able to repay their debt. Bonded labour is also referred to as debt bondage or debt slavery. Due to the heavy nature of debt, these persons effectively become the 'property' of the moneylenders or persons of influence. The bonded labour system is a social evil and exists in India despite constitutional provisions for its total eradication. The system is used for

- Providing cheap domestic labour to rich households in rural and urban areas.
- Using cheap bonded labour to work in factories producing cheap goods for international markets. Hence, bonded labour even becomes part of the worldwide supply chain.
- Bonded labour is also a means to attain societal power in rural areas through ownership of a large number of bonded labour by large landowners and people of influence.
- Caste dynamics

The International Labour Organization (ILO) has pointed out various obstacles in the path of removing bonded labour in India. These are as follows:

- Large numbers of bonded labours are Dalit in India. Hence caste rigidity and rules play a significant role in perpetrating bonded labour.
- The Dalit face other social problems such as boycott, rape, arson, robbery, etc. if they resist bonded labour.
- Extreme poverty also forces bonded labour on poor people.
- Direct or indirect involvement of private companies, as they use bonded labour to produce goods at cheap rates.

Action by Government, NGOs, and other organizations

- The Bonded Labour System (Abolition) [BLS (A)] Act, 1976 was enacted to completely outlaw this practice. The Act provides a vigilance committee at the district and sub-divisional levels in each state and Union Territory for identification, release, and rehabilitation.
- The Bandhua Mukti Morcha (BMM, an NGO) has worked closely with international and national organizations to eradicate bonded labour in India.
- Human Rights watch (another NGO) has launched various programmes in India to eradicate bonded labour in the silk industry.
- The ILO and UN have passed legislations against bonded labour.
- The Rehabilitation Scheme of 1978 has been able to free 2.82 lakh bonded labourers in 18 states comprising172 districts in the country during the past 38 years.

The Rehabilitation of Bonded Labour Scheme for bonded labour is taking the following initiatives:

1. It is making bonded labour rehabilitation a centrally sponsored scheme.
2. It proposes to increase the budget provision from INR5 crore to about INR47 crore per annum.

3. It aims to raise financial assistance to bonded labour of INR 20,000–1 lakh each.
4. The most deprived and marginalized, such as the disabled, women, children rescued from trafficking, sexually exploited, and transgender, will get higher funds.
5. It is addressing new forms of bondage such as organized begging rings, forced prostitution, and child labour, for which women, disabled persons, and transgenders are exploited.

Human Rights Institutions in India

According to the Principles Relating to the Status of National Institutions (Paris Principles, 1993), which serve as an international benchmark, independence from the government is one of the most crucial elements in building effective human rights institutions. This principle is seriously undermined whenever there is political interference in appointments and whenever the tenure and stability of these institutions is subject to the whims and fancies of the government.

The Judiciary has played its part well by revoking such arbitrary appointments, but now it is for the government to demonstrate its willingness to establish strong and independent institutions according to the rule of law.

1. National Human Rights Commission of India (NHRC)
2. National Commission for Protection of Children's Rights
3. National Disaster Management Committee
4. National Commission for Women

The problems related to the involvement of the government in appointments are as follows:

- Political parties appoint people known to them instead of merit, thereby promoting nepotism (selection on political grounds).Hence, the selection process remains opaque.
- During change of government, heads and members are removed, again based on personal agenda instead of merit.

Capital Punishment

Capital Punishment has been at the centre of the human rights debate for long. It has been practised since the dawn of civilization in the world to punish those charged with heinous crimes such as murder.

In India, capital punishment was officially recognized and codified by the British during the colonial period. It has been awarded post-independence as well, but with high caution. Even the Supreme Court has declared the 'rarest of the rare 'doctrine in the Bachan Singh case, to be considered when sentencing a criminal to capital punishment.

The 262nd Law Commission report titled 'Capital Punishment' has provided many arguments for and against capital punishment. They are as follows.

Arguments for Capital Punishment

- It deters extreme crimes.
- It keeps the society together by producing a fear of the law.
- It puts a criminal to justice in the eyes of the victim's family, which is important for their psychological being.
- It is a must to counter new problems such as terrorism.
- It is too expensive for a justice system to keep a serious criminal under bars.

Arguments against Capital Punishment

- It is against the modern principles of liberalism and humanism.
- The primary aim of the justice system is reform and not punishment. Capital punishment does not give any chance to the criminal to reform himself.
- It is practised in inhuman ways such as hanging and poisoning and even stoning to death in many societies, which is regressive.
- It does not have a place in a democratic and forward-looking society such as ours.

The human rights group, Amnesty International, has published a new report on the number of death penalty executions across the world. At least 1,634 people were executed last year, an increase of more than 50% with respect to 2014.

Family Law Reforms

Indian society is highly complex due to diversity of religions, castes and sub-castes, gender-related issues, and the coming of modern ideals of equality, liberty, and fraternity since Independence. In this respect, various communities (religious and caste) follow different customary family laws that often collide against the constitutional and legal rights of individuals.

A government-appointed high-level panel gave suggestions related to family reforms. A panel was formed for the review of women and family laws with respect to marriage, divorce, custody, inheritance, and succession. The suggestions made by the Panel are as follows:

1. The IPC on adultery (Section 497) should be amended—currently it can only be used by the husband against the person who has sexual relations with his wife.
2. Removing the gender discrimination inherent in laws that stipulate a lower legal age of marriage for a girl.
3. Ban on triple talaq and polygamy.
4. Right to maintenance for Muslim women as well as for women in live-in relationships and unmarried dependent daughters.
5. Introduction of a separate legislation for dealing with honour killings.
6. Amendment of the Special Marriages Act—the 30-day public notice enforceable under the Act should be done away with to protect couples marrying against the wishes of their parents.

7. The term 'cruelty' also needs to be redefined, since personal laws recognize cruelty as a ground for divorce.

Need for reform

1. To implement the Uniform Civil Code in India as envisioned in Article 44 of the Constitution.
2. To remove the implicit gender biases in the personal laws of various religions.
3. To create peaceful conditions for people to marry according to their choice and prevent them from societal pressure as is practised among the Khaps.
4. To help in improving the condition of women and their empowerment in the patriarchal society of India.

Minority Institutions in a Secular Country

Minority communities are communities that have a small population in the country but with a distinctive cultural, linguistic, or religious identity. For example, the National Commission for Minorities has identified Muslims, Janis, Buddhists, and other such communities as minorities in India.

Reasons for Establishment of Minority Institutions

1. Constitutional provisions: Article 30(1) provides for setting up of minority institutions and Article 30(2) provides for non-discrimination of the State in providing aid.
2. Supreme Court ruling: In the TMA Pai Foundation case, the SC has noted that institutions such as Aligarh Muslim University (AMU) have been involved in commendable work in social sciences and imparting education to Muslim youth, which can be considered as charitable work.
3. Preservation of minority beliefs, languages, literature, architecture, arts, traditions, and culture
4. Promotion of education among minorities, especially women
5. Promotion of secular ethics

Even the Sachar Committee report has encouraged the states' participation in ensuring that minority institutions are well-funded.

Judicial Pronouncement

On 10 June 2016, the Kerala High Court, in a remarkable verdict, ruled that Section 16 of the Right of Children to Free and Compulsory Education Act, 2009 (RTE Act), which mandates schools to not detain any child before s/he completes elementary education, is applicable to minority educational institutions as well (Sobha George v. State of Kerala). The Supreme Court has exempted minority schools from the purview of the RTE Act in Pramati Education and Cultural Trust v. Union of India (2014). The High Court located this obligation not in the Act but under Article 21 of the Indian Constitution, which guarantees right to life and liberty. It ruled that the no-detention policy (NDP) is in the "best interest" of the child and could independently be considered a fundamental right. How does this judgment redraw the lines of engagement between minority rights and rights to education? While this judgment is indeed innovative, is it necessarily good?

RTE Act and minority rights

Article 21A recognizes the right of all children aged between 6 and 14 to free and compulsory elementary education. The RTE Act operationalizes this right by elucidating supporting rights, identifying the duty-bearers, and establishing administrative structures to enforce these rights. The generic scope of the right to education seems to conflict with the specific contexts of the rights of minorities to establish and administer educational institutions of their choice under Article 30. That right, however, is not absolute. The freedom to 'administer' a school cannot include 'mal-administering' it. Regulations for maintaining academic standards, ensuring proper infrastructure, health and sanitation, etc. could be imposed on minority schools as well. Further, a government-aided minority school cannot discriminate against students on the grounds of religion, race, caste, and language in the matters of their admission [Article 29(2)].

The Pramati judgment was erroneous on two counts. First, it failed to notice that besides the 25% quota in Section 12(1) (c), the RTE Act also has provisions on infrastructural norms, pupil-teacher ratio, prohibition on screening tests and capitation fee, and ban on corporal punishment. Far from annihilating the 'minority character', these provisions benefit both the students and the community. Second, it did not consider the fact that government-aided minority schools stand on a different footing from their unaided counterparts and are more amenable to regulations than the latter.

Earlier, the Karnataka High Court refused to apply NDP to minority schools as it rightly considered itself bound by the Pramati judgment. Interestingly, the Kerala High Court, while it began with the same premise, ended up with the opposite result! The significance of the Sobha George verdict, therefore, lies not only in making certain provision of the RTE Act applicable to minority schools but also in the strategy employed for this. The courts reasons: "... RTE Act has no application in a minority school, whether aided or unaided. However, the Court has to examine whether Section 16 of RTE Act is a mere statutory right or can be treated as a fundamental right expressed in the form of statutory provision."

A key take away from this judgment is the recognition that certain provisions of the RTE Act have a universal appeal, even if the Act lacks it. However, it is completely within judicial discretion to determine which provisions are these. Prior to Pramati, the courts had consistently upheld those regulations that do not annihilate the 'minority character' of the school and would actually serve the interests of students and the community. As the RTE Act and rules incorporated a substantial part of these regulations, the Pramati judgment practically forecloses this line of reasoning.

A question of a clear law

While the Sobha George judgment opens possibilities of applying different provisions of the RTE Act on minority schools through the Article 21 route, it simultaneously forces a rethink on the role of judicial precedents. In the contrasting judgments of two high courts on the same issue while ostensibly paying allegiance to the same Supreme Court precedent, one could notice a snowballing effect. This makes the overall position of law unclear, arising from an erroneous opinion by the highest court. Besides fairness, certainty and stability are essential values underpinning the rule of law.

In Common Law, a lower or a latter court cannot displace the judgment given by a higher or a prior court merely because it has a different perspective. This is what makes that judgment 'binding'. However, a lower court may distinguish its case from the higher court on material facts; the latter judge could do that or, if there are compelling reasons, overrule the prior judgment of the same court.

The question here is not only about NDP. A number of studies have documented the effects of detention on the psyche of young children. The issue is the obligation of the superior court in laying down a clear binding law for all subordinate courts. The Sobha George case may immediately benefit thousands of children in Kerala, yet conflicting judgments adversely affect the realization of rights of all children equally. A 'constitutionally permissible balance' between the right to education and minority rights requires an interpretation that makes them mutually reinforcing rather than irreconcilable.

It is hoped that the Supreme Court (a) re-examines the positive (establishing and administering educational institutions for the welfare of minorities) and the negative (protection against imposition of majority language or culture) aspects of the educational rights of minorities and (b) appreciates the special case for guaranteeing the right to elementary education universally and equitably.

The problem with a judgment like Pramati is that for the issues it addresses, it either can overstay or is overruled.

Further Insights on the Shobha George Case

The Kerala High Court in 2016ruled that the "no detention policy" envisaged under the RTE Act should be applicable to minority run schools as well. The reasoning is that this policy is consistent with right to life under Article 21, as it is in the "best interest" of the child (Sobha George case). The key take away from this judgment is that some provisions of the RTE have a universal appeal and cannot be denied, as they directly fulfill fundamental rights. This runs contradictory to the Pramati judgment of the Supreme Court, in which it ruled that minority institutions are exempt from following the RTE guidelines.

The Pramati judgment is flawed because the RTE Act has some universal provisions on infrastructural norms, pupil-teacher ratio, etc., which are absolutely necessary for good education of children and cannot be exempt for even minority institutions. The universally applicable provisions of the RTE are the following:

- Article 29(2): A government-aided minority school cannot discriminate against students on the grounds of religion, race, caste, and language in the matter of admission.
- Article 21A: Making education a fundamental right in the Indian constitution.

The conflicting provisions of the RTE are as follows:

1. Cultural Trust v. Union of India (2014) and the Pramati judgment: The SC had exempted minority schools from the purview of the RTE Act.
2. No-detention policy (NDP): The obligations not in the Act but under Article 21 of the Indian Constitution and in the "best interest" of the child could independently be considered as fundamental rights.
3. Rights of minorities: The RTE conflicts with Article 30, with the specific contexts of the rights of minorities to establish and administer the educational institutions of their choice. However, it is not absolute and not misadministration. So RTE can be enforced.

A 'constitutionally permissible balance' between the right to education and minority rights is required to interpret the conflicting judgments—Sobha George and Pramati—an interpretation that makes them mutually reinforcing rather than irreconcilable.

The Pramati judgment has excluded some of the RTE provisions from application to minority schools.

RBI Governor: Appointment and Responsibilities

Appointment:

According to the RBI Act, 1935, the RBI governor is appointed by an Appointment Commission in consultation with the Prime Minister, Finance ministry, and the outgoing RBI governor. The tenure of the RBI governor is not more than 5 years. However, the tenure can be extended in certain circumstances. The powers vested with an RBI governor are as follows:

1. Since they are the head of the RBI, they play an important role in formulating RBI policies.
2. The governor regulates the interest rates on the deposits and borrowings.
3. The Foreign Exchange Management Act, 1999 is managed by the governor.
4. Since they are the banker of bankers, their decisions have the power to influence both the macro- and microeconomics enormously.
5. The stock market, the economy, and the lives of people are impacted by the governor's actions.
6. The RBI governor controls financial institutions such as SEBI and NABARD.
7. The governor's autograph appears on currency notes.

Responsibilities

1. Issuing licenses to establish new private and foreign banks.
2. Regulating the financial system of the country.

3. Monitoring the issue and destruction of currency and coins that are not fit for circulation in the public.
4. Controlling the country's monetary, currency, and credit system.

LGBT Issues

In July 2009, the Delhi High Court, recognizing the inherent injustice in the operation of Section 377, rendered a momentous verdict and found that the law, in persecuting a community purely based on the sexual orientation of its members, was patently opposed to the Constitution's essential promises. However, just over four years later, in Suresh Kumar Koushal vs. Naz Foundation, the Supreme Court reversed this finding.

Section 377, at its core, is an intention to enforce a decree against actions that are professed to be beyond the warrants of society's moral compass. Only, that in the case of criminalising homosexuality, it is the outlawing of the act that is immoral, and not the act itself. As the American philosopher Martha Nussbaum has argued, the Supreme Court's verdict in Koushal shows us that there is an almost pathological emotion of disgust at the heart of any perceived rationale for criminalizing homosexuality, when such acts cause no actual harm to any person whatsoever.

It is undeniable that a society's moral judgment must play some role in determining the extent of its criminal laws. However, "a conscientious legislator who is told a moral consensus exists," as the legal philosopher Ronald Dworkin once wrote, "must test the credentials of that consensus." The community's moral standards cannot thus be arbitrarily gleaned nor be a product simply of inexplicable revulsion and disgust. (The Hindu, 'To be equal before the law', 2016)

In the case of Section 377, any reasonable analysis would show us that to regard homosexual activity as somehow immoral violates the innate natural autonomy that every person has over his or her respective sexuality.

Armed Forces Special Powers Act

The Armed Forces Special Powers Act (AFSPA), 1958 comes into play when the government declares a particular part of NE or J&K as a 'disturbed area'.

Arguments Against the AFSPA

- It is against Article 3 (right to life) of the UN Declaration on Human Rights and also against the United Nations Convention on Human Rights, of which India is a signatory.
- It is a draconian law in our progressive society:
  - o AFSPA has been questioned largely because of the numerous human rights violations due to its draconian provisions.
  - o Section 6 of the Act says that a government officer cannot be prosecuted unless a previous sanction from the government is sought.
  - o It also enables the armed forces to fire upon or use force against any person acting against the law.

Arguments in Favour

- National security in disturbed areas: Areas of J&K and North East are highly disturbed and harbour terrorist, criminal, and secessionist groups that impact the security of these regions and the rest of India.
- Effective operation of the armed forces is only possible due to the provisions of this Act.

The government has made clear that security forces must fire only after they are clearly convinced of weapons or explosives in the hands of the other party. The B.P. Jeevan Reddy Committee has recommended that Section 6 of the AFSPA be amended.

Supreme Court Order on AFSPA

This SC order concerns the applicability of the law and immunities accorded to the armed forces personnel.

1. War

First, it is extremely significant that the Court does not agree with the argument that a law and order situation, or sustained disturbance in any area, gives rise to a situation of 'war'.

a. It categorically states that any military intervention under the proclamation that a particular area is 'disturbed' must be to supplement and help restore civil authority, and not to supplant the same completely by military administration.

b. Within the territory of the country, a constitutional government and its authority must always be the norm, and any deviation from the same cannot be unlimited, either in scope or time.

c. It is especially noticed by the court that Manipur, with the exception of the Imphal municipal area, has been constantly notified as a disturbed area since 1958. This fact signifies best that military deployment (under the guise of the Disturbed Areas Act) and immunity (under the AFSPA) often become so intertwined with the notions of order that they become permanent features of governance themselves, and not the means to an end.

2. Excessive Use of Force:

a. In all the cases of killings looked into by the Court, the shootings by military forces were not genuine and the use of force had been excessive.

b. Indeed, this is the main crux of the argument against the AFSPA, that it encourages a disregard for legal processes such as arrest and detention in favour of the use of brute force and extra-judicial executions.

3. Treatment of Indian Citizens:

a. The Supreme Court in the present case has reiterated that there is a difference in the manner in which a person who violates an order in force in a disturbed area should be treated as compared to an enemy combatant belonging to a hostile country.

b. The fact that an Indian citizen is violating a prohibitory order in a disturbed area does not give rise to an automatic right to the security forces to treat him with force or to assume that he constitutes an enemy in that situation.

c. The Court looks at the methods of practice prescribed by the army itself and states that the use of force and especially excessive and retaliatory force on citizens is unjustified.

4. **Enquiry needed in case of actions under AFSPA:**

a. Finally, the court also holds that in cases where the use of force is excessive or the encounter itself not genuine, there is nothing that precludes a criminal investigation and inquiry under ordinary criminal law.

b. Both the Army Act and the Code of Criminal Procedure (CrPC) allow for an inquiry to be conducted before a judicial magistrate for crimes committed by armed forces personnel while on duty.

The order, which will be one in a series of orders to come, as more cases being investigated reach their conclusions, has shown a much needed light on the dark underbelly of the operation of the AFSPA in several parts of the country and the effects it has had on governance and civil liberties. It is a welcome step in extending the rule of law and fundamental rights to an area where it has been much needed for decades.

Disabled People—Supreme Court's Actions

The SC's judgment along with strict implementation guidelines will certainly empower the disabled, but it needs to be examined how and in what way it would affect their condition.

SC Directives

1. 3% government jobs for disabled: Employment is a key factor in helping the disabled become self-dependent and overcome marginalization.
2. No applicability of 50% cap: This guideline would allow the state government flexibility in planning the quota accordingly.
3. Group A and Group B inclusion in reservation: The government has created a distinction between posts, and the disabled do not gain entry to Group A; however, now onwards, getting entry via direct recruitment and promotion and is considered illegal and inconsistent with the Persons with Disabilities Act of 1995 by the SC.

Challenges to overcome

1. Social barriers: Disabled people are out of jobs not because of their disability but due to the social and practical barriers that prevent them from joining the workforce. So a reservation of 3% alone may not help.

2. Identifying the right post: Although the SC has directed that the appropriate posts be identified, there have been recent cases of people selected as junior engineering candidates doing the job of sweepers.
3. Failure of the Centre and states: The Centre and states have failed to provide reservation to the blind and low-vision persons in the past. Enforcing guidelines may not have the desired impact due to the slow action of law proceedings.
4. Dignity at work: Even selected candidates may face discrimination, and workplaces rules and law creation hold significance.

Right to Privacy

The right to privacy also includes Declaration of Assets and Liabilities by Public Servants under Section 44. The question of pertinence is: Does the declaration of assets violate the right to privacy?

1. The Lokpal Act has been amended to put on hold the declaration of the assets of the spouses and kin of public servants, which includes NGO chiefs as well.
2. The United Nations Convention against Corruption (UNCAC), to which India is a signatory, requires a legal framework for the declaration of the assets of government officials.
3. Transparency International India also says that compulsory disclosure of assets by government employees is not a violation of individual privacy, since there is a direct link between the income/salary and the assets declared. Transparency International Report ranked India at 76 out of 168 countries in its latest Corruption Perception Index.
4. Also, the Supreme Court has declared in the PUCL judgment that in case of conflict between right to privacy and right to information in public interest, the latter would take precedence over the former.

JUSTICE J.S. VERMA COMMITTEE

The Justice Verma Committee was set up after the Nirbhaya rape case in Delhi. The important recommendations of the Committee are as follows:

1. Rape:

i. Retain rape as a separate offence and modify the definition of rape as any non-consensual penetration of sexual nature.

ii. Include marital rape in the definition of rape.

iii. Set up a rape crisis cell that will be notified about any FIR related to a sexual offence and will provide legal assistance to the victims.

2. **Offences against women in conflict areas:**
    i. Remove the requirement for Central Government sanction in the cases of alleged sexual offence.
    ii. Appoint commissioners in conflict areas to monitor and prosecute officials found guilty of sexual offences.
    iii. Reorient army training to inculcate strict observance in this regard.

3. **Police reforms:**
    i. Establish state security commissions to protect state police from any interference by state governments.
    ii. Police stations should have CCTV cameras in the entrance and questioning rooms.

4. **Electoral reforms:**
    i. Amend the Representation of the People Act to include sexual offences as the basis for disqualification of any candidate.
    ii. Sitting members of the Parliament with sexual offence cases booked against them must step down.

5. **Education reforms:**
    i. Sexual education should be imparted in schools, as it will make children more aware.
    ii. Adult literacy programmes should be conducted, which will lead to gender empowerment.

6. **Judicial and Other Reforms:**
    i. The number of judges should be increased with due consideration to quality.
    ii. All marriages should be registered and dowry transactions stopped.
    iii A new medical protocol must be suggested for rape victims, and the laws should cover sexual minorities.
    iv. Crackdown on the unconstitutional Khap panchayats from acting as a parallel legal system.
    v. Travelling in public transport should be made safer, especially for women.

A change in the existing patriarchal attitude is also the need of the hour. There should be a change in the way society looks upon women. Community awareness programmes and educating people on these issues will help a lot in raising the status of women in the society.

PCPNDT Act

The Pre-Conception and Pre-Natal Diagnostic Techniques (Prohibition of Sex Selection) (PCPNDT) Act, 1994 applied a blanket ban on pre-natal sex determination. This was done to:

- Stop female foeticides
- Arrest the declining sex ratio

Child sex ratio has declined from 927 in 2001 to 914 in 2011, showcasing how the implementation of this Act has not helped in the reduction of female foeticide.

Objectives

- Prohibition of sex selection techniques before or after conception.
- Regulation of pre-natal diagnostic techniques for detecting genetic, metabolic, or congenital malformations or sex-linked disorders.
- Prevention of the misuse of such techniques for the purpose of sex determination of the foetus.

Reasons for Failure of the Act

- Women are not aware of their rights under the Act.
- There is a gap between the availability of funds and their effective utilization.
- Incomplete paperwork related to the Act from clinic records, case-related documents, etc.
- Inadequate monitoring of clinics, as most of the states do not have detailed plans for strict implementation.
- Lack of witnesses and insufficient evidences, thereby resulting in low conviction rates.

However, the ban should not be lifted, as it will act as a deterrence for the doctor and he/she will not indulge himself in any wrongdoing. The onus to safeguard the foetus will then be on the mother. Further, there should be a ban on sex selection advertisements, easy detection of sex-linked disorders, congenital malformations, etc.

Way forward

- The government should provide financial support to the states and UTs for operationalization of the PNDT cells, capacity building, sensitization workshops, etc.
- Information, education, and communication campaigns and strengthening the structures for the implementation of the PCPNDT Act.
- The states should focus on districts/blocks/villages with low child sex ratio to ascertain the causes and to plan appropriate behavioural changes.
- Mobilize civil society as agents of change as well as community-level watchdogs of malpractices.

Forest Rights Act, 2006 and related Issues

The Forest Rights Act (FRA), 2006 provides the right to tribal communities for governing, using, and conserving their local forest resources and land through the provision of gram Sabhas. It provides:

a. Title rights, which cannot be reversed once given to tribals

b. Use rights

c. Relief and developmental rights

d. Forest management rights

However, this Act has been poorly implemented and enforced, and many tribal communities have faced alienation from their own land and forest resources. For example, the acquisition of traditional lands in Ghatbarra village in Chhattisgarh.

Veto by tribal gram panchayats

In May 2016, five tribal villages in Raigarh, Chhattisgarh, unanimously vetoed the plans of South Eastern Coalfields Limited (SECL), a subsidiary of Coal India Limited, to mine their forests. On similar lines, some more tribal villages in Odisha also decided not to award land to the Rungta Mines project.

Judicial Action

The NGT ruled that before constructing the hydroelectric project, the Himachal Power Corporation should place the necessary approvals before the Lippa village gram Sabha in Kinnaur. The Supreme Court also ruled in May 2016 that the Odisha Mining Corporation must seek the permission of the gram Sabhas for the mining proposal in Niyamgiri hills. Similarly, for the Vedanta mining project, permission was to be sought from the Dongaria Kondh tribe.

Provisions of the Act

- The Act provides the forest tribal communities the right to govern, use, and conserve forests through gram Sabhas.
- The process of recognition of rights needs screening and approval at the taluka level and then at the district level as well.

Some negative developments

The Maharashtra state government passed regulations that ensured that the forest department retained control over forest management, which includes the large-scale trade and sale of forest produce. Similar rules were also notified by the Madhya Pradesh government. This has posed a threat to the empowering provisions of the FRA.

UN provisions

The UN Declaration of Rights of the Indigenous People also highlights the principle of 'free and prior informed consent' enshrined in its international agreements.

Street Dog Menace

20 million people get bitten by stray dogs every year in India, and over 20,000 die of rabies every year—many of these are children, old people, and women. A large number of vehicle accidents can also be attributed to street dogs. It is estimated that there are over 50 million dogs on the roads in India, and it is financially very difficult to sterilize all of them.

Legislation

The Ministry of Culture issued Animal Birth Control Rules (ABC Rules) under the Prevention of Cruelty on Animals (PCA) Act, 1960. According to these rules, sterilization must be used to control the dog population on the streets. The other rules of the PCA Act are self-contradictory; for example, there is no guideline on how to treat dogs captured by municipalities. The Act also does not classify dogs as either wildlife or domesticated animals. Further, the rules also forbid euthanizing of rabid dogs. Internationally, dogs are routinely euthanized. The Humane Society of the United States euthanized 3.4 million stray dogs and cats. In UK, a dog that is considered dangerous can be 'destroyed'.

Budgeting in India—Constitutional Provisions

The 'budget' was first introduced in India in 1860 during the colonial rule. Later on, after Independence, provisions relating to the budget were included in the Constitution. Some features of the budget are as follows:

1. On the President's recommendation [Articles 117(1) and 117(3)], the finance minister lays down the budget before the Parliament for its approval, as the Parliament is the sole authority on the finances of the country. It legislates the taxes to be levied (Article 265) and authorizes expenditure from the consolidated fund of India (Article 266).
2. The Budget, which is referred to as the 'Annual Financial Statement' in the Constitution (Article 112), provides a statement of estimated receipts and expenditure for the financial year fewer than three accounts—Consolidated Fund of India, Contingency Fund of India, and Public Accounts.
3. The Budget consists of two parts—revenue budget and capital budget. The revenue budget covers the proceeds of taxes, interests, and dividends on investments made by the government, and the fees and other receipts for services rendered by the government. The capital budget gives details for capital receipts and payments, including loans from the public and borrowings from the Reserve Bank.

Demand for Grants

The expenditure estimates from the consolidated fund are voted for by the Lok Sabha in the form of Demand for Grants, which are arranged ministry-wise (Article 113).

Appropriation Bill

It is introduced to give authority to the government to appropriate monies out of the consolidated fund to incur expenditure.

Finance Bill

It is a money bill and is introduced along with the budget. It provides for imposition, abolition, remission, alteration, or regulation of the taxes proposed in the budget.

Vote on account, vote of credit, and exceptional grant

A vote on account deals with expenditure pending the passing of the Demand for Grants and the appropriation bill. The Lok Sabha makes grants in advance to authorize the withdrawal of money for such a period (Article 116). The vote of credit refers to the grants that the Lok Sabha makes for meeting unexpected demands.

Fiscal Responsibility and Budget Management Act, 2003

This Act was enacted to ensure that governments follow fiscal discipline. It mandates the laying down of certain additional documents relating to fiscal policy during budget presentation.

Private Distribution of Public Services

Cash transfers or 'cash relief' during famines may work better than arranging other means of relief, as it is quick (speed matters during famines) and can lead to people acquiring the goods they need to survive quickly. However, this also has the potential of leading to the creation of a monopoly of traders, hence artificially controlling the prices and defeating the purpose of such relief. The same is true for disposal of cash wages, as is done under the MGNREGA (Mahatma Gandhi National Rural Employment Guarantee Act).

Asymmetric Information

These arrangements of private distribution may not work in the case of healthcare, education, sanitation, immunization, etc. This is because of the presence of asymmetric information, for example, between patients who may know a little about the treatment they need or are given and doctors who may know much more. Here, this asymmetric information leads to the failure of the market model.

Externalities

Externalities refer to __. Examples of externalities are those associated with communicable diseases and public health—the difference between social benefits and costs is pretty large in such cases.

Inequitable Distribution

When direct cash transfers are provided for the various services, the supply side may sideline the poor. Such services need to be managed effectively on the supply side.

Consumer Sovereignty

The Liberals argue that consumers are the best judges of what they need. However, this may not be true for many people, as they may not be educated or aware about the outcomes of the various decisions in their lives. Their decisions may also get affected by aggressive advertising, herd behaviour, misplaced optimism, procrastination, and other psychological factors. For example, the government passed the IMS Act to control the marketing of infant food supplements below the age of 2 years for infants.

Case of Latin America

Cash transfers in Brazil and Mexico do not act as substitutes, but as complements for the public provision of health, education, and other basic services. Hence, cash transfers must not be treated as a golden cure for all the public programmes. Basic services in health, education, immunization, etc. are needed to make the cash transfers work.

Inquiries on Civil Servants

When civil servants are inquired upon and consequently transferred as a result of his/her superiors not being comfortable with his/her initiatives or there being disagreement between the two, the officer is impacted as follows:

- Motivation is important. The loss of morale when asked to leave behind his/her vision and a failed opportunity to bring about a change is painful.
- Uncertainty of tenure leads to fear and instability in the mind, which should be without fear for the proper delivery of services.
- Incentives encourage hard work but punishment attracts further malfunctioning, crippling the quality of governance.

Protection is provided to civil servants through Article 311 and DPSE Section 6A:

Article 311

- A civil servant cannot be dismissed by any authority that is subordinate to the one by which he/she was appointed.
- An enquiry is important to present the information of the charges he/she has been framed with and to give him the 'right to be heard'.

DSPE Section 6A

Section 6A of the Delhi Special Police Establishment (DSPE) Act, 1946 refers to prior concurrence on the registration of a case. This section was abolished by the SC, as it is against Article 14.

Recommendations by Committees

1. The A.D. Gorwala Committee Report, 1951 recommended greater understanding between ministers and civil servants.
2. The Hota Committee, 2004 recommended amendments to the following sections in the Prevention of Corruption Act, 1988 and Code of Criminal Procedure to protect honest civil servants:
    - Code of Ethics
    - Public evaluation of performances

T.S.R Subramanian vs Union of India

- Creation of an independent Civil Services Board both at the Centre and in the states for promotion and transfers of bureaucrats.
- Provision of fixed tenure in service, providing civil servants protection against transfers by politicians based on biases.
- All bureaucrats should record the directives given to them from their administrative superiors and political authorities.

Indian Administrative Service (Cadre) Rules

The Indian Administrative Service (Cadre) Rules, 1955 have been amended and following new clauses inserted:

- The Central Government, in consultation with the state government(s) concerned may determine the tenure of all or any of the cadre posts specified for the state concerned in item 1 of the Schedule to the Indian Administrative Service (Fixation of Cadre Strength) Regulation, 1955.
- A cadre officer appointed to any post for which the tenure has been so determined shall hold the minimum tenure prescribed except in the event of promotion, retirement, deputation outside the state, or training exceeding two months.
- An officer may be transferred before the minimum prescribed tenure only upon the recommendation of a Committee on Minimum Tenure, as specified in the Schedule annexed to these rules.

Steps taken by Supreme Court

The Supreme Court has advised the following measures:

- Civil servants should spend a minimum of two years in a posting before they can be transferred.
- A Civil Services Board should be set up to check political interference.
- Advices with regards to appointments and postings should be recorded, ensuring transparency and accountability.

Way Forward

- The nature of transfer should be independent and based on sound administrative grounds that are clearly spelt out.
- Fixed tenures for critical ranks such as DGPs, district SPs, and SHOs would ensure smooth functioning of the administration.
- The tenures should be directly linked to performance targets and fast-track advancements on the basis of forward-looking career management policies and techniques. These should be managed by autonomous personnel boards for assisting high-level political authorities in making key decisions.

- Civil service boards should be constituted under statutory provisions.
- Repeated shuffling is a menace for good governance and if the officer is concerned about the disruption in the flow of services due to his transfer, he should be given a chance to take his case before an Ombudsman.
- Ministers must uphold the political impartiality of the civil service and not ask civil servants to act in any way that would conflict with their duties and responsibilities.

Civil Services—Posting Officers Indiscriminately

The practice of posting civil service officers indiscriminately can be attributed to the blurred allocation of responsibility for tenures. Postings are used as a means to award punishments or to suit individual agenda.

In India, the elected representatives are accountable to the people and the civil servants are accountable to the ministers. Due to some vested interests, 'political neutrality' has paved the way for 'political interferences', which has led to the phenomena of 'politicization of the civil service'.

The cases of arbitrary and questionable moves by political masters have increased manifold and strengthened the temptation to resort to collusive practices to avoid untimely transfers and to play safe, giving rise to 'political neutrality' as a new hallmark. Some examples are as follows:

- Maria, who was heading the high-profile Sheena Bora murder case was shunted out of the post and promoted as Director General of Police Home Guards.
- "Tried hard to address corruption and bring reforms in the Transport department despite severe limitations and entrenched interests. Moment is truly painful." –Khemka remarked (after 46th transfer (from Transport Department in Haryana) in the service of 22 years).

Constitutional Provisions

1. Articles 53 and 154 vest the executive power of the Union and the states in the President or governor directly or through officers subordinate to him and these officers constitute the permanent civil service governed by Part XIV of the Constitution.
2. The President or governor is required to act according to the aid and advice of his/her council of ministers, appointed under Articles 73 and 163 of the Constitution, and this grants a political colour to the work process.
3. The minister has the mandate of the people to govern, but the secretary has an equivalent constitutional mandate to advise the minister. Once his/her advice has been suitably considered, unless the minister passes an illegal order, the secretary is bound to implement it and the minister is required to support the secretary who is implementing his/her order.

Healthcare

Targeting Recipients of Health Programmes

The Health Protection Programme (earlier Rashtriya Swasthya Bima Yojana) can easily be easily linked with Aadhaar for easy cash-free health services at hospitals.

Early Identification of Diseases

Nilekani has discussed the use of public health surveillance data for quickly identifying patterns of emergent epidemics, and understanding our rapidly changing burden of chronic diseases compared to patterns in Western Europe.

Interoperability

Perhaps the biggest win that Aadhaar can bring about is that it can accelerate the process of interoperability in healthcare. Interoperability is the seamless exchange of data across the patient care continuum, not just between the internal systems of the provider network, but also with an outside laboratory and pharmacy, and their connection with the insurance company's claims department. When systems are interoperable, patients and their families and doctors can access patient information from anywhere. This translates into no longer having to lug stacks of charts and lab and x-ray results and other documentation from doctor to doctor.

Saving Funds

At a system level, it can save precious funds. In the US, interoperability has the potential to lower healthcare costs by $30 billion annually. Currently, there is $36 billion in addressable waste within the US healthcare system, of which 97% is attributed to lack of interoperability.

Tracking Doctor Absenteeism

New ideas and initiatives are taking hold as leaders discover the possible applications of Aadhaar. One simple example is an initiative in Krishna district in Andhra Pradesh, where doctors and nurses are tracked for absenteeism using biometric markers. This has improved attendance and access by patients.

Universal Health Coverage in India

The World Health Organisation (WHO) describes UHC as a state where the health needs of all citizens are met without any of them experiencing financial hardship. It depicts UHC with three dimensions:

1. Population coverage (what proportion of people and which sections are covered)
2. Service coverage (what is the package of health services that is covered)
3. Cost coverage (what proportion of the healthcare cost is incurred as out-of-pocket spending and how much is met by the government or employer).